PROFILES OF THE PRESIDENTS

PROFILES OF THE PRESIDENTS

By Emerson Roy West

Published by
Deseret Book Company
Salt Lake City, Utah
1974

Lithographed by

DESERET PRESS

in the United States of America

DEDICATION

Affectionately dedicated to my parents, Roy A. and
Geneva Rose Day West, whose lives have been exemplary
and faith promoting.

Contents

ACKNOWLEDGMENTS

Although it is impossible to thank adequately all those who have shared their views and offered me valuable suggestions, a special note of appreciation is extended to my father, Roy A. West, who saw the need for this type of book and gave extensive guidance in preparing the book and seeing it completed.

I express thanks to William James Mortimer of Deseret Book Company for his faith and encouragement.

I want to especially thank Kay Stubbs, Dr. Glen Stubbs, Francia Stephens, Loren Cluff, Dr. T. Edgar Lyon, Edward L. Kimball, and Dr. Fred Holmstrom for their editing assistance and stimulating criticism.

Special thanks go to Diane Blake, Pat Gordon, Judy Hill, Rae Ann Merrill, Golden K. Driggs, Kenneth Foulger, Raymond Mayo, Max Parker, Leonard C. Smith, Sterling Nelson, Alan Busath, Dr. Harold Glen Clark, and Irene Mousley for their helpful suggestions.

Joseph Anderson, Assistant to the Council of the Twelve, and Henry Smith of the Church Information Service provided helpful insight into the matters of succession and the role of the President. Kathy Gilmore of the Church Historian's Office was helpful in selecting interesting pictures.

Grateful acknowledgment is further extended to my wife, Gloria, for helping type and prepare the manuscript, giving me constant support and encouragement, and making the years of researching and writing this book happy and rewarding ones.

INTRODUCTION

Presented here are brief profiles and biographies, with pictures, human interest stories, and inspiring statements, of the great men who have presided over The Church of Jesus Christ of Latter-day Saints from its organization in April 1830 until the present time.

These profiles of the Presidents are not intended to be an extensive scholarly work; rather, they are written for those readers who do not have the time for extensive reading and research but who wish to get a perspective of the men, the times, and events.

Studying the words and lives of these faithful, committed, heroic, and spiritual men can serve as patterns and testimony builders for everyone. In these latter days the Lord has raised leaders to guide the destiny of his Church according to the needs of the hour. Each man who has presided over the Church has possessed the particular aptitudes and talents that have been needed in the day of his ministry.

The statements by the Presidents pertaining to the spiritual, as well as the social, political, economic, and physical, sides of man are selected to help the reader live a full, productive life.

The purpose of this book is to give the reader some insight into the lives and words of God's prophets, seers, and revelators, in these, The Profiles of the Presidents.

"The men who have presided over this Church from the beginning have been men raised up by the Lord for the particular time during which they served, men prepared and qualified for the service they were to render and for the leadership they were to give. These men are not mediocre men; they are giants of the Lord, chosen and ordained before they came here to perform the work they have done and will do. Each is different from the others, but all are men of inspiration, of revelation, of devotion, and of faith—prophets of the living God."—Joseph Anderson, Assistant to the Council of the Twelve, *Improvement Era*, May 1970, p. 8.

Jesus Christ and His Church

Jesus is the Christ. This is the message of The Church of Jesus Christ of Latter-day Saints. It is the most important message in the world today.

Jesus Christ is the Son of God. He was chosen by God the Father as the Savior of the world. His coming was foretold centuries before his birth upon the earth. It was seen in vision by Adam, Moses, Isaiah, Ezekiel, Lehi, Nephi, King Benjamin, Alma, Samuel, and many others, including Mary, his earthly mother.

A modern prophet, the late Elder James E. Talmage of the Council of the Twelve, has declared who Jesus was and is:

> The solemn testimonies of millions dead and of millions living unite in proclaiming Him as divine, the Son of the living God, the Redeemer and Savior of the human race, the eternal Judge of the souls of men, the Chosen and Anointed of the Father—in short, the Christ.
>
> Jesus Christ was and is Jehovah, the God of Adam and of Noah, the God of Abraham, Isaac, and Jacob, the God of Israel, the God at whose instance the prophets of the ages have spoken, the God of all nations, and He who shall yet reign on earth as King of Kings and Lord of Hosts. (Talmage, *Jesus the Christ*, pp. 1, 4.)

What was the purpose of Christ's mission in life?

". . . God created man in his own image, in the image of God created he him; male and female created he them." (Genesis 1:27.) Man, created in the image of God, was placed on earth to experience mortal life, an intermediate state between premortal life and immortality.

Our first parents, Adam and Eve, disobeyed God.

By eating the forbidden fruit, they became mortal. Consequently, they and all of their descendants became subject to both mortal and spiritual death (mortal death—the separation of body and spirit; and spiritual death— the separation of the spirit from the presence of God, and death as pertaining to the things of the spirit).

In order for Adam to regain his original state (to be in the presence of God), an atonement for this disobedience was necessary. In God's divine plan, provision was made for a redeemer to break the bonds of death and, through resurrection, make possible the reunion of the spirits and bodies of all persons who had dwelt on earth.

Jesus of Nazareth was the one who, before the world was created, was chosen to come to earth to perform this service, to conquer mortal death. This voluntary action would atone for the fall of Adam and Eve and permit the spirit of man to recover his body, thereby reuniting body and spirit.

Jesus Christ has influenced humanity more than anyone else who ever lived. Born in a manger of an earthly mother and a Heavenly Father, he lived on earth for thirty-three years. He spent thirty of those years preparing for his life's mission and ministry. Then he traveled to the River Jordan to be baptized by immersion by his cousin John, called the Baptist. By participating in this symbolic ordinance, he demonstrated to all that baptism is the door into his church. From heaven, his Father acknowledged the important occasion, saying, "This is my beloved Son, in whom I am well pleased." (Matthew 3:17.)

For the next three years the Savior served mankind. He healed the sick, restored sight to the blind, cast out evil spirits, restored life to the dead, provided comfort to the oppressed, spread the good news of the gospel of love, testified of the Father, taught the eternal plan of salvation, and lay the groundwork for an organization that would provide for the salvation of man—his church. This church was not the church of John the Baptist, nor was it the church of Peter, nor of Paul, nor of any other of his followers. It was Christ's own church; he was its head.

That Christ established a church is well documented in the New Testament. In Ephesians we are told that the church of Jesus Christ was "built upon the foundation of the apostles and prophets, Jesus Christ himself being the chief corner stone." (Ephesians 2:20.) The Savior, speaking to Peter, said: "And I will give unto thee the keys of the kingdom of heaven; and whatsoever thou shalt bind on earth shall be bound in heaven; and whatsoever thou shalt loose on earth shall be loosed in heaven." (Matthew 16:19.)

In his church Christ selected twelve apostles and a council of seventy, and, having endowed them with authority, he sent them forth to preach.

> Then he called his twelve disciples together, and gave them power and authority over all devils, and to cure diseases.
> And he sent them to preach the kingdom of God, and to heal the sick. (Luke 9:1-2.)
> After these things the Lord appointed other seventy also, and sent them two and two before his face into every city and place, whither he himself would come. (Luke 10:1.)

God has said that he does not change; he is the same yesterday, today, and forever. Neither does his gospel change. His requirements for salvation are the same today as they were in the days of the apostles. Therefore, his church must always be the same in basic organization, in doctrine, and in divine authority.

Every Christian who understands the New Testament realizes that Christ's whole earthly mission was a message from God the Father to his mortal children, to reveal God's plan of salvation. Christ revealed his divinity in the flesh both before his crucifixion and after his resurrection. He performed his work with divine power and authority. And when his short mortal mission was finished, he left behind a divinely organized church, endowed with his priesthood and headed by twelve apostles who were to direct and continue his work. Thus he provided the means by which his message could be carried to the world.

In the early church, the apostles were called and commissioned as special witnesses of Jesus Christ. As vacancies occurred in their body, they were filled through the inspiration of the Lord. For example, Matthias was named an apostle to replace Judas, and though we do not have the record of their selection, Barnabas and Paul are referred to as apostles in Acts 14:14. Paul, in his epistles, introduces himself as an apostle of divine commission.

There is abundant evidence that the organization of Christ's church was a vital force during the Savior's life on earth and for some time after his resurrection and ascension. For example, on the day of Pentecost, only about a week following the ascension, three thousand new converts were added to an apparently already strong church organization.

But although the church flourished for a time, it wasn't long before changes began to appear, and by the time the apostles were killed, there was a widespread apostasy, a falling away from the teachings, laws, and ordinances of the church of Jesus Christ. The priesthood was lost, the doctrine was altered, and the organization was changed.

Paul predicted that an apostasy from the true gospel would certainly occur: ". . . for that day [Christ's return] shall not come, except there come a falling away first. . . ." (2 Thessalonians 2:3.) This fact is the justification for the claim of The Church of Jesus Christ of Latter-day Saints (Mormon) that there has been a restoration of the gospel.

Isaiah spoke about an apostasy: "And it shall come to pass in that day, that the Lord shall set his hand again the second time to recover the remnant of his people. . . ." (Isaiah 11:11.)

John the Revelator said: "And I saw another angel fly in the midst of heaven, having the everlasting gospel to preach unto them that dwell on the earth, and to every nation, and kindred, and tongue, and people." (Revelation 14:6.)

Jesus himself bore witness to a falling away and restoration: "And Jesus answered and said unto them, Elias truly shall first come, and restore all things." (Matthew 17:11.)

The Church of Jesus Christ of Latter-day Saints, then, is Christianity, or the church of Jesus Christ, restored, together with the principles and ordinances, the priesthood and authority, as taught and exercised in the primitive church in New Testament times.

If, as some claim, an apostasy did occur, where should one seek to find the kingdom of God today? The apostle Paul said:

> And he gave some, apostles; and some, prophets; and some, evangelists; and some, pastors and teachers;
>
> For the perfecting of the saints, for the work of the ministry, for the edifying of the body of Christ;
>
> Till we all come in the unity of the faith, and of the knowledge of the Son of God, unto a perfect man, unto the measure of the stature of the fulness of Christ:
>
> That we henceforth be no more children, tossed to and fro, and carried about with every wind of doctrine, by the sleight of men, and cunning craftiness, whereby they lie in wait to deceive. (Ephesians 4:11-14.)

Only in The Church of Jesus Christ of Latter-day Saints does one find the organization of the church of Christ as described in the New Testament, with the same officers that have been mentioned: deacons, teachers, priests, bishops, elders, seventies, high priests, and apostles. Without taking into consideration direct guidance by revelation, reason alone would dictate that Christ's church should be the same today as when organized under his direction.

Can the world claim that we have come to a unity of the faith? Religion cannot relate to people if it is based on the idea that God dealt with mankind only in ancient times and that the Bible is the only proof we have that God was a living, revealing, and communicating Being. If God ever communicated, he should still be communicating. He is the great I Am, not the great "He Was."

The position of The Church of Jesus Christ of Latter-day Saints has been summarized by President Joseph Fielding Smith, its tenth prophet, seer, and president:

> . . . the Lord has revealed his everlasting gospel anew to us in this day and has made The Church of Jesus Christ of Latter-day Saints the custodian and dispenser of its saving truths. . . . Our knowledge of these simple and yet profound doctrines has come to us by revelation in this dispensation.
>
> We know that our Heavenly Father is a glorified, exalted personage who has all power, all might, and all dominion, and that he knows all things. We testify that he, through his Only Begotten Son, is the Creator of this earth and of worlds without number, all of which are peopled by his spirit children. . . .
>
> We testify that the gospel of Jesus Christ is the plan of salvation; and that through our Lord's atoning sacrifice all men shall be raised in immortality, to be judged by him according to the deeds done in the flesh; and that those who believe and obey the fullness of gospel law shall be raised also unto eternal life in our Father's kingdom. . . .
>
> We proclaim that to gain salvation men must believe in the Lord Jesus Christ, repent of their sins, be baptized by immersion by one who has authority, receive the gift of the Holy Ghost by the laying on of hands, and then press forward with a steadfastness in Christ, keeping the commandments and enduring to the end. . . .
>
> We know Joseph Smith is a prophet; that the Father and the Son appeared to him in the spring of 1820 to usher in this final gospel dispensation; that he translated the Book of Mormon by the gift and power of God; that he received keys and authority from angels sent for this very purpose; and that the Lord revealed to him the doctrines of salvation.

We announce that The Church of Jesus Christ of Latter-day Saints is the kingdom of God on earth, the only place where men may come to learn the true doctrines of salvation and find the authority of the holy priesthood. (*Ensign*, June 1971, pp. 2, 4.)

Because the church was established by Christ during his ministry, we must assume that it is essential for men and not an elective. His life and ministry were to set the pattern and create the model. The things established by him were given with the admonition that we follow them. We hear him saying, "Come, follow me."

Let us examine a few of the fruits and important aspects of The Church of Jesus Christ of Latter-day Saints:

1. Belief in modern revelation.
2. Doctrine of eternal progression—we lived before we were born; we live after death.
3. Religious scripture, including the Bible, the Book of Mormon, the Doctrine and Covenants, and the Pearl of Great Price.
4. The Holy Ghost—the Comforter, Testifier, and Revelator whose companionship is a great gift that mortal man can enjoy.
5. Individual testimony of the truth of the gospel and the Church.
6. The same church organization as found in the New Testament, with prophets, apostles, bishops, elders, seventies, and other officers.
7. Free agency—the privilege of choosing what we shall believe, do, and become.
8. A belief in different degrees of rewards for life after death, based on faithfulness as mortals.
9. The priesthood, the authority to act in God's name, held by every worthy male member (no professional clergy).
10. Eternal nature of the family, with temples wherein marriages are solemnized for time and eternity and vicarious work is performed for the dead.
11. Tithing, the basic means of financing the programs of the Church.
12. Emphasis on seeking after truth and a good education, reiterated in the admonitions that "a man is saved no

faster than he gains knowledge," and "the glory of God is intelligence."

13. A belief in being hopeful, buoyant, and happy, with an affirmative attitude toward life. The goal of the Church is salvation; "men are that they might have joy."

14. The Welfare Plan—a practical program for caring for the poor and the needy; a plan to insure against want.

15. A great voluntary missionary system.

16. The Word of Wisdom, a divine law of health, which advocates the partaking of only good things into the body, and avoiding strong drinks, tobacco, and harmful drugs.

17. Religious education for young people through seminaries and institutes of religion at buildings near their campuses; several colleges, and a great university.

18. Opportunities for service and responsibility for everyone.

19. Great emphasis on recreation and cultural development.

20. A youth program to develop talents in sports, drama, speech, music, and dance.

21. Family home evening—a program to provide for family members an opportunity to share together experiences in teaching, learning, and living the gospel truths in the home, giving strength to family unity.

22. Home teaching—a program whereby families are fellowshipped by other Church members each month.

23. Opportunities for women, exemplified by the Relief Society, which trains wives and mothers for better homemaking, cultivates talents and interests, provides cultural advancement, and provides compassionate service to the sick and needy.

24. A great pioneer heritage, honoring thousands of Saints who moved west because of their faith and testimonies.

25. A belief in God, the God of the scriptures—a belief that is basic to all others.

Count Leo Tolstoi (1828-1910), the famous Russian novelist, once stated:

The Mormon people teach the American religion; their principles teach the people not only of heaven and its attendant glories, but how to live so that their social and economic relations with each other are placed on a sound basis. If the people follow the teachings of this Church, nothing can stop their progress—it is limitless. . . . If Mormonism is able to endure, unmodified, until it reaches the third and fourth generation, it is destined to become the greatest power the world has ever known. (*Improvement Era,* February 1939, p. 94.)

The restored church of Jesus Christ now has reached the third and fourth generations among the descendants of its first pioneers. Members of The Church of Jesus Christ of Latter-day Saints are commonly called Mormons. Numbering more than three million, they can be found throughout North, Central, and South America, western Europe, Africa, the islands of the Pacific, Australia, and the Orient. Tolstoi's prediction appears to be on the brink of fulfillment.

What Is a Prophet?

God communicates with mankind through his chosen servants, the prophets. These are the men whom he has called to give guidance, inspiration, and instruction. Through them, he points the way to all truth and salvation; the voice of a prophet is the voice of God to all generations, past, present, and future.

In ancient times, such prophets as Adam, Noah, Moses, and Isaiah received revelation from God for the guidance of the people of their day. In our own day, the President of The Church of Jesus Christ of Latter-day Saints is a modern-day prophet who just as surely receives revelations for the guidance of the people. He possesses the same characteristics as did the ancient prophets.

An overriding message of the Bible, in both the Old and the New Testaments, is: "Surely the Lord God will do nothing, but he revealeth his secret unto his servants the prophets." (Amos 3:7.) Prophets will always be found in the church of Christ.

No one who believes the holy scriptures could hope to find the gospel plan upon the earth without a prophet to direct it, for there is no scriptural warrant that God has ever had a church or a movement without one. Many of the Christian reformers understood this important truth. Martin Luther, John Wesley, John Calvin, John Knox, and others knew that God dealt with his people through prophets in ancient times, and they lamented their own lack of divine guidance.

Since God spoke anciently through his prophets, is

it unreasonable to believe that he speaks today? Members of The Church of Jesus Christ of Latter-day Saints testify that God *does* speak today through the voice of prophets. The Lord reestablished this ancient pattern with the Prophet Joseph Smith in 1830, and since then the line of communication has been unbroken.

The Lord gave a commandment to the members of the Church with respect to their prophet-president. Said he, ". . . thou shalt give heed unto all his words and commandments which he shall give unto you as he receiveth them, walking in all holiness before me; For his word ye shall receive, as if from mine own mouth, in all patience and faith." (D&C 21:4-5.) The need for divine guidance may be even greater in today's complex world than it was in ancient times. The role of a modern prophet of God is to give that guidance—to guide the people and encourage them to live the gospel of Jesus Christ, as well as to prophesy of the future. A prophet speaks and teaches as a representative of God and administers the saving ordinances among the people.

What characteristics distinguish both ancient and modern prophets? The following may provide us with a "prophet profile."

A prophet is ordained of God. He is called as a prophet by God himself. He is called and commissioned to act as God's messenger and watchman and as interpreter of God's will to man. He learns the desires of God under the inspiration of the Holy Spirit. President Harold B. Lee says:

> A prophet does not become a spiritual leader by studying books about religion, nor does he become one by attending a theological seminary. One becomes a prophet, a divinely called religious leader, by actual spiritual contacts. He gets his diploma, as it were, directly from God. (*Improvement Era*, February 1970, p. 46.)

A prophet declares that God speaks to him. He teaches mankind the character of God. He has the right, the power, and the authority to speak the mind and will of God to his people, saying, "Thus saith the Lord."

A prophet is often a foreteller of future events. Although he warns of impending judgments, he offers hope and a way to salvation for those who repent.

A prophet is a man of unshakable faith in God. He holds all the keys of priesthood authority. He bears witness that he knows by personal revelation from the Holy Ghost that God lives and that Jesus Christ is the Son of God, "for the testimony of Jesus is the spirit of prophecy." (Revelation 19:10.)

A prophet is a preacher of righteousness. He calls men to repentance and declares his message courageously, without compromising gospel standards. His mission is to fellowship people, to purify their minds and souls, to direct them back to God. He shows the offender that he is still loved by the Lord. He enjoys teaching righteousness to the righteous.

A prophet has two major commitments: to God and to mankind. He is the "conscience of the people." He seeks confrontation with them. He is a reformer. He seeks to relate to man, to weld men into a brotherhood, to build a better society. He is a champion of human rights.

A prophet is an interpreter of the scriptures. He declares their meaning and application. His own teachings are in strict harmony with scripture, and his words and writings may become scripture when he speaks under the influence of the Holy Ghost.

A prophet is an instructor in Church policy. He is well versed in such policy and directs and instructs others in it.

A prophet is humble. He readily admits his limitations. He is human, with imperfections common to mankind in general.

A prophet is charismatic. He has a special spiritual endowment and holds special powers, such as those held by Ezekiel. He is identified as a man of love, compassion, and mercy, as were Moses and John the Beloved.

A prophet is self-denying, to the point of enduring great suffering or even death for the message. When these trials come, he is loyal, courageous, and faithful.

A prophet is a leader actively engaged in the political and economic life of his people. If the conditions of society are not favorable, men cannot achieve the spiritual goals God desires, for his children cannot live the "good life" in the face of war, depression, ignorance, poverty, illness, sin, unemployment, or disunity among the people and government. A prophet seeks ways to alleviate these conditions.

President Spencer W. Kimball has stated:

> To be a prophet of the Lord, one does not need to "be everything to all men." He does not need to be youthful and athletic, an industrialist, a financier, nor an agriculturist; he does not need to be a musician, a poet, an entertainer, nor a banker, a physician, nor a college president, a military general, nor a scientist.
>
> He does not need to be a linguist to speak French and Japanese, German and Spanish, but he must understand the divine language and be able to receive messages from heaven.
>
> He need not be an orator, for God can make His own. The Lord can present His divine messages through weak men made strong. He substituted a strong voice for the quiet, timid one of Moses, and gave to the young man Enoch power which made men tremble in his presence. (*Church News*, May 8, 1971, p. 14.)

A prophet is known by the fruits of his message. He may possess all other qualifications, but if his message does not stand up under this test, he cannot justify a claim to the divine call. The prophet Jeremiah gave this challenge as a test of a true prophet: "When the word of the prophet shall come to pass, then shall the prophet be known, that the Lord hath truly sent him." (Jeremiah 28:9.)

And finally, a prophet is unique in his own individual

fashion. As the late Elder James E. Talmage of the Council of the Twelve declared:

> The true prophet is no imitator, blindly following step-by-step the footprints of a predecessor; he is, perforce, pathfinder and path-maker himself; for though he travels as others have done, as yet others will do, toward destination fixed and known, his special duties often lead him over ground before untrodden. Originality, relative originality at least, is essentially associated with the prophetic calling. The Hebrew equivalents of our word prophet signified one from whom inspired utterances bubbled forth spontaneously, as water from a fountain; one who was a source of right counsel, a well-spring of truth. The prophet of God is without predecessor or successor in his own particular mission; yet his words and his works must be consistent with those of the prophets before him, and of assured agreement with the prophecies that shall appear as the scroll of futurity unrolls. Through ordination one may be installed in the place of a prophet who has departed this life; yet, in the labors and official administration of each, a marked individuality as to the work and its execution appears. (*Improvement Era*, December 1956, pp. 897-98.)

Jesus Christ is the foundation of The Church of Jesus Christ of Latter-day Saints. He personally visited Joseph Smith and called him to be a prophet in His name, to receive the fullness of the gospel, to restore His church, and to do His will. Joseph Smith was the first prophet of the restored church. He has been succeeded by other prophets, men called of God and ordained to this holy office and work, and these prophet-presidents have been associated with other apostles and prophets.

Members of the Church sustain these prophets as spokesmen for God, revelators, and emissaries, as leaders called to interpret and to do God's will among men.

Succession in the Presidency

God . . . has fashioned every man whom he has ever called to lead his people, even from Moses of old till now. No man ever comes to lead God's people whom he has not trained for his task. (J. Reuben Clark, Jr., *Deseret News*, May 15, 1945, p. 1.)

Suppose the President of the Church were to die today. Who would become the new President? Would he be elected by the membership of the Church, selected by the General Authorities, or has he already been chosen by the Lord? Is succession based on tradition and practice, or does the Church have a definite, inspired procedure for selecting a new President?

President Joseph Fielding Smith answers the question of succession with the following statement:

The Prophet, in anticipation of his death, conferred upon the Twelve all the keys and authorities which he held. He did not bestow the keys on any one member, but upon them *all*, so that *each held the keys* and authorities. All members of the Council of the Twelve since that day have also been given all of these keys and powers. But these powers cannot be exercised by any one of them *until*, if the occasion arises, he is called to be the *presiding officer* of the Church. The Twelve, therefore, in the setting apart of the President do not give him any additional priesthood, but *confirm* upon him that which he has *already* received; they *set him* apart to the office, which it is their right to do.

On the death of the President, the Council of the Twelve becomes the presiding quorum in the Church *until* by their action they organize again the First Presidency. This is a consistent order. If only one man held this binding and loosing power, then the Lord would be under the necessity of restoring it each time a new President of the Church was called.

There is no mystery about the choosing of the successor to

the President of the Church. The Lord settled this a long time ago, and the *senior apostle automatically becomes the presiding officer of the Church,* and he is so sustained by the Council of the Twelve which becomes the presiding body of the Church when there is no First Presidency. The president is *not elected,* but he has to be *sustained* both by his brethren of the Council and by the members of the Church. . . .

The Twelve Apostles have been sustained as prophets, seers, and revelators ever since the time of the dedication of the Kirtland Temple. *There is only one man at a time who holds the keys of revelation for the Church.* The Twelve Apostles may receive revelation to guide them *in their labors* and to assist them in setting in order the priesthood and organizations of the Church. When they are sent out into a stake by authority, they have all the power to receive revelation, to make changes, and to conduct the affairs according to the will of the Lord. But they do not receive revelations for the guidance of the whole Church, only wherein one of them may succeed to the Presidency. In other words the right to receive revelation and guidance for the whole Church is vested in each one of the Twelve which he could exercise should he succeed to the Presidency. But this power is *dormant* while the President of the Church is living. (*Doctrines of Salvation,* vol. 3, pp. 155-57.)

President Joseph F. Smith, sixth President of the Church, stated in 1895 the safeguards the Lord has taken so that the Church continues:

If the Presidency were to be killed off, then the Council of the Twelve Apostles would stand in their place and preside until the Presidency should be restored; and if they and the First Presidency were all killed off, then the seventies would come forward and they would establish the order of Zion and renew the order of the priesthood upon the earth; and if all the seventies were killed off, and yet there was one elder possessing the Melchizedek Priesthood, he would have authority to organize the Church, under the command of God and the guidance of His Holy Spirit, as Joseph did in the beginning; that it should be re-established in its perfect form. So you can see that this organization is well-nigh undestructible. (*Liahona,* or *Elders Journal,* vol. 4 [1895], pp. 45-46.)

It is important to review Church history briefly in order to recall certain past events pertaining to succession in the presidency. For instance, the Lord gives us insight into the role of the twelve apostles.

For unto you, the Twelve, and those, the First Presidency, who are appointed with you to be your counselors and your leaders, is the power of this priesthood given, for the last days and for the last time, in the which is the dispensation of the fulness of times.

Which power you hold, in connection with all those who have received a dispensation at any time from the beginning of the creation;

For verily I say unto you, the keys of the dispensation, which ye have received, have come down from the fathers, and last of all, being sent down from heaven unto you. (D&C 112:30-32.)

Who were the members of the Council of the Twelve who were chosen in 1835? The following list shows how members of the Council of the Twelve were arranged by Joseph Smith according to their ages; at that time age was the basis for seniority (birthdates are in parentheses):

1. Thomas B. Marsh (Nov. 1, 1799)
2. David W. Patten (Nov. 14, 1799)
3. Brigham Young (June 1, 1801)
4. Heber C. Kimball (June 14, 1801)
5. Orson Hyde (Jan. 8, 1805)
6. William E. McLellan (1806)
7. Parley P. Pratt (April 12, 1807)
8. Luke S. Johnson (Nov. 3, 1807)
9. William B. Smith (March 13, 1811)
10. Orson Pratt (Sept. 19, 1811)
11. John F. Boynton (Sept. 20, 1811)
12. Lyman E. Johnson (Oct. 24, 1811)

Thomas B. Marsh and David W. Patten preceded Brigham Young in seniority. In 1838, Patten was killed by mobbers. Marsh, senior member and President of the Twelve, apostatized and was excommunicated in 1839. Brigham Young then became the senior member of the Council of the Twelve.

In a meeting of the Council of the Twelve in Preston, England, Brigham Young was unanimously sustained as President of the Twelve. This was sanctioned by Joseph Smith.

When Brigham Young heard of the death of Joseph Smith in June 1844, he was at Petersboro, New Hampshire. As the questions of succession occurred to him, he had this reaction:

> The first thing that I thought of was whether Joseph had taken the keys of the kingdom with him from the earth. Brother Orson Pratt sat on my left, we were both leaning back in our chairs. Bringing my hand down on my knee, I said, the keys of the kingdom are right here with The Church. (Tullidge, *Life of Brigham Young,* p. 106.)

On August 7, 1844, Brigham Young met with the Council of the Twelve, the high council of Nauvoo Stake, and the high priests. Speaking of the Twelve, he said:

> Joseph conferred upon our heads all the keys and powers belonging to the apostleship which he himself held before he was taken away, and no man or set of men can get between Joseph and the Twelve in this world or the world to come. How often has Joseph said to the Twelve, "I have laid the foundation and you must build thereon, for upon your shoulders the kingdom rests." (*Millennial Star*, vol. 25, p. 232.)

Following Joseph Smith's death in 1844, the procedure was established that the senior member and President of the Council of Twelve would be the new President of the Church unless otherwise directed by the Lord. John Taylor, the third President, gives his viewpoint about succession in the presidency with this statement:

> I occupied the senior position in the Quorum and occupying that position, which was thoroughly understood by the Quorum of the Twelve, on the death of President Young, as the Twelve assumed the Presidency, and I was their President, it placed me in a position of President of the Church. . . . (Taylor, *Gospel Kingdom*, p. 192.)

In 1887, shortly before John Taylor's death, while Wilford Woodruff was the President of the Twelve,

Elder Heber J. Grant of the Twelve asked if the President of the Twelve would become the next President of the Church and if this would always be the procedure. On March 28, 1887, President Woodruff wrote his answer in a letter:

When the President of the Church dies, who then is the Presiding Authority of the Church? It is the Quorum of the Twelve Apostles (ordained and organized by the revelations of God and none else). Then while these Twelve Apostles preside over the Church, who is the President of the Church? It is the President of the Twelve Apostles. And he is virtually as much the President of the Church while presiding over Twelve men as he is when organized as the Presidency of the Church, and presiding over two men.

As far as I am concerned it would require . . . a revelation from the same God who had organized the Church and guided by inspiration in the channel in which it has traveled for 57 years, before I could give my vote or influence to depart from the paths followed by the Apostles since the organization of the Church and followed by the inspiration of Almighty God, for the past 57 years, by the apostles, as recorded in the history of the Church. (*Improvement Era*, June 1970, p. 29.)

Since the time of Brigham Young there has been no deviation from this procedure.

Appointment of the senior apostle as President places at the head of the Church the apostle who has been longest in service and is thus most familiar with Church government. It also eliminates any politics from operating within the council. President Spencer W. Kimball says:

We may expect the Church President will always be an older man; young men have action, vigor, initiative; older men, stability and strength and wisdom through experience and long communion with God. (*Improvement Era*, June 1970, p. 93.)

President Harold B. Lee gave additional clarification to the question of succession in his general conference talk of April 1970, at the solemn assembly when Joseph Fielding Smith was sustained as President of the Church.

To those who ask the question: How is the President of the Church chosen or elected? the correct and simple answer should be a quotation of the fifth Article of Faith: "We believe that a man must be called of God, by prophecy, and by the laying on of hands, by those who are in authority to preach the Gospel and administer in the ordinances thereof."

The beginning of the call of one to be President of the Church actually begins when he is called, ordained, and set apart to become a member of the Quorum of the Twelve Apostles. Such a call by prophecy, or in other words, by the inspiration of the Lord to the one holding the keys of presidency, and the subsequent ordination and setting apart by the laying on of hands by that same authority, places each apostle in a priesthood quorum of twelve men holding the apostleship.

Each apostle so ordained under the hands of the President of the Church, who holds the keys of the kingdom of God in concert with all other ordained apostles, has given to him the priesthood authority necessary to hold every position in the Church, even to a position of presidency over the Church if he were called by the presiding authority and sustained by a vote of a constituent assembly of the membership of the Church.

The Prophet Joseph Smith declared that "where the president is not, there is no First Presidency." Immediately following the death of a President, the next ranking body, the Quorum of the Twelve Apostles, becomes the presiding authority, with the President of the Twelve automatically becoming the acting President of the Church until a President of the Church is officially ordained and sustained in his office.

Early in this dispensation, because of certain conditions, the Council of Twelve continued to preside as a body for as long as three years before the reorganization was effected. As conditions in the Church became more stabilized, the reorganization was effected promptly following the passing of the President of the Church.

All members of the First Presidency and the Twelve are regularly sustained as "prophets, seers, and revelators". . . . This means that any one of the apostles, so chosen and ordained, could preside over the Church if he were "chosen by the body [which has been interpreted to mean, the entire Quorum of the Twelve], appointed and ordained to that office, and upheld by the confidence, faith, and prayer of the church," to quote from a revelation on this subject, on one condition, and that being that he was the senior member, or the president, of that body. (See D&C 107:22.)

Occasionally the question is asked as to whether or not one

other than the senior member of the Twelve could become President. Some thought on this matter would suggest that any other than the senior member could become President of the Church only if the Lord reveals to that President of the Twelve that someone other than himself should be selected.

The Lord revealed to the first prophet of this dispensation the orderly plan from the Church leadership by a predetermined organization of the earthly kingdom of God. He gave these specific guidelines, as we might speak of them:

"Of the Melchizedek Priesthood, three Presiding High Priests, chosen by the body, appointed and ordained to that office, and upheld by the confidence, faith, and prayer of the church, form a quorum of the [First] Presidency of the Church."

"The twelve traveling councilors are called to be the Twelve Apostles, or special witnesses of the name of Christ in all the world—thus differing from other officers in the Church in the duties of their calling.

"And they form a quorum, equal in authority and power to the three presidents previously mentioned." (D&C 107:22-24.) (*Improvement Era*, June 1970, pp. 28-29.)

Let us review a recent succession in the presidency to see exactly what transpires. In his general conference address of April 1970, at the solemn assembly, President Spencer W. Kimball, Acting President of the Council of the Twelve, gave us specific insight into the actual process of succession. Here he referred to the deceased David O. McKay and to the new President of the Church, Joseph Fielding Smith.

The work of the Lord is endless. Even when a powerful leader dies, not for a single instant is the Church without leadership, thanks to the kind Providence who gave his kingdom continuity and perpetuity. As it already has happened eight times before in this dispensation, a people reverently close a grave, dry their tears, and turn their faces to the future.

The moment life passes from a President of the Church, a body of men become the composite leader—these men already seasoned with experience and training. The appointments have long been made, the authority given, the keys delivered. For five days, the kingdom moves forward under this already authorized council. No "running" for position, no electioneering, no stump speeches. What a divine plan! How wise our Lord, to organize so perfectly beyond the weakness of frail, grasping humans.

Then dawns the notable day (January 23, 1970), and 14 serious men walk reverently into the temple of God—this, the Quorum of the Twelve Apostles, the governing body of The Church of Jesus Christ of Latter-day Saints, several of whom have experienced this solemn change before.

When these 14 men emerge from the holy edifice later in the morning, a transcendently vital event has occurred—a short interregnum ends, and the government of the kingdom shifts back again from the Quorum of the Twelve Apostles to a new prophet, an individual leader, the Lord's earthly representative, who has unostentatiously been moving toward this lofty calling for 60 years. He now presides over the Church.

Not because of his name, however, did he accede to this high place, but because when he was a very young man, he was called of the Lord, through the then living prophet, to be an apostle—member of the Quorum—and was given the precious, vital keys to hold in suspension pending a time when he might become the senior apostle and the President.

In that eventful temple meeting, when he has been "ordained and set apart" as the President of the Church by his brethren, the Twelve, he chooses his counselors—two mighty men of valor: Elder Harold B. Lee and Elder Nathan Eldon Tanner, with their rich background as teachers, businessmen, public officials, and especially Church leaders.

And a presidency of three and a newly constituted Council of Twelve walk humbly to their offices without fanfare or ostentation, and a new administration moves into a new period with promise of great development and unprecedented growth. (*Improvement Era*, June 1970, p. 92.)

A new President of the Church is sustained by the voting of Church membership in a solemn assembly. Representatives of priesthood quorums in stakes, wards, and missions assemble in the Tabernacle on Temple Square in Salt Lake City for this inspiring and memorable occasion.

In several revelations to the Prophet Joseph Smith, the Lord instructed him to "call your solemn assembly." (D&C 95:7; see also sections 88 and 109.) This voting pattern has been used since the sustaining of President

John Taylor, third President, in the 1880 general conference. The appointment and sustaining of a new President is not done in secret; rather, it is done publicly at a general conference or at a special conference. For example, special conferences for the sustaining of a new President by the people were held (1) when Lorenzo Snow died on October 10, 1901, and Joseph F. Smith was sustained in November 1901; (2) when Joseph F. Smith died on November 19, 1918, and Heber J. Grant was sustained in June 1919 (the delay was due to a flu epidemic during the spring of that year).

The following is the procedure that has developed from Joseph Smith to the present, presented so that understanding and certainty may replace guesswork.

1. When the President of the Church dies, the First Presidency is dissolved and the counselors lose their presiding authority and are automatically released and returned to their former quorums of priesthood activity.

2. The presiding power resides in the Council of the Twelve, and during that interim period they are virtually the Presidency of the Church, the presiding quorum. Each member of the Council of the Twelve has equal priesthood authority and may hold any office in the Church, even presiding over the Church if so called by the presiding authority and sustained by the membership of the Church.

3. To become President of the Church, a man must be an apostle (member of the Council of the Twelve), called of God, approved by the Council of the Twelve, and sustained by members of the Church in the solemn assembly.

4. Seniority begins automatically when a man becomes a member of the Council of the Twelve. Each new apostle may become the senior apostle (senior by length of service but not by age) if he remains faithful and outlives those apostles who have seniority in service in the Council.

5. The President of the Council of the Twelve becomes the President of the Church when the First Presidency is reorganized upon the death of the former President. Following the death of a President, the senior apostle automatically becomes the presiding officer and the sole spokesman of God for the entire church.

6. The new President is selected by a "call by prophecy and by the laying on of hands by those who are in authority." This is done in a meeting in the temple, where members of the Council of the Twelve are assembled in prayer and fasting. Each man, guided by inspiration, declares his belief, judgment, and testimony as to whom the Lord has chosen. Usually they speak starting with the junior member. After all the apostles have spoken, a vote is taken.

7. With the approval and the sustaining vote of the Twelve, the senior apostle is ordained and set apart as President by the laying on of hands by the Council of the Twelve. The new President of the Twelve is the voice of the Twelve during this sacred occasion. Later, in solemn assembly, the membership of the Church votes.

8. The person who has held apostleship longest (next to the President of the Church) is appointed and sustained as the President of the Council of the Twelve. He officiates in this position unless he is called into the First Presidency and is excused from these duties. If this occurs, he still retains his apostleship, seniority, and presidency of the Council of the Twelve.

9. If the New President of the Church selects the senior member of the Twelve (the President of the Council of the Twelve) as his counselor, the next member of the Twelve in seniority usually becomes the Acting President of the Twelve.

10. The President of the Church selects his own counselors, who need not be apostles but who must be high priests. It is essential that they be approved and sus-

tained by the Council of the Twelve and the Church membership. Normally he selects two counselors.

11. This procedure of succession (senior apostle becoming President of the Church) has been followed in every instance, with no deviation, since the Church was organized, and will continue to be the order of the Church unless the Lord speaks and commands a change. The Lord could change the procedure, but such a change would be received through revelation by the senior apostle or by the President before his death.*

In summary, Elder John A. Widtsoe of the Council of the Twelve wrote:

Men are called to the prophetic office of the President of the Church through inspiration from God. The call does not come by chance, or merely by attaining seniority in the councils of the Church. There must be fitness in the man, to be placed in the foremost office in God's latter-day Church. (*Improvement Era*, May 1948, p. 224.)

---

*Some of the ideas for the principles of succession came from the following sources: interviews with Joseph Anderson, Assistant to the Twelve (secretary to the First Presidency for many years); Henry Smith, of the Church Information Service; *Succession in the Church* by Reed C. Durham, Jr., and Steven H. Heath (Bookcraft, 1970), pp. 177-79.

The quorum of the First Presidency set the pattern for voting in Solemn Assembly held October 6, 1972, in the Salt Lake Tabernacle. This procedure of voting has been the pattern since the sustaining of President John Taylor in 1880.

Succession in the Presidency

Line of Authority

THE LORD JESUS CHRIST

PETER, JAMES, AND JOHN
were ordained apostles by the Lord Jesus Christ.
(John 15:16.)

JOSEPH SMITH, JR., and
OLIVER COWDERY
received the Melchizedek Priesthood in 1829 under
the hands of Peter, James, and John.

THE THREE WITNESSES
were called by revelation to choose the Twelve
Apostles and on February 14, 1835, they were "blessed
by the laying on of the hands of the Presidency,"
Joseph Smith, Jr., Sidney Rigdon, and Frederick G.
Williams, to ordain the Twelve Apostles.
(*Documentary History of the Church*, vol. 2, pp. 187-88.)

BRIGHAM YOUNG
was ordained an apostle February 14, 1835, under the
hands of the Three Witnesses, Oliver Cowdery,
David Whitmer, and Martin Harris.

GEORGE Q. CANNON
was ordained an apostle August 26, 1860, by
Brigham Young.

HEBER J. GRANT
was ordained an apostle October 16, 1882, by
George Q. Cannon.

SPENCER W. KIMBALL
was ordained an apostle October 7, 1945, by
Heber J. Grant.

The Role of the President

In order to fully understand the powers and duties of the President of the Church, his special responsibilities and functions, it is necessary to recognize that he is the spiritual leader who receives revelation for the Church. One must also recognize that he is a lawgiver, judge, and prophet, and the Lord's earthly representative in all things pertaining to the Church.

He is the oracle of the Lord, the man raised up to guide the destiny of the Church. Heber J. Grant, seventh President of the Church, once said: "You need have no fear, my dear brothers and sisters, that any man will ever stand at the head of the Church of Jesus Christ unless our Heavenly Father wants him to be there." Each man who has presided over the Church has possessed those particular aptitudes and talents that have been needed in the day of his ministry.

The President of the Church is by divine direction appointed from among the members of the High Priesthood to preside over the entire Church. He is to "set in order all the affairs of this church and kingdom." (D&C 90:16.) He is known as "President of the High Priesthood of the Church; Or, in other words, the Presiding High Priest over the High Priesthood of the Church." (D&C 107:65-66.) His duty is "to preside over the whole church, and to be like unto Moses—Behold, here is wisdom; yea, to be a seer, a revelator, a translator, and a prophet, having all the gifts of God which he bestows upon the head of the church." (D&C 107:91-92.)

The late Elder John A. Widtsoe of the Council of the Twelve said:

The President of the Church holds all the keys of authority of the Priesthood and of the Church upon the earth. He acts as the earthly head of the Church of which the Lord Jesus is the Eternal Head. There is only one man at a time upon the earth who holds these keys. He is the Prophet, Seer and Revelator of the Church, the only one authorized to receive revelation for the Church. The President of the Church is the living oracle of God to whom the Lord reveals whatever is necessary for the conduct of the Church. (Widtsoe, *Priesthood and Church Government*, p. 131.)

Thus, the President of the Church is the spokesman for God on earth. The Lord has said concerning the office of president of his church: ". . . thou shalt give heed unto all his words and commandments which he shall give unto you as he receiveth them, walking in all holiness before me; For his word ye shall receive, as if from mine own mouth, in all patience and faith." (D&C 21: 4-5.)

The Presidents Receive Revelation in the Latter Days

The presiding officer or President of the Church is the only person who holds the keys to revelation for the Church. The men who have been called in the latter days as prophets, seers, and revelators have all received visions, revelations, and guidance from our Heavenly Father. (See Mosiah 8:15-18 for the distinction between prophet, seer, and revelator.)

Man's circumstances and needs change. As he is confronted with new questions and new problems, he needs new answers or new applications and interpretations of former revelations. President John Taylor, third President of the Church, understood this need when he said:

A good many people, and those professing Christianity, will sneer a good deal at the idea of present revelation. Whoever heard of true religion without communication with God? . . . The principle of present revelation . . . is the very foundation of our religion.

The Bible is good; and Paul told Timothy to study it, that he might be a workman that need not be ashamed, and that he might be able to conduct himself aright before the living Church, the pillar and ground of truth. The church-mark, with Paul, was the foundation, the pillar, the ground of truth, the living church, not the dead letter. The Book of Mormon is good; and the Doctrine and Covenants, as land-marks. But a mariner who launches into the ocean requires a more certain criterion. He must be acquainted with heavenly bodies and take his observations from them in order to steer his barque aright. Those books are good for example, precedent, and investigation, and for developing certain laws and principles. But they do not, they cannot, touch every case required to be adjudicated and set in order.

We require a living tree—a living fountain—living intelligence, proceeding from the living priesthood in heaven, through the living priesthood on earth. . . . And from the time that Adam first received a communication from God, to the time that John, on the Isle of Patmos, received   his communication, or Joseph Smith had the heavens opened to him, it always required new revelations adapted to the peculiar circumstances in which the churches or individuals were placed. Adam's revelations did not instruct Noah to build his ark; nor did Noah's revelation tell Lot to forsake Sodom; nor did either of these speak of the departure of the children of Israel from Egypt. These all had revelations for themselves, and so had Isaiah, Jeremiah, Ezekiel, Jesus, Peter, Paul, John, and Joseph. And so must we, or we shall make a shipwreck. (Taylor, *Gospel Kingdom*, p. 34.)

Three types of revelation come through the President of the Church.

First, there are revelations pertaining to the organization of the Church.

Second, there is revelation relating to the doctrine of the Church. These revelations, for the salvation of man, initially were received in this dispensation by the Prophet Joseph Smith. Additional revelations may be given by the Lord as he deems appropriate. These revelations will serve only to increase understanding and will not change the present basic principles of the Church. "In case of difficulty respecting doctrine or principle, if there is not a sufficiency written to make the case clear to the minds of the council, the president may inquire and obtain the mind of the Lord by revelation." (D&C 102:23.)

Third, these revelations pertain to the welfare and

progress of the Church and are continually given because current problems need current solutions.

The President of the Church is the instrument through which the Lord speaks for the edification and guidance of the Church. By inspiration he interprets God's word and makes relevant application for present-day social, political, moral, and economic conditions. He warns of evils, indicates the "best" way, and clarifies truth.

Official prophetic declarations to the Church by the President are usually spoken at the general conference of the Church or appear in signed statements. Any individual can review Church history and verify that revelation has been in continuous force. The fact that the revelations are not printed in compiled scripture form and available to the public does not diminish their truthfulness. When the prophet speaks to Latter-day Saints in an official assembly or in an official printed document signed by the First Presidency, his signature and his voice bring to them the will of God.

Examples of Presidents Receiving Revelation

The following examples are from the lives of some of the presidents of the Church.

Joseph Smith: He was the first prophet in this dispensation who received revelations contained in the Doctrine and Covenants.

Brigham Young: Section 136 of the Doctrine and Covenants, "The Word and Will of the Lord, given through President Brigham Young at the Winter Quarters," January 14, 1847.

John Taylor: A revelation at Salt Lake City, Utah Territory, April 14, 1883, in answer to the question: "Show unto us thy will, O Lord, concerning the organization of the seventies."

Wilford Woodruff: A revelation in 1890 officially discontinuing the practice of plural marriage. (D&C, pp. 256-57.)

Lorenzo Snow: A personal visitation from the Lord Jesus Christ. "Brother Snow told us that he was instructed by the Lord in the Temple the night after President Woodruff died to organize the Presidency of the Church at once." In 1889 Lorenzo Snow also received a renewed revelation on tithing.

Joseph F. Smith: A marvelous vision in 1918 pertaining to the redemption of the dead; the building of temples in Hawaii and Canada.

Heber J. Grant: A revelation in 1936 to help meet the economic or temporal needs of the Church members. It is now called the Welfare Plan. The plans for the Arizona, Idaho Falls, and Los Angeles temples.

David O. McKay: The building of temples in foreign lands (Switzerland, New Zealand, England); family home evenings; correlation program; Regional Representatives of the Twelve.

Joseph Fielding Smith: Mission Representatives appointed.

The Duties, Powers, and Responsibilities of the President

1. Only the President holds the "keys of the kingdom." (D&C 81:2.) The "keys of the kingdom" are the governing power and authority to preside over and to administer in all spiritual and temporal affairs of the Church. He has the authority and power to delegate and exercise these keys to others of the General Authorities, temple presidents, mission presidents, stake presidents, bishops, patriarchs, and others as holders of the special or particular keys pertaining to specific offices in certain geographical areas. Through his authority, salvation becomes available to the people of the world.

2. He alone is the spokesman for the Lord to the Church and receives revelations for its guidance. He declares official edicts that concern the entire Church and sets policies for it. He says "why, when, where, who, and how" with regard to setting Church policy.

3. He has the gift of the Holy Ghost and of prophecy.

4. He has full responsibility for the welfare of the Church. He reads and hears reports pertaining to the progress and problems of the Church. He is concerned about the temporal and spiritual welfare of his people. He preserves order in the Church.

5. He is the only one who holds keys to the sealing ordinance and temple work. He may delegate these powers to others. However, he is the only one who can sign and grant a temple divorce, the cancellation of the sealing. He may delegate the research on specific cases to others. All the temples are under his direct supervision.

6. He is trustee-in-trust for the Corporation of the President, which holds or may hold title to all properties of the Church.

7. He is the president of Zion's Securities Corporation, a corporation of the President that holds title to and operates such properties as are subject to taxation, such as property indirectly used for Church purposes.

8. He acts as chairman or president of most of the industrial, mercantile, agricultural, and welfare enterprises of the Church. He is also the president of the Church board of education. He inspects or directs the inspection of Church farms, ranches, landholdings, and proposed new real estate.

9. He is responsible for the preparation and procedures of general conference.

Joseph F. Smith, sixth President of the Church, summarized the powers and duties of the President in the following statement:

> I have the right to bless. I hold the keys of the Melchizedek Priesthood and of the office and power of patriarch. It is my right to bless; for all the keys and authority and power pertaining to the government of the Church and to the Melchizedek and Aaronic Priesthood are centered in the presiding officers of the Church. There is no business, nor office, within the Church that the Presi-

dent of the Church may not fill, and may not do, if it is necessary, or if it is required of him to do it. He holds the office of patriarch; he holds the office of high priest and of apostle, of seventy, of elder, of bishop, and of priest, teacher and deacon in the Church; all these belong to the Presidency of the Church of Jesus Christ of Latter-day Saints, and they can officiate in any and in all of these callings when occasion requires. (*Conference Report,* 1915, p. 7.)

The Activities of the President

With the exception of Joseph Smith and Brigham Young, the men who have been appointed to preside over the Church have been older men. In order to bear the heavy burdens of the office, these men must be sustained by the Lord.

The nature of his work requires the President to be up early and to be earnestly involved in the work of the day. He spends many hours in prayer, meditation, and study of the scriptures. The pressures and schedules of the office of President would exhaust many younger men. His work requires attending many meetings, reading and answering a great deal of correspondence, answering numerous phone calls and signing papers, and preparing many speeches and articles.

Official letters from the President and the First Presidency are personally signed by the President. In addition, he signs calls to full-time missionaries, letters approving appropriations for properties and building projects, and letters to stake presidents and bishops. He answers questions on points of doctrine and policy and signs letters dealing with sealing cancellations and approvals for the divorced to reenter the temple. To all such matters, as well many others, the President of the Church gives his personal attention.

The President is assisted by at least two counselors, and together they form the First Presidency. They meet regularly with the Council of the Twelve on Thursday in the Salt Lake Temple, where decisions are made concerning the affairs of the Church. The President acts in concert with his two counselors and the Council of the Twelve; his decisions are mostly quorum decisions. (See D&C 90:12-18; 107:22, 79.) President Spencer W. Kimball has described this meeting:

> When in a Thursday temple meeting, after prayer and fasting, important decisions are made, new missions and new stakes are created, new patterns and policies initiated, the news is taken for granted and possibly thought of as mere human calculations. But to those who sit in the intimate circles and hear the prayers of the prophet and the testimony of the man of God; to those who see the astuteness of his deliberations and the sagacity of his decisions and pronouncements, to them he is verily a prophet. To hear him conclude important new developments with such solemn expressions as "the Lord is pleased"; "that move is right"; "our Heavenly Father has spoken", is to know positively.
>
> . . . The Lord definitely calls prophets today and reveals His secrets to them; as He did yesterday, as He does today and as He will do tomorrow—that is the way it is. (*Instructor*, August 1960, p. 257.)

This spiritual leader commits himself to preaching and teaching the gospel and bears testimony of its truthfulness. He exercises kindness, patience, long-suffering, charity, and love—in short, all the godly virtues prompted by the Spirit of the Lord for the blessing and advancement of all mankind.

He normally has a schedule that requires many speeches. For example, he speaks at general conference, general priesthood meetings, conferences of the Church auxiliaries, and stake conferences, firesides, funerals, youth conferences, missionary meetings, civic, governmental, and patriotic assemblies, and universities, colleges, and schools.

He dedicates chapels, temples, and other Church buildings. He ordains and sets apart various Church officers. He meets with many people in his extensive travels and in his office. He shakes hands, answers questions, gives counsel and advice, and enjoys having dialogue with people. He greets the notables of the world who come to Salt Lake City. He also meets with educators and with civic and government leaders of the city and state. These activities are in addition to his regular duties in directing and regulating the affairs of the Church through regular meetings of the First Presidency, the Council of the Twelve, and others.

From the time of Joseph Smith right up to the present, the role of the President has been basically the same. However, there has been a change of attitude toward the Church and its President by the people of the world. It was difficult during the early years to preside over the Church in the face of mobs, severe persecution, suffering, and with much inadequate means of communication and transportation. Today, however, the President of the Church presides over a worldwide Church organization numbering over three million members. The senseless persecution of the past has largely disappeared. With the spread of the news and communications media, the Church has been able to tell its story more effectively. Thousands of missionaries all over the free world are preaching the gospel. Important also is the increase in modes of travel throughout the earth. Millions of tourists and travelers visit Salt Lake City and Church visitor centers each year. These visitors see for themselves the fruits of the Church and then pass on their findings to their friends.

When the President of the Church gives conference addresses today, millions of people throughout the world may hear and see him by means of radio and television. His messages are translated into several languages and are also printed in Church publications that may be read by hundreds of thousands of Saints and nonmembers throughout the world. The importance of learning the teachings of the Presidents and following their counsel is critical to the eternal salvation of man. Studying the

teachings of the President and other Church leaders gives
the Saints insight as to what the Lord would have them do
at the present time. President Harold B. Lee emphasized
this important idea when he said:

> If you want to know what the Lord has for this people at the
> present time, I would admonish you to get and read the discourses
> that have been delivered at this conference, for what these brethren
> have spoken by the power of the Holy Ghost is the mind of the Lord,
> the will of the Lord, the voice of the Lord, and the power of God unto
> salvation. (*Ensign*, July 1973, p. 74.)

The President has the important responsibility of
keeping the Church members everywhere united in the
gospel of Jesus Christ. He has many other important roles
and duties. President Spencer W. Kimball offers this
insight:

> We have the assurance that we are carrying forward the work
> of the Lord Jesus Christ, who is the head of this church. We are but
> his earthly helpers.
> . . . we have in this church the answer to all questions, for
> the Lord . . . has given us . . . a program that will overcome the evils
> of the day.
> Our message is what it has always been . . . the home, chastity,
> honor, integrity, and all of the virtues that men recognize, but do not
> always follow. (*Church News*, January 5, 1974, pp. 3, 14.)

Joseph Smith, First President (1805–1844)

JOSEPH SMITH, JR.

First President of the Church

Born: December 23, 1805, Sharon, Windsor County, Vermont

Died: June 27, 1844, Carthage, Illinois (age 38)

First Elder of the Church: April 6, 1830, to January 25, 1832 (1 year, 9 months)

President of the Church: January 25, 1832, to June 27, 1844 (12½ years)

Physical Characteristics: Six feet tall, weighed 200-210 pounds, light complexion, light brown hair, athletic build, heavy in shoulders, piercing blue eyes, military carriage, distinguished appearance

Areas of Distinction: Prophet, colonizer, missionary, writer, army general, linguist, poet, athlete, mayor, judge, politician, educator, historian, translator, philosopher, scientist, economist, humanitarian

Family: Son of Joseph and Lucy Mack Smith. Married Emma Hale on January 18, 1827 (she died April 30, 1879); eleven children. He practiced plural marriage. (A complete and accurate list of wives is not available.)

Profile of Joseph Smith

In the year 1820, God the Father and his Son Jesus Christ revealed themselves to a fourteen-year-old boy who recorded:

> . . .I saw a pillar of light exactly over my head, above the brightness of the sun, which descended gradually until it fell upon me.
> . . .When the light rested upon me I saw two Personages, whose brightness and glory defy all description, standing above me in the air. One of them spake unto me, calling me by name and said, pointing to the other—*This is My Beloved Son. Hear Him!* (Joseph Smith 2:16-17.)

Later angelic messengers came with information and instructions and explained the same story, the same gospel, the same church that Jesus had established while he labored in mortality. The purpose of Joseph's life was to bring these truths back to earth. He was the Prophet of the restoration of the church of Jesus Christ.

That first marvelous vision clarified that God the Father and Jesus Christ are personal, separate beings who communicate with mankind, and further, that no creed then in Christendom had the true plan of salvation. (Joseph Smith 2:19.) Other visions acquainted Joseph with numerous immortal beings. In addition to God the Father and his Son Jesus Christ, he received visitations from Moroni, Peter, James, John, John the Baptist, Moses,

Elias, Elijah, and others, who brought all the powers and keys needed for the restoration of Christ's true church.

Joseph Smith's concept and presentation of God's eternal plan for the happiness and salvation of his children may be summed up in this declaration: "to bring to pass the immortality and eternal life of man." (Moses 1:39.)

The man Joseph Smith was a commanding individual with a magnetic personality. Brigham Young once stated: "I feel like shouting hallelujah, all the time, when I think that I ever knew Joseph Smith." Others who knew him personally made similar observations: "One of the most remarkable men of the present, or in fact of any other age." "An extraordinary man." "One of God's noblemen." "I stood face to face with the greatest man on earth." "I never saw a nobler looking or acting man than Joseph Smith." "I have seen him on a white horse wearing the uniform of a general. . . . He was leading a parade of the Legion and looked like a god."

People instinctively liked him, because he instinctively liked people. Some of his qualities included a strong sense of humor, open-mindedness, humility, teachableness, meekness, and willingness to make his will conform to the will of the Lord.

Paul H. Dunn of the First Council of Seventy wrote:

As one looks more deeply into his personality, experiences, and character, one can see a remarkable blend of Christ-like qualities. His peers spoke of his solemnity in sacred moments, yet are much pleased at his prophetic wit, his love of music, poetry, drama, and, very notably, his hearty laughter. They were continually amazed at his versatility in changing pace. He could move from studying the scriptures or any of his four foreign languages to playing ball, wrestling, jumping at a mark, and back again to studying. All people could recognize his easy jovial appearance when he was engaged in activities of fun, but they were quick to note his dislike of anything that was degrading or vulgar.

The Prophet Joseph Smith (right) with his brother
Hyrum, who was martyred with him at Carthage
Jail June 27, 1844

He could reprove betimes with sharpness and always showed forth afterwards an increase of love. "I am determined," he said, "while I lead this church to lead it right."

Joseph Smith was a rugged and free outdoor man. He delighted in physical work and taught that it was a God-given principle to keep our bodies strong. During the building of the Nauvoo Temple, he would often work in the rock quarry. Many people learned of the restoration of the gospel while working at his side in the quarry, in the forest, or the hayfield. (*Improvement Era*, June 1970, p. 70.)

There are no authentic portraits of Joseph Smith, and there is no one living now who saw him. Parley P.

Pratt, who, as a young man, knew the Prophet well, left perhaps the best word picture of the Prophet's person and character.

President Joseph Smith was in person tall and well built, strong and active; of light complexion, light hair, blue eyes, very little beard, and of an expression peculiar to himself, on which the eye naturally rested with interest and was never weary of beholding. His countenance was ever mild, affable, beaming with intelligence and benevolence; mingled with a look of interest and an unconscious smile, or cheerfulness, and entirely free from all restraint or affectation of gravity; and there was something connected with the serene and steady penetrating glance of his eye, as if he would penetrate the deepest abyss of the human heart, gaze into eternity, penetrate the heaven and comprehend all worlds.

He possessed a noble boldness and independence of character; his manner was easy and familiar; his rebuke terrible as the lion; his benevolence unbounded as the ocean; his intelligence universal, and his language abounding in original eloquence peculiar to himself—not polished—not studied—not smoothed and softened by education and refined by art; but flowing forth in its own native simplicity, and profusely abounding in variety of subject and manner. He interested and edified, while, at the same time, he amused and entertained his audience; and none listened to him who were ever weary with his discourse. I have even known him to retain a congregation of willing and anxious listeners for many hours together, in the midst of cold or sunshine, rain or wind, while they were laughing at one moment and weeping the next. Even his most bitter enemies were generally overcome, if he could once get their ears. . . .

In short, in him the character of a Daniel and a Cyrus were wonderfully blended. The gifts, wisdom and devotion of a Daniel were united with the boldness, courage, temperance, perseverance and generosity of a Cyrus. And had he been spared a martyr's fate till mature manhood and age, he was certainly endowed with powers and ability to have revolutionized the world in many respects, and to have transmitted to posterity a name associated with more brilliant and glorious acts than has yet fallen to the lot of mortal. (*The Historical Record*, VII, January 1888, pp. 575-76.)

Joseph Smith lived on a farm away from the cultural influences of a great city. He never went to high school or college; he was without a formal education in the ordinary sense of the word. He was taught by heavenly messengers, and his mind, uncluttered by the false notions of the day, made him easy to teach, ready and eager to learn.

Teachable but also a teacher, he freely shared what he learned. Wilford Woodruff, fourth President of the Church, made this statement: "He seemed a fountain of knowledge from whose mouth streams of eternal wisdom flowed. As he stood before the people, he showed clearly that the authority of God was upon him." (Cowley, *Wilford Woodruff*, p. 68.)

Further, he was a man of action. He had the kind of faith that motivates and sustains appropriate action. He acted decisively without concern for the consequences to himself.

It is difficult to study the life of this religious leader without being impressed with the fact that he possessed a quality of true greatness, the source of which is found in a desire to know God's will and to follow it.

Carthage Jail
Where Joseph and Hyrum
Smith were Martyred
June 27, 1844

Carthage Jail, where the Prophet Joseph Smith and his brother Hyrum were martyred

And where did it lead him? Bold in his challenge to the religious world, Joseph was fearless in rejecting the existing religious creeds as unauthoritative, and he declared many of their doctrines absolutely false. He stood against the world without flinching, withstood terrible persecution, and endured great suffering. He was driven from four states, shared in the loss of six children at birth, was tarred and feathered, was poisoned, spent months in vile prisons, and appeared more than forty times in court on false charges. Finally, he was shot to death at the age of thirty-eight by a mob at Carthage Jail, Hancock County, Illinois, on June 27, 1844.

But think of all his callings and accomplishments: First, he was God's prophet, seer, and revelator, receiver of the powers and keys to reestablish the true church of Christ. He was first president of The Church of Jesus Christ of Latter-day Saints, a teacher of gospel principles, a translator, giving to the world books of scripture—both ancient and modern. He built temples and cities.

Great men were his friends. Abraham Lincoln, Governor Thomas Ford, and Senator Stephen Douglas were men who respected him and visited with him frequently at the Mansion House in Nauvoo.

He was a candidate for the presidency of the United States; he was lieutenant general of the Nauvoo Legion; he was mayor and justice of Nauvoo. He was a poet, a linguist, an orator, an athlete, a leader of men—all of these during his short life of thirty-eight years. Brigham Young was right when he said that Joseph Smith lived one thousand years in thirty-eight.

The *New York Times*, one of the great papers of the world, said of Joseph Smith on September 4, 1843:

This Joe Smith must be set down as an extraordinary character—a prophet-hero, as Carlyle might call him. He is one of the great men of this age, and in future history he will be ranked with those who, in one way or another, have stamped their impress strongly upon society.

After the Prophet's death, the Lord caused to have written and included as scripture the following: "Joseph Smith, the Prophet and Seer of the Lord, has done more, save Jesus only, for the salvation of men in this world, than any other man that ever lived in it. . . ." (D&C 135:3.)

The Prophet's life and the Church, which he restored under the direction of God, stand as evidence that Jesus the Christ is the Son of God: ". . .this is the testimony, last of all, which we give of him: That he lives!" (D&C 76:22.)

Interesting Facts and Contributions
of Joseph Smith

1. "**New Scripture.** In addition to his corrections on the Bible, the Prophet translated records and papyri bringing forth the Book of Mormon and Writings of Abraham. His ever-inquiring mind caused him to appeal in prayer over many problems of doctrine, ordinances, and organization. The Book of Moses and Doctrine and Covenants contain revelations in answer to prayers."

2. "**Prophecy.** The Civil War, Stephen Douglas, Rocky Mountains, and his own martyrdom prophecies are but a few of the many which came from Joseph Smith."

3. "**Doctrine.** The true knowledge of the Godhead and their relationship to mankind was revealed. Life's purposes and its relationship to future estates were made clear. Also, the following: care of the body, information on the pre-mortal existence, Divine authority, salvation for the dead, eternal family relationships, degrees of glory, the place of little children, the fall and atonement, etc."

4. "**Ordinances.** Blessing of infants, baptism, confirmation, ordination to the priesthood, ordinances for the living and dead in temples, marriage, sacrament of the Lord's Supper, anointing the sick, dedication of lands, properties, chapels, temples, consecrating of oil for administrations to the sick, and etc., were all restored through the Prophet Joseph Smith's being commissioned by Jesus Christ."

5. "**Authority.** Until Joseph and Oliver were visited by John the Baptist, the priesthood—whether Aaronic or

Melchizedek—did not exist on this mortal earth. The priesthood had been taken away after the death of the early Christians in the first and second centuries.

"Peter, James, John, Elias, Moses, and Elijah all gave certain powers or rights to the Prophet Joseph Smith. Therefore, through the visitation of these authorized beings, Joseph Smith was fully empowered to organize the Church and lead its people under the direction of Jesus Christ." (Brooks, *LDS Encyclopedia*, pp. 464-65.)

6. Thousands of converts and their descendants testify that he was and is a prophet of God. He was also accepted as a prophet by his own family.

7. He had the ability to lead and gather people of all ages, languages, customs, races, and attitudes and move them from state to state.

8. He organized The Church of Jesus Christ of Latter-day Saints. He was a capable leader who cared for both the spiritual and the temporal needs of his people.

9. Forty-eight lawsuits were filed against him. From each he was completely acquitted except one (much of this came over the fourteen years after the Church was organized).

10. He was greatly persecuted and the only Church President to be martyred.

11. His teachings and speeches motivated men and women of all walks of life to live the good life.

12. In 1834 he led a group of 205 Mormon soldiers on a 1,000-mile march from Kirtland, Ohio, to Independence, Missouri. This group, known as Zion's Camp, sought the reestablishment of the Saints in their homes from which they had been driven by mobs. At a later time, he became a general in the Illinois state militia and commander of the Nauvoo Legion.

13. So great was his mission that holy prophets spoke of him by name thousands of years before his mortal birth.

14. He never had a high school or college education. He pioneered an adult education program. He established the School of the Prophets, America's first school for adults. He helped to establish the University of Nauvoo. He studied foreign languages, law, and many other subjects.

15. He wrote a comprehensive history of the Church that numbers over three thousand pages in printed form. He was the editor of the Church's periodical, *Times and Seasons*, for about a year.

16. He was a builder of Zion. His plans were used as the basis for the laying out of Nauvoo, "The city beautiful." His plan for the proposed City of Zion also served as a model for many of the western cities established by the members of the Church.

17. In 1842 he was mayor of Nauvoo, the largest city in Illinois. In 1844 he announced his candidacy for the presidency of the United States.

18. He established the United Order, a unique plan of living, in various communities in 1831. He devised a special banking system that helped resolve the needs of the Saints in Kirtland in 1836-37. He established farms, stores, and manufacturing enterprises in Nauvoo.

19. He was constantly concerned about the well-being of mankind. He wanted freedom for the slaves and advocated women's rights (Relief Society) and the elimination of social classes.

20. He was a great proselyter.

21. He was a man of great physical strength and participated in many sports activities.

22. He read the New Testament in Hebrew, Greek, Latin, and German.

23. "There is general agreement that he was an extraordinary talented and imaginative man with brilliant organizational abilities. The religion that he founded was essentially eclectic. The 19th Century idea that man

is capable of eternal progress was fundamental to his theology, and he elaborated it by teaching that there were progressive stages of salvation. A man of audacity and courage, he proved himself to be one of the most successful American religious leaders." (*Colliers Encyclopedia*, vol. 21 [1966], p. 94.)

24. In March, 1842, at the request of John Wentworth, editor and proprietor of the *Chicago Democrat*, Joseph Smith wrote a letter of nearly six pages in which he told of the rise, progress, persecution, and faith of the Church members. Near the end of his letter he stated in clear, simple, but comprehensive terms the religious creed that has since become known as the Articles of Faith of The Church of Jesus Christ of Latter-day Saints. These statements illustrate the divine inspiration that he possessed.

Significant Dates and Events in Lifetime of
Joseph Smith*

Church Membership, 1830: 12   1844: 35,000 (est.)

1844—Stakes: 9   Missions: 3   Temples: 2

U.S. Population, 1844: 19 million (est.)

World Population, 1844: 1.1 billion (est.)

U.S. Presidents, 1820-44: James Monroe, John Quincy Adams, Andrew Jackson, Martin Van Buren, William Henry Harrison, John Tyler

1805   Joseph was born December 23 at Sharon, Windsor County, Vermont.

1811   Joseph and his brothers and sisters were stricken with typhus fever; had an operation due to infection in bones; lame for few years.

1814   The Smith family moved to Palmyra, New York, for about four years, after which Manchester became their home.

1819-20 Manchester was scene of great religious excitement, with Methodists, Baptists, and Presbyterians contending for adherents. Joseph started seeking to know which of these churches he should join.

1820   Joseph received vision of the Father and the Son in grove of trees on Smith farm in the spring, at age 15.

Slavery in U.S. became stronger, more profitable; Missouri Compromise settled slavery problem in new states for next 30 years. Nathaniel Brown Palmer, American, discovered the Antarctic continent.

---

*Items set in italics indicate United States and world events during these years.

1820–44   *The following became states: Maine, Arkansas, Missouri, Michigan.*

1821   *First public high school in U.S. established in Boston. Central American republics separated from Spain.*

1822   *Santa Fe Trail opened Southwest to trade. Brazil became independent of Portugal. Greece became independent of Ottoman Empire.*

1823   Joseph was visited by the Angel Moroni (September 21, 22); continued to receive instructions for next four years.

Monroe Doctrine guaranteed independence of the Americas against any European interference.

1824   *Mexico became a republic. Jim Bridger explored the Great Salt Lake. Latin American wars of independence ended.*

1825   In Harmony, Pennsylvania, Joseph was employed in search of old Spanish mines, resided at home of Isaac Hale, met Emma Hale.

Erie Canal was completed, speeding settlement of Midwest.

1826   *Jedediah S. Smith, first explorer of the Great Basin, led a party of 17 men to the Rocky Mountains and California.*

1826–28   *Russia invaded Persia and won land north of the Arak River, which now forms boundary between Iran and Russia.*

1827   Joseph married Emma Hale on January 18, age 22; received the plates from the Angel Moroni, September; commenced to translate Book of Mormon at Harmony, Pennsylvania, December.

1828   Martin Harris took a copy of Book of Mormon characters to Dr. Charles Anthon in New York City, February. Joseph translated 116 pages of Book of Mormon manuscript with assistance of Martin Harris, primarily between April 12 and June 14; Martin lost 116 pages of the book on June 14.

First passenger railroad in America, Baltimore & Ohio Railroad, was established.

1829   John the Baptist restored the Priesthood of Aaron (Aaronic Priesthood) on banks of Susquehanna River between Harmony and Colesville (now Ninevah), New York, May 15; Melchizedek Priesthood was restored a month later by Peter, James, and John. Joseph was baptized by Oliver

Cowdery on May 15. Joseph finished translation of Book of Mormon, June. Three Witnesses received revelations of Book of Mormon at Fayette, New York, and saw plates (June); Eight Witnesses were shown plates by Joseph shortly after Three Witnesses had seen them, at Smith home at Palmyra.

1830   First edition of Book of Mormon was printed by E. B. Grandin, March 30. Church was organized at Peter Whitmer's home at Fayette, April 6. Oliver Cowdery preached first public discourse for Church at meeting in Fayette, April 11. First missionaries were sent out. First chapter of Book of Moses (Pearl of Great Price) was revealed to Joseph at Harmony, June. First Lamanite mission was opened in Missouri by Oliver Cowdery and companions, September.

1831   Joseph moved to Kirtland, Ohio, January. Revelation was given on law of consecration. First bishop was ordained, February. Church headquarters was moved to Kirtland. First high priests were ordained, June. Zion was founded at Independence, Missouri, and Joseph dedicated temple site, August. Portion of Prophecy of Enoch, now part of Book of Moses in Pearl of Great Price, was revealed at Fayette. First conference in Jackson County was held, August 4. Joseph worked on revising and clarifying Bible.

Invention of reaping machine brought sweeping changes in agriculture.

1832   Joseph was sustained as President of Church at conference at Amherst, Lorain County, Ohio, January 25. Vision of the glories (D&C 76) was received at Hiram, Ohio. Joseph was mobbed, tarred, feathered, and beaten after being dragged from bed at night at Hiram, Ohio, March 24-25. Emma lost twin babies at birth; Joseph and Emma adopted two children (twins). Joseph received revelation known as "Revelation and Prophecy on War," concerning Civil War, December 25.

1833   Book of Commandments, in process of printing, was destroyed by a mob. Word of Wisdom was given to the Church, February. Missionary work was begun in Canada. First Presidency was organized March 18, with Joseph as President, Sidney Rigdon and Frederick G. Williams as counselors; Joseph Smith, Sr., was ordained as Patriarch on December 18. Joseph completed first translation and review of New Testament. School of Prophets was started in Kirtland. Joseph served mission to Canada, October 5–November 4. Saints were driven from Jackson County, Missouri, by mob. Saints were commanded to build Kirtland Temple, May 6.

1834   High council and first stake were organized in Kirtland, February 17. Joseph organized Zion's Camp to help Saints in Missouri, February 26. Exiled Saints crossed Missouri River to Clay County at gun point. Zion's Camp marched from Kirtland to Missouri, May 8. Joseph served mission to eastern states with Hyrum Smith, Sidney Rigdon, Oliver Cowdery.

1835   Council of the Twelve (February 14) and First Quorum of the Seventy (February 28) were organized. Joseph began practice of plural marriage, February 28. Michael A. Chandler exhibited mummies with rolls of papyrus covered by hieroglyphics in Kirtland, July; Joseph commenced to translate the records (Book of Abraham) July 3. Doctrine and Covenants was approved by general assembly of the Church, August.

1836   Kirtland Temple was dedicated by Joseph March 27. Savior appeared to Joseph and Oliver Cowdery in Kirtland Temple; Moses, Elias, and Elijah also appeared.

1837   Kirtland Safety Society Bank failed. British Mission, first permanent mission, was opened July 20 and missionaries were sent to England. Period of apostasy for the Church.

Great depression paralyzed the U.S. economy.

1838   Adam-Ondi-Ahman, near Grand River, Missouri, was named. Mob violence against the Saints in Missouri, by order of governor. Joseph and five companions were imprisoned in Liberty Jail, Clay County, Missouri, for six months (escaped April 15, 1839). Haun's Mill Massacre, with 18 murdered, including many children. The Church of Jesus Christ of Latter-day Saints was officially named.

1838-45   *John C. Fremont carried on extensive western exploration in North America.*

1839   Armed militia mobs, carrying out the governor's orders, expelled Mormons from Missouri. Joseph Smith and other leaders appealed to President Van Buren for redress from further Missouri persecutions. Joseph preached in Philadelphia and Washington before returning to Nauvoo in February 1839. Saints settled in Nauvoo. Wards headed by bishops were first created in Nauvoo October 6.

First photograph made in the United States was taken by Samuel F. B. Morse.

1840   First immigrants arrived from England. Missionary work was started in Australia. *Millennial Star,* monthly periodical, was started in England. Joseph Smith, Sr., died, September 14. Orson Hyde was sent to Palestine to dedicate land for return of the Jews, April 15. Baptisms for the dead were inaugurated, August.

1841   Saints were commanded to build temple at Nauvoo. Joseph gave instructions on subject of baptism for the dead. Work began on the Nauvoo Temple, April 6. Joseph gave instruction to Saints at October conference on baptism for the dead. Nauvoo Temple baptismal font was dedicated and first baptisms were performed, November. Joseph announced plans for immigration agency to be established for Church immigrants in England, December 24.

David Livingstone began exploring Africa. The Oregon Trail opened the way for settlement of the Pacific Northwest.

1842   Relief Society was organized, March 17. Book of Abraham was published. Joseph wrote Wentworth letter (of which the Articles of Faith formed the conclusion) for John Wentworth, editor of the *Chicago Democrat.* Endowment ceremonies were inaugurated in private office of Joseph's store, May 4. Joseph became mayor of Nauvoo, May 19. Joseph prophesied Saints would move to Rocky Mountains, August 6. Joseph was arrested as accessory in attempt on Governor Boggs' life by extradition proceedings, but was later released, August 8; submitted to voluntary arrest and was taken to Springfield, Illinois, for trial; later released.

1843   Brief period of peace in Nauvoo. Joseph gave revelation for eternal marriage and plurality of wives, July 12. Conspiracy against Joseph by some Church members. Joseph stated before Nauvoo City Council, "I am exposed to far greater danger from traitors among ourselves than from enemies without."

1844   Joseph delivered King Follett address at April conference, a revelation of eternal truths concerning glories of immortality; became presidential candidate on independent ticket; was arrested for destruction of the *Expositor* and tried before municipal court in Nauvoo, acquitted, June 12; delivered last sermon, June 18. Joseph left Nauvoo with Hyrum Smith and Willard Richards, crossed Mississippi River, intending to journey to the West; returned to Nauvoo June 23. Nauvoo Legion was ordered to surrender arms, June 24. Joseph and Hyrum were arrested and charged with treason; were accompanied by Willard Richards and John Taylor to Carthage Jail, June 25; were granted interview with Governor Ford, who pledged full protection and left next day with troops for Nauvoo. Joseph and Hyrum were killed by mob at Carthage Jail about 5:15 p.m., June 27. The Prophet was 38 years of age at the time of his death.

1830-47   *Significant inventions: reaper (U.S.), Portland cement (England), revolver (U.S.), ether (U.S.), steel plow (U.S.), photography (U.S.), telegraph (U.S.), safety match (Sweden), gas refrigeration (U.S.), vulcanized rubber (U.S.), dynamo (England), electroysis (England), bicycle (Scotland), steam hammer (Scotland), chloroform (U.S.), ice-making machine (U.S.), platform scales (U.S.), typewriter (U.S.), Braille printing (France), stereoscope (England), calotype photography (England), daguerreotype photography (France), blueprint (England).*

The First Presidency
During Joseph Smith's Administration

First Counselor	President	Second Counselor
*Sidney Rigdon 1833-44	**Joseph Smith 1830-44	*Frederick G. Williams 1833-37
		**Hyrum Smith 1837-41
	Assistant President	
	**Oliver Cowdery 1834-37	*William Law 1841-44
	**Hyrum Smith 1841-44	

Additional Counselors	Assistant Counselors
*John Cook Bennett 1841-42	**Oliver Cowdery 1837-38
Amasa M. Lyman (1842) 1843-44	*Joseph Smith, Sr. 1837-40
	**Hyrum Smith Sept.-Nov. 1837
	*John Smith 1837-44

Excommunicated

1838—Oliver Cowdery
(rebaptized 1848)

1839—Frederick G. Williams
(restored to fellowship,
1840)

1842—John Cook Bennett

1844—Sidney Rigdon

1844—William Law

---

*Never ordained an apostle.
**An apostle but not a member of the Council of the Twelve.
Note: Joseph Smith and Oliver Cowdery were ordained apostles in 1829 by
Peter, James and John. See D&C 20:2; 27:12; also see Durham and Heath, *Succession in the Church*, pp. 2-3 and 12-29.

Council of the Twelve (all ordained in 1835)

Thomas B. Marsh   Parley P. Pratt
David W. Patten   Luke S. Johnson
Brigham Young   William B. Smith
Heber C. Kimball   Orson Pratt
Orson Hyde   John F. Boynton
William E. McLellan   Lyman E. Johnson

Excommunicated:

1837—John F. Boynton
1838—William E. McLellan
1838—Luke S. Johnson (rebaptized 1846)
1838—Lyman E. Johnson
1839—Thomas B. Marsh (rebaptized 1857)
1839—Orson Hyde (disfellowshipped
          in May; restored in June)
1842—Orson Pratt (rebaptized
          in 1843)

Died

1838—David W. Patten

Added

John E. Page (1838)   Willard Richards (1840)
John Taylor (1838)   Lyman Wight (1841)
Wilford Woodruff (1839)   Amasa M. Lyman (1842)
George A. Smith (1839)

Council of the Twelve—1844

Brigham Young (1835)   John E. Page (1838)
Heber C. Kimball (1835)   John Taylor (1838)
Orson Hyde (1835)   Wilford Woodruff (1839)
Parley P. Pratt (1835)   George A. Smith (1839)
William B. Smith (1835)   Willard Richards (1840)
Orson Pratt (1835)   Lyman Wight (1841)

Note: Dates in parentheses indicate date ordained member of the Council of the Twelve.

Testimony of Joseph Smith

The full text of Joseph Smith's own story appears in tract form and is also included in the Pearl of Great Price. The following are excerpts from these references.

Manchester, New York, in the early 1800s, was the scene of many religious revivals. Joseph Smith's family were God-fearing and Bible-reading people. As a result of these influences, Joseph developed early in his life a strong desire to know which church to join. He records the following:

> While I was laboring under the extreme difficulties caused by the contests of these parties of religionists, I was one day reading the Epistle of James, first chapter and fifth verse, which reads: *If any of you lack wisdom, let him ask of God, that giveth to all men liberally, and upbraideth not; and it shall be given him.*
>
> Never did any passage of scripture come with more power to the heart of man that this did at this time to mine. It seemed to enter with great force into every feeling of my heart. I reflected on it again and again, knowing that if any person needed wisdom from God, I did; for how to act I did not know, and unless I could get more wisdom than I then had, I would never know; for the teachers of religion of the different sects understood the same passages of scripture so differently as to destroy all confidence in settling the question by an appeal to the Bible.
>
> At length I came to the conclusion that I must either remain in darkness and confusion, or else I must do as James directs, that is, ask of God. I at length came to the determination to "ask of God," concluding that if he gave wisdom to them that lacked wisdom, and would give liberally, and not upbraid, I might venture.
>
> So, in accordance with this, my determination to ask of God, I retired to the woods to make the attempt. It was on the morning of a beautiful, clear day, early in the spring of eighteen hundred and twenty. It was the first time in my life that I had made such

an attempt, for amidst all my anxieties I had never as yet made the attempt to pray vocally.

After I had retired to the place where I had previously designed to go, having looked around me, and finding myself alone, I kneeled down and began to offer up the desires of my heart to God. I had scarcely done so, when immediately I was seized upon by some power which entirely overcame me, and had such an astonishing influence over me as to bind my tongue so that I could not speak. Thick darkness gathered around me, and it seemed to me for a time as if I were doomed to sudden destruction.

But, exerting all my powers to call upon God to deliver me out of the power of this enemy which had seized upon me, and at the very moment when I was ready to sink into despair and abandon myself to destruction—not to an imaginary ruin, but to the power of some actual being from the unseen world, who had such marvelous power as I had never before felt in any being—just at this moment of great alarm, I saw a pillar of light exactly over my head, above the brightness of the sun, which descended gradually until it fell upon me.

It no sooner appeared that I found myself delivered from the enemy which held me bound. When the light rested upon me I saw two Personages, whose brightness and glory defy all description, standing above me in the air. One of them spake unto me, calling me by name, and said, pointing to the other—*This is My Beloved Son. Hear Him!*

My object in going to inquire of the Lord was to know which of all the sects was right, that I might know which to join. No sooner, therefore, did I get possession of myself, so as to be able to speak, than I asked the Personages who stood above me in the light, which of all the sects was right—and which I should join.

I was answered that I must join none of them, for they were all wrong; and the Personage who addressed me said that all their creeds were an abomination in his sight; that those professors were all corrupt; that "they draw near to me with their lips, but their hearts are far from me, they teach for doctrines the commandments of men, having a form of godliness, but they deny the power thereof."

He again forbade me to join with any of them; and many other things did he say unto me, which I cannot write at this time. When I came to myself again, I found myself lying on my back, looking up into heaven. . . .

Joseph learned he had been chosen to be an instrument in God's hands, "to bring about some of his purposes in this glorious dispensation." (*DHC*, vol. 4, p. 537.)

After this marvelous experience, Joseph returned to his home and told his mother and others about the manifestation. His family accepted his testimony; they knew it to be true. Others, however, rejected his story and harassed and persecuted him.

Three and a half years later, on September 21, 1823, Joseph prayed to know concerning his status before the Lord. He records the experience he had that night:

. . . on the evening of the above-mentioned twenty-first of September, after I had retired to bed for the night, I betook myself to prayer and supplication to Almighty God for forgiveness of all my sins and follies, and also for a manifestation to me, that I might know of my state and standing before Him; for I had full confidence in obtaining a divine manifestation, as I previously had one.

While I was thus in the act of calling upon God, I discovered a light appearing in my room, which continued to increase until the room was lighter than at noonday, when immediately a personage appeared at my bedside, standing in the air, for his feet did not touch the floor.

He had on a loose robe of most exquisite whiteness. It was a whiteness beyond anything earthly I had ever seen; nor do I believe that any earthly thing could be made to appear so exceedingly white and brilliant. His hands were naked, and his arms also, a little above the wrist; so, also, were his feet naked, as were his legs, a little above the ankles. His head and neck were also bare. I could discover that he had no other clothing on but this robe, as it was open, so that I could see into his bosom.

Not only was his robe exceedingly white, but his whole person was glorious beyond description, and his countenance truly like lightning. The room was exceedingly light, but not so very bright as immediately around his person. When I first looked upon him, I was afraid; but the fear soon left me.

He called me by name, and said unto me that he was a messenger sent from the presence of God to me, and that his name was Moroni; that God had a work for me to do; and that my name should be had for good and evil among all nations, kindreds, and tongues, or that it should be both good and evil spoken of among all people.

He said there was a book deposited, written upon gold plates, giving an account of the former inhabitants of this continent, and the source from whence they sprang. He also said that the fulness of the everlasting Gospel was contained in it, as delivered by the Savior to the ancient inhabitants;

Also, that there were two stones in silver bows—and these stones, fastened to a breastplate, constituted what is called the Urim and Thummim—deposited with the plates; and the possession and use of these stones were what constituted "seers" in ancient or former times; and that God had prepared them for the purpose of translating the book.

Moroni appeared to Joseph three times during the night and then again the next day. He met the boy at the Hill Cumorah but would not let him have the plates. Joseph was instructed to go to the same hill each year on September 22 for three years, and he did as he was instructed. Then on September 22, 1827, the time arrived for the Angel Moroni to deliver up the plates for translation. Joseph records the following:

At length the time arrived for obtaining the plates, the Urim and Thummim, and the breastplate. On the twenty-second day of September, one thousand eight hundred and twenty-seven, having gone as usual at the end of another year to the place where they were deposited, the same heavenly messenger delivered them up to me with this charge: that I should be responsible for them; that if I should let them go carelessly, or through any neglect of mine, I should be cut off; but that if I would use all of my endeavors to preserve them, until he, the messenger, should call for them, they should be protected.

Joseph Smith bore constant and consistent testimony of the restoration and the gospel of a living Redeemer. His testimony, along with that of Sidney Rigdon, is recorded in one of the most powerful sections of the Doctrine and Covenants (76:22-24).

And now, after the many testimonies which have been given of him, this is the testimony, last of all, which we give of him: That he lives!

For we saw him, even on the right hand of God; and we heard the voice bearing record that he is the Only Begotten of the Father—

That by him, and through him, and of him, the worlds are and were created, and the inhabitants thereof are begotten sons and daughters unto God.

Personal Experience of Joseph Smith

Across the river and past the long, narrow island extending up and down the stream, was a sort of town, called Montrose. It consisted mostly of log cabins in an abandoned barracks, which had once been used by Uncle Sam's soldiers while guarding the frontiers of the rapidly growing nation.

In one of these cabins were two families—Brigham Young's and Orson Pratt's. A few doors away, in another cabin, lived Wilford Woodruff, by this time an apostle, who tells the all but incredible tale.

On this twenty-second day of July there came across the river to Montrose, in the ferry-boat, a group of five men. They were Joseph Smith, Parley P. Pratt, Sidney Rigdon, Hyrum Smith, and Heber C. Kimball. Silently they walked to where Young lived. He was in bed, sick of a fever, and had been for some days. The Prophet touched him, spoke to him, and the sick man rose, dressed, and joined the group. Passing by Woodruff's door, Joseph called out to him, "Brother Wilford, follow me." This "Brother Wilford" was glad to do.

Without speaking, the seven men crossed the quadrangle and came to the home of one, Elijah Fordham. Fordham was on what every one believed his death-bed. He was no longer aware of his surroundings. He had been dying for an hour. Already the death glaze was in his eyes. The Prophet went to the bed. One hand holding his hat, he took the sick man's hand with the other. He said:

"Brother Fordham, do you know me?"

There was no answer.

"Brother Elijah," Joseph said again, "don't you know who I am?"

Something began to play on the dying man's features. It was as if he were coming out of a sound sleep. Very feebly he answered, "Yes."

"Have you faith to be healed?"

"I'm afraid it is too late"—very faintly; "if you had come sooner, Brother Joseph, I think I might have been healed."

"Do you believe that Jesus is the Christ?"

"I do, Brother Joseph, I do."

Thereupon the Prophet, standing erect, his face luminously pale, said in a very loud voice: "Elijah, in the name of Jesus of Nazareth, I command you to arise and be made whole!"

In an instant Elijah Fordham leaped from his bed like a man rising from the grave. A healthy color was in his face, and life in every movement. His feet had been done up in poultices of meal. These he kicked off vigorously, ate a bowl of bread and milk, and went out into the street with the visitors to take part in the healing of others.

Before coming across the river to Montrose, the Prophet had healed all those who were sick on the east side of the stream—first those in his own house and dooryard, then those on the river bank. And now he did the same thing for those on the west side who were fever-stricken.

Woodruff says that, while they were waiting for the ferryboat to take them back to Commerce, a stranger came up to the Prophet and begged him to come to his home and heal his sick babies. The man had heard of the extraordinary things that had happened.

Joseph hesitated a moment, then he said to Wilford: "You go with the man. Take this handkerchief and wipe the faces of the children, as you administer to them, and they will be healed."

Woodruff says that he did as directed—with the desired result. The handkerchief, a red silk, is still in the Woodruff family treasure chest.

The twenty-second day of July, 1839, therefore, has come down in Mormon history as "a day of God's power"—and, incidentally, of Joseph Smith's. (Evans, *Joseph Smith, an American Prophet*, pp. 147-49.)

Quotations from Joseph Smith

AMERICA

The whole of America is Zion itself from north to south, and is described by the Prophets, who declare that it is the Zion where the mountain of the Lord should be.

BAPTISM

Baptism is a sign to God, to angels, and to heaven that we do the will of God, and there is no other way beneath the heavens whereby God hath ordained for man to come to Him to be saved, and enter into the kingdom of God, except faith in Jesus Christ, repentance, and baptism for the remission of sins, and any other course is in vain; then you have the promise of the gift of the Holy Ghost.

BIBLE

In the Bible a rule of conduct is laid down for [man]; in the Old and New Testaments the law by which he is to be governed, may be found. If he violates that law, he is to be punished for the deeds done in the body.

BOOK OF MORMON

These records were engraven on plates which had the appearance of gold, each plate was six inches wide and eight inches long, and not quite so thick as common tin. They were filled with engravings, in Egyptian characters, and bound together in a volume as the leaves of a book, with three rings running through the whole. The volume was something near six inches in thickness, a part of which was sealed. The characters on the unsealed part were small, and beautifully engraved. The whole book exhibited many marks of antiquity in its construction, and much skill in the art of engraving. With the records was found a curious instrument, which the ancients called "Urim and Thummim," which consisted of two transparent stones set in the rim of a bow fastened to a breast plate. Through the medium of the Urim and Thummim I translated the record by the gift and power of God.

CHARACTER

No man is safe unless he is master of himself, and there is no tyrant so merciless or more to be dreaded than an uncontrollable appetite or passion.

CONSTITUTION

The Constitution of the United States is a glorious standard; it is founded in the wisdom of God. It is a heavenly banner; it is to all those who are privileged with the sweets of liberty, like the cooling shades and refreshing waters of a great rock in a thirsty and weary land. It is like a great tree under whose branches men from every clime can be shielded from the burning rays of the sun.

CREATION

You ask the learned doctors why they say the world was made out of nothing, and they will answer, "Doesn't the Bible say He *created* the world? And they infer, from the word create, that it must have been made out of nothing. Now, the word create came from the word *baurau*, which does not mean to create out of nothing; it means to organize; the same as a man would organize materials and build a ship. Hence we infer that God had materials to organize the world out of chaos—chaotic matter, which is element, and in which dwells all the glory. Element had an existence from the time He had. The pure principles of element are principles which can never be destroyed; they may be organized and re-organized, but not destroyed. They had no beginning and can have no end.

DEATH

The Lord takes many away, even in infancy, that they may escape the envy of man, and the sorrows and evils of this present world; they were too pure, too lovely, to live on earth; therefore, if rightly considered, instead of mourning we have reason to rejoice as they are delivered from evil, and we shall soon have them again.

FALL OF MAN

I believe that a man is a moral, responsible, free agent; that although it was foreordained he should fall, and be redeemed, yet after the redemption it was not foreordained that he should again sin.

FAMILY

Wives, submit yourselves unto your own husbands, as it is fit in the Lord. Husbands, love your wives, and be not bitter against them. Children, obey your parents in all things, for this is well pleasing unto the Lord. Fathers, provoke not your children to anger, lest they be discouraged.

FATHER
To be a successful father or mother is greater than to be a successful general or a successful statesman.

FRIENDSHIP
Friendship is one of the grand fundamental principles of "Mormonism"; [it is designed] to revolutionize and civilize the world, and cause wars and contentions to cease and men to become friends and brothers.

GENEALOGY
The greatest responsibility in the world that God has laid upon us is to seek after our dead. It is one of the greatest and most important subjects that God has revealed. He should send Elijah to seal the children to the fathers, and the fathers to the children. . . . without us, they could not be made perfect, nor we without them, the fathers without the children, nor the children without the fathers.

GODHEAD
God himself was once as we are now, and is an exalted man, and sits enthroned in yonder heavens! . . . I am going to tell you how God came to be God. We have imagined and supposed that God was God from all eternity. I will refute that idea, and take away the veil, so that you may see. . . . It is the first principle of the gospel to know for a certainty the character of God, and to know that we may converse with Him as one man converses with another, and that He was once a man like us; yea, that God himself, the Father of us all, dwelt on an earth, the same as Jesus Christ Himself did; and I will show it from the Bible. . . .

Here, then, is eternal life—to know the only wise and true God; and you have got to learn how to be gods yourselves, and to be kings and priests to God, the same as all gods have done before you, namely, by going from one small degree to another, and from a small capacity to a great one; from grace to grace, from exaltation to exaltation, until you attain to the resurrection of the dead, and are able to dwell in everlasting burnings, and to sit in glory, as do those who sit enthroned in everlasting power. . . . [Such persons are] heirs of God and joint heirs with Jesus Christ. What is it? To inherit the same power, the same glory and the same exaltation, until you arrive at the station of a god, and ascend the throne of eternal power, the same as those who have gone before.

GOSPEL
We believe in the gift of the Holy Ghost, the power of faith, the

enjoyment of the spiritual gifts according to the will of God, the restoration of the house of Israel, and the final triumph of truth.

HOLY GHOST
The gift of the Holy Ghost by the laying on of hands, cannot be received through the medium of any other principle than the principle of righteousness, for if the proposals are not complied with, it is of no use, but withdraws.

HUMILITY
Let not any man publish his own righteousness, for others can see that for him; sooner let him confess his sins, and then he will be forgiven, and he will bring forth more fruit.

JESUS CHRIST
And now, after the many testimonies which have been given of him, this is the testimony, last of all, which we give of him: That he lives! For we saw him, even on the right hand of God; and we heard the voice bearing record that he is the Only Begotten of the Father— That by him, and through him, and of him, the worlds are and were created, and the inhabitants thereof are begotten sons and daughters unto God. (D&C 76:22-24.)

JUDGMENT
[God] will judge them, "not according to what they have not, but according to what they have," those who have lived without law, will be judged without law, and those who have a law, will be judged by that law.

KNOWLEDGE
A man is saved no faster than he gets knowledge, for if he does not get knowledge, he will be brought into captivity by some evil power in the other world, as evil spirits will have more knowledge, and consequently more power than many men who are on the earth.

LAW
[God] never has—He never will institute an ordinance or give a commandment to His people that is not calculated in its nature to promote that happiness which He has designed.

LEADERSHIP
The way to get along in any important matter is to gather unto yourselves wise men, experienced and aged men, to assist in council in all times of trouble.

POLITICS

There is one thing more I wish to speak about, and that is political economy. It is our duty to concentrate all our influence to make popular that which is sound and good, and unpopular that which is unsound. 'Tis right, politically, for a man who has influence to use it, as well as for a man who has no influence to use his. From henceforth I will maintain all the influence I can get.

PRIESTHOOD

Where there is a priest of God—a minister who has power and authority from God to administer in the ordinances of the gospel and officiate in the priesthood of God, there is the kingdom of God. . . . Where there is no kingdom of God there is no salvation. What constitutes the kingdom of God? Where there is a prophet, a priest, or a righteous man unto whom God gives His oracles, there is the kingdom of God; and where the oracles of God are not, there the kingdom of God is not.

PROGRESSION

If you wish to go where God is, you must be like God, or possess the principles which God possesses, for if we are not drawing towards God in principle, we are going from Him and drawing towards the devil.

RELIGION

But meddle not with any man for his religion: all governments ought to permit every man to enjoy his religion unmolested. No man is authorized to take away life in consequence of difference of religion, which all laws and governments ought to tolerate and protect, right or wrong. Every man has a natural, and, in our country, a constitutional right to be a false prophet, as well as a true prophet.

REPENTANCE

All sins shall be forgiven, except the sin against the Holy Ghost; for Jesus will save all except the sons of perdition. What must a man do to commit the unpardonable sin? He must receive the Holy Ghost, have the heavens opened unto him, and know God, and then sin against him. After a man has sinned against the Holy Ghost, there is no repentance for him.

RESURRECTION

The expectation of seeing my friends in the morning of the resurrection cheers my soul and makes me bear up against the evils of life. It is like their taking a long journey, and on their return we meet them with increased joy.

REVELATION
We believe all that God has revealed, all that He does now reveal, and we believe that He will yet reveal many great and important things pertaining to the Kingdom of God.

SALVATION
Salvation means a man's being placed beyond the power of all his enemies.

TEACHING
I teach them correct principles, and they govern themselves.

TRUST
Whatever God requires is right, no matter what it is, although we may not see the reason thereof until long after the events transpire.

ZION
Men and angels are to be co-workers in bringing to pass this great work, and Zion is to be prepared, even a new Jerusalem, for the elect that are to be gathered from the four quarters of the earth, and to be established an holy city, for the tabernacle of the Lord shall be with them.

Brigham Young, Second President (1801-1877)

BRIGHAM YOUNG

Second President of the Church

Born: June 1, 1801, Whittingham, Windham County, Vermont

Died: August 29, 1877, Salt Lake City, Utah (age 76)

President of the Church: December 27, 1847, to August 29, 1877 (30 years)

Physical Characteristics: Five feet ten inches tall, weighed 188-200 pounds, reddish to gray hair, wore a beard in later years, strong jaw, rugged and stocky physique

Areas of Distinction: Prophet, pioneer, colonizer, statesman, governor, writer, missionary, carpenter, joiner, painter, glazier, humanitarian

Family: Son of John and Abigail Howe Young. Married Mariam Works October 8, 1824 (she died in September 1832). He practiced plural marriage; following is a complete list of his wives:

Mariam Works, Mary Ann Angell, Lucy Ann Decker, Harriet E. C. Cook, Augusta Adams, Clara Decker, Olive Grey Frost, Louissa Beaman, Clarissa Ross, Emily Partridge, Emmeline Free, Margaret Maria Alley, Susan Snivley, Margaret Pierce, Ellen Rockwood, Maria Lawrence, Martha Bowker, Zina Dintha Huntington, Naomah K. J. Carter, Mary Jane Bigelow, Lucy Bigelow, Eliza R. Snow, Eliza Burgess, Hariet Barney, Hariet Amelia Folsom, Mary Van Cott, Ann Eliza Webb. Had 56 children.

*Source: Genealogical Society

Profile of Brigham Young

According to the opinions of many newspaper editors, much of the general public, and even some Mormons, the deaths of Joseph and Hyrum Smith marked the end of Mormonism. But the Lord had raised up another prophet to lead his church and his people. In 1925, a famous American biographer, not a member of the Church, wrote these words about Brigham Young:

> As a statesman, Brigham Young is one of the few Americans deserving of the adjective "great." In a situation of precariousness and importance, he showed himself a man of resourcefulness and sturdiness, and his personality contributed as much as that of any one man of the development of the western half of the United States. (Werner, *Brigham Young*, p. 1.)

Sidney Rigdon, Joseph Smith's former counselor, believed that he was to lead the Church. But as Brigham Young spoke to the people, the mantle of Joseph fell upon him, and it was said that he looked and sounded like the Prophet Joseph. A vote was taken, and the people sustained Brigham Young as their new leader. From that day, for over thirty-three years, he led the Church as prophet, seer, and revelator.

Like many great men in his time of history, Brigham Young was a self-made man. The ninth of eleven children, he cut wood, plowed on his father's farm, and found little time for school or recreation. He later said that he had gone to school no more than eleven and a half days. However, his mother had taught him to read, his father had taught him from the Bible, and he was able to observe and relate events in the world around him.

Brigham Young as governor of Utah Territory, 1850

Brigham Young's original contact with the Church came as a result of newspaper accounts he read of the publication of the Book of Mormon. He later read the book—a copy that had been sold to his brother, Phineas, and shared with others of his family—and received a testimony of its truthfulness. This testimony was reinforced by the testimonies of missionaries who came to his brother's home and again by other missionaries whom he traveled to hear.

Perhaps his greatest testimony came from his first meetings and his continued relationship with the Prophet Joseph Smith, for no man affected his life as deeply as did the Prophet, of whom he became a staunch disciple and for whom he would have given his life. He was Joseph Smith's most trusted lieutenant, filling several effective missions, preaching, baptizing, organizing branches, participating in the march of Zion's Camp and the exodus from Missouri to Illinois, and helping to establish Nauvoo.

Brigham Young learned from Joseph Smith and through prophecy that the destiny of his people lay far to the west, beyond the limits of civilization, in the tops of the Rocky Mountains. By 1845 it had become impossible for the Saints to live in peace among the "gentiles." Ill-equipped as they were for such a long trek, the Mormons turned their backs on their Illinois homes and set out toward the western horizon.

Brigham Young led the first company of the migration. With courage and farsightedness he selected the forbidding Salt Lake Valley as the new home of the Saints. "This is the place," he said upon seeing it in July 1847.

That exodus of 15,000 people in covered wagons across the plains is an epic of human industry and endurance unexcelled in American history. Never before had such a large mass of people braved the hostile wilderness and attempted to cross the prairies and then the Rocky Mountains.

Brigham Young and his people founded a great commonwealth in the tops of the mountains. They worked hard planting crops, building homes and meeting-houses, digging irrigation ditches, laying out farms, starting schools and factories, and beginning construction on temples. Brigham sent people to found towns and cities in many places in Utah, Idaho, Nevada, Arizona, and California, and more than two hundred cities were established in this territory. In the years to come he laid the groundwork for agricultural and industrial development, established peaceful coexistence with the Indians, served as territorial governor, and for thirty-three years directed the spiritual and temporal affairs of the Church, bringing thousands of colonists from all parts of the world to settle in the West. When criticized for not allowing the mining of the region's wealth until irrigation had brought the rich land under cultivation, he replied:

> The time has not come for the Saints to dig gold. It is our duty first to develop the agricultural resources of this country, for there is no country on earth that is more productive than this. ... . If the mines are opened first, we are a thousand miles from any base of supplies, and the people would rush in here in such great numbers that they would breed a famine; and gold would not do us or them any good if there were no provisions in the land. People would starve to death with barrels of gold; they would be willing to give a barrel of gold for a barrel of flour rather than starve to death. . . . This people will stand mobbing, robbing, poverty, and all manner of persecution, and be true. But my greater fear for them is that they cannot stand wealth; and yet they have to be tried with riches, for they will become the richest people on this earth. (Hinckley, *The Faith of Our Pioneer Fathers*, pp. 12-13.)

Brigham Young planned and built Salt Lake City as the "new Zion" of the Saints. This beautiful city is a most effective monument to him. But others of his accomplishments are equally impressive. He was the prime mover in the building of the Union Pacific and the telegraph lines to local points in the state. He founded Deseret University, now the University of Utah; Brigham Young Academy, now Brigham Young University; and Brigham Young College.

During his administration as President of the Church, he made frequent and extensive tours, accompanied by his associates, to the settlements of the Saints. A powerful and persuasive preacher, he knew how to reach his audiences and, with his great doctrinal sermons, to motivate men to do God's will.

A philanthropist to all who would receive his counsel and kind acts, he was "Brother Brigham" to thousands. People had great faith and confidence in what he asked them to do. They believed that if one went against President Young's advice, failure would be the end result.

He had a sound understanding of his environment and human nature. He possessed practical judgment, wisdom, and good common sense. He believed in the strictest industry, that it was false policy to feed men in idleness

President Brigham Young and his 17 sons

if work could be provided for them. Part of his success as a master builder was founded on these traits.

He was the husband of many wives like some of the husbands of the Old Testament, and the father of fifty-six children. He also provided means of support and education for orphans and others.

A friend to the Indians, his policy that "it is better to feed them than to fight them" paved the way for lasting friendships and a peace with these people that might not otherwise have been achieved.

Like his predecessor, Joseph Smith, and indeed nearly all great men, he had bitter enemies. In the face of opposition and challenge, he was calm and serene, and

HEBER C. KIMBALL
1847-1868

BRIGHAM YOUNG
1847-1877

WILLARD RICHARDS
1847-1854

THE FIRST PRESIDENCY
1847-1854

The First Presidency 1847-54: Brigham Young (center) and counselors Heber C. Kimball and Willard Richards

he bore persecution with patience. He was a man of great faith—in God, in the gospel he preached and taught, and in the work with which he was entrusted.

During World War II the United States government

—which had once set an army against him—honored President Young by naming one of the liberty ships in the Navy after him. In 1950, in honor of his work, his statue was placed in the Capitol Building in Washington, D.C. The following summation of that work is made by the English historian and author, Harold J. Sheptstone:

> In the development of those desert wastes, Brigham Young dug canals, imported plants, and animals, built railways and telegraphs; established industries and banks, constructed theatres and universities; and encouraged literature, music, and art. The hand press for the first newspaper and the machinery for the first sugar factory were brought by ox teams, across a thousand miles of desert sand. He planned and erected temples and tabernacles, still used by his people today; they are the wonder of modern architects. He was the founder of a hundred cities and settlements and the Governor of one of the territories of the United States.

President J. Reuben Clark, Jr., made this observation:

> Brigham Young—a pioneer, unmatched in this whole hemisphere; a statesman, with a planned intermountain commonwealth of empire proportions; a friend of the poor, a lover of his fellowman, moving from Missouri the mob-driven, sick and destitute Saints; an unexcelled leader of men, trekking his people a thousand miles over plains, through mountain vastness, into barren valleys, holding them there, intact, while gold seekers eddied about and flowed through and past them; a spiritual giant, loved, honored, obeyed, and trusted as in very deed the prophet, seer, and revelator of his people. (Hinckley, *The Faith of Our Pioneer Fathers*, p. 19.)

Brigham Young died at his home at Salt Lake City on August 29, 1877. His last words were as if the Prophet Joseph Smith had come to take him into the spirit world, for he said: "Joseph! Joseph! Joseph! Joseph!" Brigham Young had finished his work.

Interesting Facts and Contributions

of Brigham Young

1. When Joseph Smith was murdered in 1844, Brigham's leadership kept the scattered and frightened Saints together.

2. He became President at the age of forty-six—the second youngest next to Joseph Smith.

3. His administration, which lasted thirty years, is the longest in Church history.

4. He organized the strategic evacuation of the Saints from Missouri into Hancock County, Illinois, where Nauvoo was established.

5. He directed the colonization of the Mountain West and brought thousands of colonists from all over the world to settle in the West. He directed the settlement of more than 200 villages, towns, and cities. "He was the prime mover in the great development of the West." (*Encyclopedia Americana*, p. 649.)

6. He established the provisional State of Deseret in 1849; it became a territory in 1850.

7. He was appointed first governor of the Territory of Utah and served for eight years.

8. A great missionary himself, he sent missionaries to China, Siam, India, and Chile. His promoting of the European missions resulted in the immigration of thousands to America.

9. He was a leader in education. He established the University of Utah and Brigham Young University.

10. He built roads and canals, and founded numerous social, economic, and cultural institutions, including the Salt Lake Theatre.

11. William H. Seward, Secretary of State under Abraham Lincoln, stated that America had never produced a greater statesman than Brigham Young.

12. The fact that he often faced opposition with calmness and serenity and bore persecution with submission and patience stamped him as a great hero.

13. Temple sites were dedicated under his direction in Salt Lake City, St. George, Logan, and Manti. He lived to see the St. George Temple completed. He also supervised the building of the Salt Lake Tabernacle.

14. He supervised the building of extensive telegraph lines and railroads.

15. Three of his sons—John W., Joseph S., and Brigham, Jr.—were apostles (only Brigham, Jr., was a member of the Council of the Twelve). John W. and Brigham, Jr., also served in the First Presidency. He was the only President to have sons serve in the First Presidency while he was President.

16. A leader in experimental agriculture, he conducted an experimental farm on the outskirts of Salt Lake City to determine which crops would best accommodate themselves to the Utah climate. His work in irrigation set patterns for years to come.

17. He was a friend to the Indians and established a policy toward them that paved the way to peace.

18. An outstanding city planner, he directed the laying out of Salt Lake City in ten-acre blocks. Other cities in the West now also follow this plan.

19. He was called the "Lion of the Lord."

20. He was a genial and benevolent man who had strong family affections, and loved dancing, singing, music, and the theater. He encouraged his people to enjoy themselves and improve themselves while they built up the kingdom: "The people must have amusement as well as religion," he said.

21. He opposed liquor, gambling, and card playing and abhorred waste.

22. He taught the Saints to protect themselves against those who would have destroyed them and to be self-sustaining.

23. In 1940, Twentieth Century-Fox made movie of his life, titled *Brigham Young*. It has been shown frequently on television throughout the nation in recent years.

24. ". . . he brought his religious, social, and economic system, the Mormon Church, to successful operation and preserved its identity against a hostile nation and against the main currents of American social evolution in the nineteenth century. . .the measure of Young's greatness." (*Dictionary of American Biography*, vol. 20, p. 623.)

Significant Dates and Events in Lifetime of

Brigham Young

Church Membership 1844: 35,000 (est.) 1877: 155,000 (est.)
1877—Stakes: 20   Missions: 9   Temples: 1
U.S. Population, 1877: 48 million (est.)
World Population, 1877: 1.3 billion (est.)
U.S. Presidents (1844-77): John Tyler, James K. Polk, Zachary Taylor, Millard Fillmore, Franklin Pierce, James Buchanan, Abraham Lincoln, Andrew Johnson, Ulysses S. Grant

1801	Brigham Young was born in Whittingham, Windham County, Vermont, June 1.
1815	Mother died; Brigham began to earn his own way in life, eventually becoming a carpenter.
1822	Joined the Methodist Church, September.
1824	Married Miriam Works, Aurelius, New York, October 8.
1829	Moved to Mendon, New York, where his father and most of his brothers and sisters lived.
1830	Samuel H. Smith, as a missionary, left copy of Book of Mormon at home of Phineas Young, brother to Brigham; Phineas read book and then Brigham read it.
1832	Baptized into Church by Eleazar Miller, who ordained him an elder, April 14. Brigham converted all his brothers and sisters, his father, and his wife. Brigham arrived at Kirtland with his brother Joseph and Heber C. Kimball; they met with the Prophet Joseph Smith, September.

1832-33   Served mission to Canada and later led many converts to Kirtland.

1833   Moved to Kirtland with his two daughters.

1834   Married Mary Ann Angell, February; joined in march of Zion's Camp.

1834-35   Worked on Kirtland Temple, supervising carpentry work.

1835   Ordained an apostle by Oliver Cowdery, David Whitmer, Martin Harris, February 15; was member of original Quorum of the Twelve (age 33).

1836   Helped complete Kirtland Temple; did missionary work in Eastern States.

1837   Fled to Missouri with Joseph Smith due to persecution.

1838   Became senior member of Council of the Twelve; directed the Church while Joseph Smith was in prison; led exodus from Missouri.

1839-41   Served mission to Great Britain.

1840   Was sustained as President of Council of the Twelve, April 14, at age 38.

1843   Served short mission to Eastern States.

1844   Martyrdom of Prophet Joseph Smith. Brigham spoke to the Saints on August 4 and was transfigured before them; the Saints accepted him as their leader.

1844-77   Missions were opened in Wales, California, France, Scandinavia, Italy, Switzerland, the Sandwich Islands, Australia, India, Malta, Gibraltar, Germany, Europe, South Africa, Siam, the Netherlands, the Eastern and Southern States, and Indian Territory.

The following became states: Florida, Iowa, California, Oregon, West Virginia, Nebraska, Texas, Wisconsin, Minnesota, Kansas, Nevada, Colorado.

1846   Brigham directed exodus of Saints from Nauvoo, February. Nauvoo Temple was dedicated, May 1. Mormon Battalion organized, July 16. Nauvoo Temple captured by mob, September.

1846-47   Brigham formulated policy for treatment of Indians: "It is cheaper to feed the Indians than to fight them."

Donner Party, westbound settlers, suffered disaster in the Sierra Nevadas when caught by snow; 47 survived out of 487.

1846-48   *United States at war with Mexico.*

1847   Brigham received revelation giving instructions for westward exodus of the Saints, January 14. First pioneers left Winter Quarters April 5, arrived in Salt Lake Valley, July 24. Mormons began irrigation of land in Utah. Brigham selected site for Salt Lake Temple, July 28; organized Salt Lake Stake, October 3; was sustained President of Church at general conference on the Missouri River, December 27.

1847-69   85,000 pioneers made trek to Utah.

1848   Seagulls saved crops from destruction by crickets, June 5.

Mexico ceded Utah to U.S. in Treaty of Guadalupe-Hildago. Communist Manifesto was written.

1848-49   *Revolutions swept Europe.*

1849   Church organized provisional State of Deseret and adopted first state constitution. First Sunday School in Rocky Mountains was started, December. Gold rush to California made Utah a national highway to gold fields, established a number of non-Mormon merchants in Salt Lake City.

1849-73   *David Livingstone, African explorer, discovered source of Zambezi River, Victoria Falls, Lake Ngami.*

1850   University of Deseret was established (now University of Utah). Perpetual Immigration Fund was incorporated to assist in gathering of Saints. Congress approved organizing Territory of Utah, and Brigham Young became governor. *Deseret News* was established. Sugar beet industry was started in Utah in 1850s.

Compromise of 1850 postponed war between North and South for ten years.

1851   Pearl of Great Price was published.

Cholera epidemic swept Canada.

1851-52   *Slavery issue, quieted briefly by the Compromise of 1850, flared up with new fury after publication of "Uncle Tom's Cabin."*

1852   Church publicly announced practice of plural marriage, August 28. Branch of Church was organized at Poonah, India, September 12.

South African Republic was established. Direct rail service began between New York City and Chicago. Henri Gifford flew first successful airship. School attendance became compulsory in Massachusetts, first law in country requiring children to go to school.

1853   Brigham Young laid cornerstone for Salt Lake Temple. Walker War with Ute Indians began over slavery among Indians (settled in 1854). First missionaries were sent to Hong Kong, Siam, Hindustan, Spain, South Africa.

Matthew C. Perry opened Japan to world trade.

1854   First of grasshopper plagues endangered crops of Saints.

1855   Utah Militia was ordered for protection from Indians, October 15. Brigham Young ordained his son, John W. Young, an apostle.

1856   First handcart companies arrived in Salt Lake Valley.

1857   Emigrants journeying to California were killed at Mountain Meadows in southern Utah by Indians, and Mormons were blamed. President Buchanan removed Brigham Young from governorship and ordered troops to Utah to suppress alleged rebellion of Mormons, resulting in Utah War. Elder Parley P. Pratt was murdered in Arkansas.

1858-61 U.S. Army in Utah.

1858   Publication of *Deseret News* transferred to Fillmore, Utah, temporarily.

Lincoln-Douglas debates focused U.S. attention on question of slavery. Great Britain took over rule of India.

1859   First issue of newspaper *Mountaineer* was published in Salt Lake City, August. Brigham Young was interviewed by Horace Greeley, editor of *New York Tribune.*

Charles Darwin published theory of evolution.

1860   Last handcart company entered Salt Lake Valley, September 24.

Pony Express operated through Utah (ended when transcontinental telegraph line was completed in 1861).

1860s   Brigham Young took part in construction of Union Pacific Railroad from Omaha, Nebraska, to Ogden, Utah.

1861   Brigham supervised construction of Salt Lake Theatre;

instructed Saints he did not wish them mixed up with secession movement.

Overland telegraph was completed through Salt Lake City. Confederate States organized. Civil War began April 12 when Confederate guns fired on Fort Sumter, South Carolina. First paper money was issued by U.S. Government. French troops invaded Mexico.

1862   Salt Lake Theatre opened in Salt Lake City. Congress rejected new State of Deseret constitution. Washington asked Church for cavalry to protect mail route. Congress passed anti-bigamy law.

1863   Construction started on Salt Lake Tabernacle. Mining in Utah brought in more non-Mormons.

Emancipation Proclamation was issued by President Lincoln, declared slaves to be free in states that were in rebellion.

1864   Brigham Young ordained his sons Joseph and Brigham, Jr., as apostles, February 4.

1864-65   Brigham Young visited settlements of Saints north and south of Salt Lake City.

1865   Church voted to construct telegraph from Salt Lake City. Ute Black Hawk War ended major Indian conflicts in Utah; peace treaty was made with Indians at Spanish Fork, Utah.

Civil War ended. Abraham Lincoln was assassinated. 13th Amendment freed remaining slaves.

1866   *Juvenile Instructor,* official organ of Sunday School, was established. Relief Societies were organized Churchwide.

1867   Salt Lake Tabernacle was completed, with first general conference held there October 6; dedication of Tabernacle October 9. Deseret Telegraph line opened to St. George from Salt Lake City. Union of local Sunday Schools was organized.

Alaska was purchased from Russia by U.S.

1868   ZCMI Department Store was established, with Brigham Young as first president.

14th Amendment made all persons born or naturalized in U.S., including Negroes, citizens. Earthquake in Peru and Ecuador killed 25,000 persons.

1869   Retrenchment Society (later YWMIA) was organized,
            November 28.

            Union Pacific and Central Pacific railroads completed trans-
            continental line with driving of golden spike at Promontory, Utah.
            Suez Canal opened.

1870   *15th Amendment insured citizens right to vote, regardless of race.*
            J. Wilson Shaffer became governor of Utah Territory, most bitter
            and bigoted anti-Mormon governor Utah ever had. Salt Lake
            Tribune *was established.*

1870-71   *Franco-Prussian War resulted in unification of Germany.*

1871   Brigham Young was indicted by grand jury for "lewd and
            lascivious cohabitation," became prisoner in own home
            until case was dismissed by Supreme Court.

            Henry M. Stanley found David Livingstone near Lake Tanganyiku
            in Africa. Chicago fire killed estimated 250 persons, made nearly
            100,000 persons homeless, destroyed over 17,000 buildings.

1873-74   Church attempted to establish United Order.

1874   George Reynolds was indicted for violation of bigamy law
            of 1862 in test case; was later convicted and sentenced but
            appealed to Supreme Court of Utah Territory and had case
            dismissed.

1875   Brigham Young Academy (now University) was established
            in Provo, Utah, and Brigham Young College was established
            in Logan, Utah. Young Men's MIA was organized, June.
            Two hundred Indians were baptized at St. George, Utah.
            Brigham Young met Ulysses S. Grant.

1876   John W. Young was called by his father to serve as first
            counselor in the First Presidency.

            General Custer and troops were massacred by Indians in Battle
            of Little Big Horn.

1877   St. George Temple was dedicated, April 6. Brigham Young
            gave last public discourse at Brigham City, Utah, on August
            19, and organized Box Elder Stake; died in Salt Lake City,
            August 29, at age 76.

1847-77   *Significant inventions: airship (France); gas burner (Germany);*
            gasoline carburetor (Germany); celluloid (U.S.); rubber dental
            plate (U.S.); dynamite (Sweden); brake elevator (U.S.); gasoline
            engine (U.S.); steel furnace (Germany); glider (England); ice-

*making machine (U.S.), linoleum (England); cylinder lock (U.S.);
electric locomotive (U.S.); machine gun (U.S.); Mason jar (U.S.);
lawn mower (U.S.); oleomargarine (France); phonograph (U.S.);
player piano (France); web printing press (U.S.); sewing machine
(U.S.); spectroscope (Germany); pneumatic tool (England); typewriter (U.S.); barbed wire (U.S.).*

The First Presidency
During Brigham Young's Administration

First Counselor	President	Second Counselor
Heber C. Kimball (1835) 1847-68	Brigham Young (1835) 1847-77	Willard Richards (1840) 1847-54
George A. Smith (1839) 1868-75		**Jedediah M. Grant 1854-56
**John W. Young 1876-77		**Daniel H. Wells 1857-77

Counselors in the First Presidency	Assistant Counselors (1874-77)
Joseph F. Smith (1867) 1866-67	**John W. Young 1874-76
Lorenzo Snow (1849) 1873-74	Lorenzo Snow (1849) 1875-77
Brigham Young, Jr. (1868) 1873-74	George Q. Cannon (1860) 1875-77
Albert Carrington (1870) 1873-74	Brigham Young, Jr. (1868) 1875-77
George Q. Cannon (1860) 1873-74	Albert Carrington (1870) 1875-77
**John W. Young 1873-74	

Note: Dates in parentheses indicate date ordained member of the Council of the Twelve.

*Never ordained an apostle.

**An apostle but not a member of the Council of the Twelve.

Council of the Twelve—October 1848

Orson Hyde (1835)   George A. Smith (1839)
Parley P. Pratt (1835)   Lyman Wight (1841)
Orson Pratt (1835)   Amasa M. Lyman (1842)
John Taylor (1838)   Ezra T. Benson (1846)
Wilford Woodruff (1839)

Excommunicated   **Died**

1845—William B. Smith   1854—Willard Richards
1846—John E. Page   1857—Parley P. Pratt
1848—Lyman Wight   1869—Ezra T. Benson
1870—Amasa M. Lyman (deprived of apostleship in 1867)

Added

Charles C. Rich (1849)   George Q. Cannon (1860)
Lorenzo Snow (1849)   Joseph F. Smith (1867)
Erastus Snow (1849)   Brigham Young, Jr. (1868)
Franklin D. Richards (1849)   Albert Carrington (1870)

October 1877

John Taylor (1838)   Erastus Snow (1849)
Wilford Woodruff (1839)   Franklin D. Richards (1849)
Orson Hyde (1839)***   George Q. Cannon (1860)
Orson Pratt (1843)***   Joseph F. Smith (1867)
Charles C. Rich (1849)   Brigham Young, Jr. (1868)
Lorenzo Snow (1849)   Albert Carrington (1870)

***In 1875 Brigham Young took him from his original position in the Quorum and placed him in the order he would have been in when he was restored to fellowship.
See Durham and Heath, *Succession in the Church*, pp. 73-76.

Testimony of Brigham Young

Permit me, my hearers, brethren and strangers, to say to you, there is not that man that hears the sound of my voice this day, that can say that Jesus lives, whether he professes to be His disciple or not; and can say at the same time, that Joseph Smith was not a Prophet of the Lord.

There is not that being that ever had the privilege of hearing the way of life and salvation set before him as it is written in the New Testament, and in the Book of Mormon, and in the Book of Doctrine and Covenants, by a Latter-day Saint, that can say that Jesus lives, that His Gospel is true; and at the same time say that Joseph Smith was not a Prophet of God. That is strong testimony, but it is true. No man can say that this book (laying his hand on the Bible) is true, is the word of the Lord, is the way, is the guide-board in the path, and a charter by which we may learn the will of God; and at the same time say, that the Book of Mormon is untrue; if he has had the privilege of reading it, or of hearing it read, and learning its doctrines. There is not that person on the face of the earth who has had the privilege of learning the Gospel of Jesus Christ from these two books, that can say that one is true, and the other is false. No Latter-day Saint, no man or woman, can say the Book of Mormon is true, and at the same time say that the Bible is untrue. If one be true, both are; and if one be false, both are false. If Jesus lives, and is the Savior of the world, Joseph Smith is a Prophet of God, and lives in the bosom of his father Abraham. Though they have killed his body, yet he lives and beholds the face of his Father in heaven; and his garments are pure as the angels that surround the throne of God; and no man on the earth can say that Jesus lives, and deny at the same time my assertion about the Prophet Joseph. This is my testimony and it is strong.

Permit me to say that I am proud of my religion. It is the only thing I pride myself in, on the earth. I may heap up gold and silver like the mountains; I may gather around me property, goods, and chattels, but I could have no glory in that, compared with my religion; it is the fountain of light and intelligence; it swallows up the truth contained in all the philosophy of the world, both heathen and Christian; it circumscribes the wisdom of man; it circumscribes all the wisdom and power of the world; it reaches to that within the veil. Its bounds, its circumference, its end, its height, and depth, are beyond the comprehension of mortals.

I wish to bear my testimony, before this congregation, to the religion which is called "Mormonism," and preached by the Elders of the same profession in all the world; and that, we believe, is the Gospel of salvation, and calculated to save all the honest in heart who wish to be saved.

This is my testimony concerning it—It is the power of God unto salvation to all who believe and obey it.

I bear my testimony that the Gospel you have embraced is the way of life and salvation to every one that believes it, and then obeys it with an honest intent. The inquiry may arise in the minds of some, as to how far they shall obey it. Every son and daughter of God is expected to obey with a willing heart every word which the Lord has spoken, and which He will in the future speak to us. It is expected that we hearken to the revelations of His will, and adhere to them, cleave to them with all our might; for this is salvation, and anything short of this clips the salvation and the glory of the Saints. (Green, *Testimonies of Our Leaders*, pp. 38-39.)

Personal Experience of Brigham Young

When the pioneers left the confines of civilization, we were not seeking a country on the Pacific Coast, neither a country to the north or south; we were seeking a country which had been pointed out by the Prophet Joseph Smith in the midst of the Rocky Mountains, in the interior of the great North American continent. When the leader of that noble band of pioneers set out with his little company from the Missouri River, they went, as did Abraham, when he left his father's house—knowing not whither he went—only God had said, Go out from your father's house unto a land which I will show you.

That band of pioneers went out, not knowing whither they went, only they knew that God had commanded them to go into a land which he would show them. And whenever the Prophet Brigham Young, the leader of that band of pioneers, was asked the question: "Whither goest thou?" the only answer he could give was: "I will show you when we come to it." The prayers of that band of pioneers, offered up day and night, continually unto God, were to lead us, as he had promised, unto a land which, by the mouth of his servant Joseph, he had declared he would give us for an inheritance. Said the Prophet Brigham: "I have seen it, I have seen it in vision, and when my natural eyes behold it, I shall know it." They, therefore, like Abraham of old, journeying by faith, knowing not whither they went, only they knew that God had called them to go out from among their brethren, who had hated, despised, and persecuted them, and driven them from their possessions, and would not that they should dwell among them.

And when they reached this land the Prophet Brigham said—"This is the place where I, in vision, saw the ark of the Lord resting; this is the place whereon we will plant the soles of our feet, and where the Lord will place his name amongst his people." And he said to that band of pioneers—"Organize your exploring parties, one to go south, another north, and another to go to the west, and search out the land, in the length and the breadth thereof, learn the facilities for settlement, for grazing, water, timber, soil and climate, that we may be able to report to our brethren when we return;" and when the parties were organized, said he unto them—"You will find many excellent places for settlement. On every hand in these mountains are locations where the people of God may dwell, but when you return from the south, west and north to this place, you will say with me, "this is the place which the Lord has chosen for us to commence our settlements, and from this place we shall spread abroad and possess the land." (Erastus Snow, in *Journal of Discourses*, vol. 16, p. 207.)

Quotations from Brigham Young

AMERICA
To accuse us of being unfriendly to the government is to accuse us of hostility to our religion, for no item of inspiration is held more sacred with us than the Constitution under which America acts.

APOSTASY
We may apostatize from the faith, and go out of the church and kingdom of God, and be lost; but this will have no effect upon the progress of the Lord's work, neither can all the powers of hell combined accomplish aught against it.

BOOK OF MORMON
There is not another nation under heaven, in whose midst the Book of Mormon could have been brought forth. The Lord had been operating for centuries to prepare the way for the coming forth of the contents of that book from the bowels of the earth, to be published to the world, to show to the inhabitants thereof that he still lives, and that he will, in the latter days, gather his elect from the four corners of the earth.

CHILDREN
Teach your children from their youth, never to set their hearts immoderately upon any objects of this world. Bring them up in the love and fear of the Lord; study their dispositions and deal with them accordingly, never allowing yourself to correct them in the heat of passion; teach them to love you rather than to fear you, and let it be your constant care that the children that God has so kindly given you are taught the importance of the oracles of God, and the beauty of the principles of our holy religion.

CHRIST
Jesus Christ, the only begotten Son of the Father, who came in the meridian of time, performed his work, suffered the penalty and paid the debt of man's original sin by offering up himself, was resurrected from the dead, and ascended to his Father. The Lord has revealed to us a plan by which we may be saved both here and hereafter. God

has done everything we could ask, and more than we could ask. The errand of Jesus to earth was to bring his brethren and sisters back into the presence of the Father; he has done his part of the work, and it remains for us to do ours. There is not one thing that the Lord could do for the salvation of the human family that he has neglected to do; and it remains for the children of men to receive the truth or reject it; all that can be accomplished for their salvation, independent of them, has been accomplished in and by the Savior.

DRAMA
Upon the stage of a theater can be represented in character, evil and its consequences, good and its happy results and rewards; the weakness and follies of man, the magnanimity of virtue and the greatness of truth. The stage can be made to aid the pulpit in impressing upon the minds of a community an enlightened sense of a virtuous life, also a proper horror of the enormity of sin with its thorns and pitfalls, its gins and snares can be revealed and how to shun it.

EDUCATION
Our education should be such as to improve our minds and fit us for increased usefulness; to make us of greater service to the human family; to enable us to stop our rude methods of living, speaking, and thinking. . . . I would advise you to read books that are worth reading, read reliable history, and search wisdom out of the best books you can procure.

EXALTATION
You cannot give any person their exaltation, unless they know what evil is, what sin, sorrow, and misery are, for no person could comprehend, appreciate, and enjoy an exaltation upon any other principle.

EXAMPLE
Experience has taught me, that example is the best method of preaching to any people. . . . If we teach righteousness, let us also practice righteousness in every sense of the word; if we teach morality let us be moral, let us see that we preserve ourselves within the bounds of all the good which we teach to others.

FASTING
We wish the Latter-day Saints to meet at their respective houses, erected for that purpose on the day appointed for a fast, and take with them of their substance to feed the poor and the hungry among us, and if it is necessary, to clothe the naked.

FREE AGENCY
What is the foundation of the rights of men? The Lord Almighty has organized man for the express purpose of beoming an independent being like unto Himself, and has given him his individual agency.

GOVERNMENT
There is no other platform that any government can stand upon and endure, but the platform of truth and virtue.

HOLY GHOST
We can tell when the speakers are moved by the Holy Ghost only when we ourselves are moved upon by the Holy Ghost. Therefore, it is essential that the membership of the Church be just as diligent in their faith as their leaders.

HOME
Bring up your children in the love and fear of the Lord; . . .teach your children by precept and example, the importance of addressing the throne of grace; teach them how to live, how to draw from the elements the necessaries of life, and teach them the laws of life that they may know how to preserve themselves in health and be able to minister to others. And when instructing them in the principles of the Gospel, teach them that they are true, truth sent down from heaven for our salvation, and that the Gospel incorporates every truth . . . and teach them too that we hold the keys of eternal life, and that they must obey and observe the ordinances and laws pertaining to this holy Priesthood, which God has revealed and restored for the exaltation of the children of men.

MAN
Man, the noblest work of God, was in his creation designed for an endless duration, for which the love of all good was incorporated in his nature. It was never designed that he should naturally do and love evil.

MONEY
If you wish to get rich, save what you get, a fool can earn money. But it takes a wise man to save and dispose of it to his own advantage.

OPPOSITION
Every trial and experience you have passed through is necessary for your salvation.

PATRIOTISM
The love of mankind is an exalted sentiment, and patriotism for home and country is worthy of a place in the bosoms of the greatest and best of mankind.

PRAYER

It matters not whether you or I feel like praying; when the times come to pray, pray. If we do not feel like it, we should pray till we do. You will find that those who wait till the Spirit bids them pray will never pray much on this earth.

RECREATION

Recreation and diversion are as necessary to our well-being as the more serious pursuits of life. There is not a man in the world but what, if kept at any one branch of business or study, will become like a machine. Our pursuits should be so diversified as to develop every trait of character and diversity of talent.

REVELATION

This Church has been led by revelation, and unless we forsake the Lord entirely, so that the priesthood is taken from us, it will be led by revelation all the time. The question arises with some, who has the right to revelation? . . . Every member has the right of receiving revelation for himself. It is the very life of the Church of the living God, in all ages of the world.

RESURRECTION

I think it has been taught by some that as we lay our bodies down, they will rise again in the resurrection with all the impediments and imperfections that they had there; and that if a wife does not love her husband in this state she cannot love him in the next. This is not so. . . . If you can, by faithfulness in this life, obtain the right to come up in the morning of the resurrection, you need entertain no fears that the wife will be dissatisfied with her husband, nor the husband with the wife; for those of the first resurrection will be free from sin and from the consequence of sin.

SABBATH DAY

Six days are enough for us to work, and if we wish to play, play within the six days; if we wish to go on excursions, take one of these six days, but on the seventh day, come to the place of worship, attend to the Sacrament, confess your faults one to another and to our God, and pay attention to the ordinances of the house of God.

WAR

Of one thing I am sure; God never institutes war; God is not the author of confusion or of war; they are the results of the acts of the children of men. Confusion and war necessarily come as the results of the foolish acts and policy of men; but they do not come because God desires they should come. If the people, generally, would turn to the Lord, there would never be any war. Let men turn from their iniquities and sins, and instead of being covetous and wicked, turn to God and seek to promote peace and happiness throughout the land, and wars would cease.

WELFARE

My experience has taught me, and it has become a principle with me, that it is never any benefit to give, out and out, to man or woman, money, food, clothing, or anything else, if they are able-bodied, and can work and earn what they need, when there is anything on the earth for them to do. This is my principle, and I try to act upon it. To pursue a contrary course would ruin my community in the world and make them idlers. People trained in this way have no interest in working, "but," say they, "we can beg, or we can get this, that, or the other."

WORK

Wealth is generally the representation of labour, industry, and talent. If one man is industrious, enterprising, diligent, careful, and saves property, and his children follow in his steps, and accumulate wealth; and another man is careless, prodigal, and lazy, and his children inherit his poverty, I cannot conceive upon what principles of justice, the children of the idle and profligate have a right to put their hands into the pockets of those who are diligent and careful, and rob them of their purse. Let this principle exist, and all energy and enterprise would be crushed.

John Taylor, Third President (1808-1887)

JOHN TAYLOR

Third President of the Church

Born: November 1, 1808, Milnthorpe, England

Died: July 25, 1887, Kaysville, Utah (age 78)

President of the Church: October 10, 1880, to July 25, 1887 (6 years and 9 months)

Physical Characteristics: Five feet eleven inches tall, 180 pounds, clean-cut appearance, gray eyes, beard, white hair, handsome

Areas of Distinction: Prophet, writer, pioneer, missionary, legislator, judge, linguist, farmer, woodturner, educator, publisher

*Family: Son of John and Agnes Taylor. Married Leonora Cannon January 28, 1833 (died December 9, 1868); Elizabeth Kaighin, December 12, 1843 (died August 31, 1895); Jane Ballantyne, February 25, 1844 (died December 26, 1900); Mary Ann Oakley, January 14, 1846 (died August 21, 1911); Sophia Whitaker, April 23, 1847 (died February 27, 1887); Harriet Whitaker, December 4, 1847 (died July 16, 1882); Margaret Young, September 26, 1856 (died May 3, 1919). Had 35 children.

---

*Source: Roberts, *Life of John Taylor*, pp. 464-465.

Profile of John Taylor

In 1877 the Church was in a period of persecution. Intolerance concerning plural marriage had broken up hundreds of families as husbands and fathers were sent to prison. Leaders had to flee in many towns, and the Saints lost the right to vote. Called to face these and other problems was sixty-nine-year-old John Taylor, third President of the Church.

A Britisher by birth, John Taylor was known as an English gentleman. His appearance and bearing gave the impression of nobility. He had been a Methodist preacher, but he became dissatisfied because he felt it didn't espouse the complete truth.

He found his complete truth in Mormonism and joined the Church in Canada, where he had emigrated from England. He then spent the rest of his life serving the Lord and his people.

John Taylor traveled thousands of miles without purse or scrip to do the work of the Church. He served two missions to Britain and opened parts of France and Germany to the teaching of the gospel. His travels in the United States alone cover the entire route of early Church history from Ohio to Missouri, to Nauvoo to Utah, to the Eastern States Mission and back to Utah.

A powerful writer, he published many tracts and several larger works, and wrote many hymns and poems.

He edited the *Times and Seasons* and the *Nauvoo Neighbor,* and his editorials and newspaper articles in the defense of Zion and her interests achieved much good.

In civic affairs, he served several times as a member of the Utah legislature and as speaker of the house. He also served as probate judge of Utah County.

As an extemporaneous speaker, he was deliberate in speech, almost slow. His voice was clear, strong, and resonant. His gestures were few but significant, and he preached righteousness. The Saints were impressed by his commanding presence, his personal magnetism, and the vigor and power of his discourses.

Cautious in his business methods and scrupulously honest, he once remarked: "I prefer a faded coat to a faded reputation." "President Taylor was a man who could not get down to grovel with the low-lived, the vicious, the ribald, nor any who indulged in the follies and vanities of moral life." (Roberts, *Life of John Taylor,* p. 455.)

He was a family man: a kind and noble father, a gentle and loving husband. He possessed superb self-control, which, with his sense of justice and honor, enabled him to be remarkably successful in the patriarchal order of marriage. Each of his seven wives was treated as the equal of the others, and with her children shared equally in the blessings and material goods he was able to give them.

He enjoyed family and social gatherings with his neighbors and friends. He was a good conversationalist, a vocalist, and had an inexhaustible fund of humor. His skill as a teller of faith-promoting stories also helped ease the ordeal of crossing the plains.

B. H. Roberts describes his character in the following passages:

In person President Taylor was nearly six feet in height and of fine proportion, that combination which gives activity and strength.

President John Taylor, 1853

His head was large, the face oval and the features large, strong and finely chiseled. The forehead was high and massive, the eyes gray, deepset, and of a mild, kindly expression, except when aroused, and then they were capable of reflecting all the feelings that moved his soul, whether of indignation, scorn or contempt. The nose was aquiline, the mouth well formed and expressive of firmness, the chin powerful and well rounded. In early life he was of a fair complexion, but with age the face grew swarthy, and even in middle life his abundant hair turned to a silvery whiteness, which but added beauty to his brown and made his appearance venerable.

In his manner he was ever affable and polite, easy and gracious, yet princely in dignity. In his intercourse with others he was familiar but never vulgar. He was not a man whom a friend, however intimate, would slap familiarly on the back or turn and twist about when shaking hands; such proceedings with him would have been as much out of place as with the proudest crowned monarch in the presence-chamber. Yet there was no affectation in his deportment, no stiffness; his dignity was that with which nature clothes her noblest sons. It did not spring from self-conceit, or self-sufficiency. . . .

A universal benevolence, powerful intellect, splendid courage, physical as well as moral, a noble independence of spirit, coupled with implicit faith and trust in God, a high sense of honor, unimpeachable integrity, indomitable determination, and a passionate love of liberty, justice and truth marked the outlines of his character. . . .

President Taylor believed absolutely in the universal Fatherhood of God and the brotherhood of man. From that grand cardinal doctrine sprang his liberal views as to the hand dealings of God with His children. He despised anything that savored of narrow-mindedness or bigotry. . . .

Of the deep religious convictions of President Taylor it is scarcely necessary to speak. His whole life demonstrates how deep was the religious soil in his nature, into which the seeds of truth were sown to bring forth an hundred fold. His devotion to his re-

The John Taylor residence in Nauvoo, Illinois, 1844

ligion was not only sincere, it was without reserve. He gave himself and his whole life to it. His faith, his trust and confidence in God were complete. "I do not believe in a religion that cannot have all my affections," he would sometimes remark, "but I believe in a religion that I can live for, or die for." (Roberts, *Life of John Taylor*, pp. 419-21.)

John Taylor was with the Prophet Joseph on the day the Prophet was martyred in Carthage Jail, June 27, 1844. At the Prophet's request he sang the hymn "A Poor Wayfaring Man of Grief," while the mob gathered around the jail. John Taylor's life was spared, despite the fact that he was shot four times, and the fifth shot struck the watch in his vest. He carried with him to the grave scars of the savage wounds.

GEORGE Q. CANNON
1880-1887

JOHN TAYLOR
1880-1887

JOSEPH F. SMITH
1880-1887

THE FIRST PRESIDENCY
1880-1887

The First Presidency, 1880-87: President John Taylor (center) and counselors George Q. Cannon and Joseph F. Smith

A man of great faith and conviction with strong feelings about injustice and freedom, he defended Joseph Smith and the Saints numerous times. From his defenses of the Saints' rights during the persecutions in Missouri, he was called "The Champion of Liberty."

The persecution and intolerance continued to grow. When the United States Army came to Utah in 1857, John Taylor encouraged the Saints to fight for their religious liberty. At a meeting of the Saints he asked, "Are you all willing to set fire to your property and lay it in ashes rather than submit to oppression?" The Saints all voted, "Yes."

Still acting according to their understanding of the religious liberties granted to all Americans by the Constitution of the United States, about two to three percent of the Church members practiced polygamy. John Taylor had been President of the Church for seven years when the United States passed the Edmunds-Tucker law, which made it unlawful to live with more than one wife. As the crusade against plural marriage came to be waged with more and more bitterness, President Taylor counseled some Saints to move to Mexico to avoid prosecution. Then, since nothing more could be done then to prevent trouble, and in order to place himself beyond prosecution for an infraction of the law, he went into exile for about two and a half years until his death. The law had made persecution legal.

John Taylor as President lived mostly in exile, and that is how he died.

Today he occupies the place of a double martyr. President John Taylor has been killed by the cruelties of the officials who have in his territory misrepresented the Government of the United States. There is no room for doubt that if he had been permitted to enjoy the comforts of his home, the ministrations of his family, the exercise to which he had been accustomed, all of which he was denied, he would have lived for many years yet. His blood stains the clothes of the men who in insensate hate have offered rewards for his arrest and have hounded him to his grave. History will yet call their deeds by their right names, but one greater than the combined voices of all historians will pronounce their dreadful sentence. (Roberts, *Life of John Taylor*, p. 414.)

Daniel H. Wells of the First Presidency spoke these words at his funeral:

> He lived a fearless, noble and God-like life—let those who still live seek to emulate his noble example. President Taylor has been a friend to himself, a friend to his family, a friend to this people and a friend to God. He has been the champion of human rights, the champion of liberty, truth and freedom. He has lived a noble, useful life, full of honor and credit to himself and family, a satisfaction to the people and a glory to God. . . . I knew him to be a man determined to do right, to see justice administered, truth upheld, and honor sustained among this people. He has lived to see this people pass through many changes. (Roberts, *Life of John Taylor,* p. 447.)

He lived, worked, and died an exemplification of his favored motto: "The kingdom of God or nothing."

Interesting Facts and Contributions

of John Taylor

1. He is mentioned in the Doctrine and Covenants three times: (1) when he was called to be a member of the Twelve Apostles (section 118); (2) when that appointment was reaffirmed (section 124); and (3) when he was identified with Willard Richards as being a witness to the murder of the Prophet Joseph Smith and Hyrum when they were killed at Carthage (section 135).

2. His missionary efforts included trips to England, where he assisted in the publication of the first hymnbook there.

3. He was shot four times when Joseph and Hyrum Smith were killed in Carthage Jail, but he recovered and rejoined the Saints, journeyed west, and spent the remainder of his life in building the Lord's kingdom.

4. His seven years as President were marked by bitter persecutions aroused because of plural marriage practices. He died in seclusion in Kaysville, Utah.

5. He was a colonel in the Nauvoo Legion and a member of the Board of Regents for Nauvoo University.

6. He nominated Joseph Smith for President of the United States.

7. He was a strong supporter of freedom and constitutional law.

8. An ingenious mechanic, he built one of the first saw mills in Utah and worked in it himself.

9. He was one of the associate judges of the provisional State of Deseret.

10. He directed the translation of the Book of Mormon into French and German.

11. He was active in his efforts to secure admission of the State of Deseret into the Union.

12. He organized numerous branches of the Church and published many tracts and several larger works that introduced the gospel to new countries.

13. He made innovations in his administration that included quarterly stake conference, weekly bishop's meeting, and monthly stake priesthood meeting.

14. He served as a member of the Utah territorial legislature for twenty years, and for five successive sessions was elected speaker of the house.

15. He wrote numerous articles and pamphlets in America and Europe defending the Church.

16. He personally edited the *Times and Seasons* for three years, the *Nauvoo Neighbor* for two and a half years, the *Wasp* for six months, the *Mormon* for two and a half years, and contributed liberally to *Etoile du Deseret* (Star of Deseret) and *Zion's Panier* (Zion's Banner) in Paris and Hamburg, respectively.

17. He was noted for his famous paper *Reply to Colfax*, a lengthy debate between himself and Vice President of the United States, Schuyler Colfax, on the subject of plural marriage.

18. He wrote numerous poems, mostly on gospel themes.

19. He set the precedent of having the quorums of priesthood separately sustain the new First Presidency.

20. He was instrumental in helping unify the Saints preparatory to the anti-Mormon storm that attempted to render the Church helpless.

21. He defended the Saints numerous times and was called the "Champion of Liberty."

22. "A man of great spiritual gifts, Taylor had a strong faith in divine revelation. He did not add materially to Church dogma or organization, but ably carried on the traditions established by his two predecessors. He was

a very effective speaker, and his most noteworthy contribution was his active proselyting." (*Dictionary of American Biography*, vol. 18, p. 334.)

Significant Dates and Events in Lifetime of

John Taylor

Church Membership 1877: 155,000 (est.)   1887: 192,000 (est.)

1887—Stakes: 31   Missions: 12   Temples: 3

U.S. Population, 1887: 55 million (est.)

World Population, 1887: 1.4 billion (est.)

U.S. Presidents (1877-87): Rutherford B. Hayes, James A. Garfield, Chester A. Arthur, Grover Cleveland

1808	Born in Milnthorpe, Westmoreland County, England, November 1.
1822	Went to work as a cooper, later as a woodturner.
1824	Joined Methodist Church.
1825	Received impression that he would preach the gospel in America.
1827-32	Became Methodist preacher.
1830	Family moved to Canada; he stayed in England to settle family affairs.
1832	Emigrated from England.
1833	Married Leonora Cannon.
1836	Was baptized by Parley P. Pratt; wife also baptized. Placed in charge of Church in Canada (age 28).
1837	Visited with Joseph Smith in Canada and was ordained a high priest. In the fall, received word from Joseph to join the Saints in Missouri.
1838	Arrived in Far West, Missouri, after spending some time working in order to secure funds for the journey. Later

fled from Missouri to Illinois. Was ordained an apostle by Brigham Young and Heber C. Kimball at Far West on December 19 (age 30).

1839-41   Served mission to England.

1841   Appointed with Elias Higbee as committee to petition Congress for redress of wrongs in Missouri; appointed by the Prophet Joseph to present the petition in October.

1842   Became Judge Advocate of Nauvoo Legion, a member of the Nauvoo city council, and regent of the University of Nauvoo.

1842-46   Editor of *Times and Seasons.*

1843-45   Editor of *Nauvoo Neighbor.*

1844   Was in Carthage Jail with Prophet and Hyrum Smith and was seriously wounded, June 27.

1846   Assisted in organizing Mormon Battalion at Winter Quarters.

1846-47   Served second mission to England.

1847   Led company of Saints from Winter Quarters to Salt Lake City, fall.

1849   Chosen associate judge of Supreme Court of the Provisional State of Deseret, March.

1849-52   Served mission to France and Germany. While in France he became acquainted with process of sugar manufacturing; under his direction machinery was purchased and shipped to Utah. Had the Book of Mormon published in French and German and also published the papers *Etoile du Deseret* and *Zion's Panier.*

1851   Published *The Government of God.*

1854   Elected member of the territorial legislature, but resigned to fill mission in New York.

1855-57   Presided over Eastern States Mission; published the *Mormon.*

1857-76   Member of Utah territorial legislature.

1868-70   Probate judge of Utah County.

1869   Entered nationally publicized written debate over plural marriage with Schuyler Colfax, Vice President of the United States.

1877   Elected territorial superintendent of district schools in Utah; became President of the Council of the Twelve, October 6 (age 69).

1877-87   Missions opened: Northwestern States, Mexican, Indian Territory, East Indian, Turkish.

Russo-Turkish War.

1878   Primary Association organized, August 25.

Business began to improve when gold returned to circulation.

1879   *War of the Pacific began.*

1880   Women's auxiliary organizations completed at special conference, June 19. At general conference October 10, John Taylor, George Q. Cannon, and Joseph F. Smith were sustained in the First Presidency. Jubilee year (fiftieth anniversary) for the Church. Church struck off one-half of indebtedness held by Perpetual Emigration Fund Co., against individuals classed as worthy poor.

1881   Orson Pratt, last surviving member of original Council of the Twelve, died. John Taylor made extended trips to northern and southern settlements.

President James A. Garfield assassinated. Estimated 300,000 persons died in typhoon in Haiphong, Vietnam.

1882   John Taylor published *Mediation and Atonement of Our Lord and Savior Jesus Christ.* Anti-Mormon legislation passed by Congress (Edmunds Law), making punishable contracting of plural marriage and polygamous living; many Church members were apprehended and forced to serve terms in prison. John Taylor issued statement at general conference in April concerning persecutions because of plural marriage; told the people to obey the law, but they should be granted their rights as citizens. Church members 21 years of age and older required to take test oath testifying they were not violating the laws of the United States prohibiting bigamy or polygamy. Most communities practicing United Order abandoned the project. Deseret Hospital dedicated by John Taylor.

Great Britain invaded and occupied Egypt. Italy joined Germany, Austria, and Hungary to form Triple Alliance.

1883   *Standard time established across United States. Brooklyn Bridge completed. Geologists in Ontario found world's largest copper-nickel reserves. Volcano Krakatoa in the Sunda Strait destroyed two-thirds of island; death toll, 60,000 to 120,000.*

1884   Logan Temple dedicated by President John Taylor, May 17. A mob attacked and killed a number of Saints in Tennessee who were meeting at home of James Condor for religious worship. Rudger Clawson was first person to be tried under Edmunds Law; he was found guilty and was fined and imprisoned. Many Church leaders went into exile because of persecution. John Whittaker Taylor was ordained an apostle by his father.

World's first skyscraper, Home Insurance Building, built in Chicago.

1885   Millard Academy opened at Fillmore, Utah. Mormon colonies began spreading to Mexico and Canada. John Taylor made last public appearance before withdrawing to voluntary exile in view of laws against plural marriage.

1886   *Statue of Liberty dedicated—a gift from France. Earthquake in Charleston, South Carolina, destroyed most of the city.*

1887   Congress passed Edmunds-Tucker Law dissolving Corporation of The Church of Jesus Christ of Latter-day Saints and turning its properties over to the Federal Government. The members appealed through the courts but lost (March). Escheatment proceedings conducted by the Federal Government; U.S. marshal took charge of real and personal property of the Church (July 30). John Taylor died at Kaysville, Utah, July 25, age 78.

Yellow River in China overflowed its banks and submerged eleven cities in a raging sea; more than 900,000 persons were known to have drowned in Honan Province; as many as 7,000,000 casualties.

1877-87   *Significant inventions: glider (Germany); automobile (Germany); steam turbine (England); air-inflated rubber tire (Scotland); submarine (U.S.); manganese steel (England); milk bottle (U.S.); transformer (U.S.); microphone (U.S.); linotype (U.S.); fountain pen (U.S.); flexible roll film (U.S.); vacuum milling machine (U.S.); incandescent light (U.S.); machine gun (England); cash register (U.S.); comptometer (U.S.).*

The First Presidency

During John Taylor's Administration

First Counselor	President	Second Counselor
George Q. Cannon	John Taylor	Joseph F. Smith
(1860)	(1838)	(1867)
1880-87	1880-87	1880-87

Council of the Twelve—October 1880

Wilford Woodruff (1839)   Brigham Young, Jr. (1868)
Orson Pratt (1843)   Albert Carrington (1870)
Charles C. Rich (1849)   Moses Thatcher (1879)
Lorenzo Snow (1849)   Francis M. Lyman (1880)
Erastus Snow (1849)   John Henry Smith (1880)
Franklin D. Richards (1849)

Died   ## Added

1878—Orson Hyde   George Teasdale (1882)
1881—Orson Pratt   Heber J. Grant (1882)
1883—Charles C. Rich   John W. Taylor (1884)

Excommunicated

1885—Albert Carrington (baptized
        again prior to death in 1889)

July to October 1887

Wilford Woodruff (1839)   Moses Thatcher (1879)
Lorenzo Snow (1849)   Francis M. Lyman (1880)
Erastus Snow (1849)   John Henry Smith (1880)
Franklin D. Richards (1849)   George Teasdale (1882)
Brigham Young, Jr. (1868)   Heber J. Grant (1882)
                              John W. Taylor (1884)

Note: Dates in parentheses indicate date ordained member of the Council of the Twelve.

Orson Hyde and Orson Pratt (reference to seniority in the Council of the Twelve—see Durham and Heath, *Succession in the Church*, pp. 73-76).

Testimony of John Taylor

If it were not for the religion I profess, which gives me to know something about the matter, by revelation for myself, I would not have anything to do with religion at all. I would worship God the best way I knew how, and act justly and honorably with my neighbor; which I believe thousands of that class of men called infidels do at the present day. But I never would submit to be gulled with the nonsense that exists in the world, under the name of religion.

We believe in the restoration of all things. We believe that God has spoken from the heavens. If I did not believe He had, I would not be here. We believe that angels have appeared, that the heavens have been opened. We believe in eternal principles, in an eternal Gospel, an eternal Priesthood, in eternal communications and associations. Everything associated with the Gospel that we believe in is eternal. If it were not so, I would want nothing to do with it. I do not want to make a profession, and worship a God because this one, that one, or the other one does it, and I not know whether I am right, and those whom I imitate not know, any more than myself, whether they are right or wrong.

I profess to know for myself, and if I did not know for myself, I would have nothing to do with it. Acting upon this principle, I associated myself with the Latter-day Saints. I preach that doctrine which I verily believe with my whole soul. I believe in its principles, because there is something intelligent about it. For instance—if I am an eternal being, I want something that is calculated to satisfy the capacious desires of that eternal mind. If I am a being that came into the world yesterday, and will leave it again tomorrow, I might as well have one religion as another, or none at all; let us eat and drink; for tomorrow we die. If I am an eternal being, I want to know something about that eternity with which I am associated.

If there is a God, I want a religion that supplies some means of certain and tangible communication with Him. If there is a heaven, I want to know what sort of a place it is. If there are angels, I want to know their nature, and their occupation, and of what they are composed. If I am an eternal being, I want to know what I am to do when I get through with time.

I believe that we as "Mormons" have the truth, and for this reason I have traveled extensively in most of the States of the Union, and in Canada; also in England, Ireland and Scotland; in the Isle of Man, Jersey, and other islands of the sea; in France, Germany, Belgium, and other parts of the earth; and I have not yet seen a man that could find one error in doctrine or principle connected with the religion of the Latter-day Saints.

Then if you have a thing that nobody can overturn, but can be sustained everywhere; that defies the wisdom and intelligence of the world to find one fault in it, you must say it is right, until it is proven to be wrong.

We believe that God has set His hand in these last days to accomplish His purposes, to gather together His elect from the four winds, even to fulfill the words which He has spoken by all the holy Prophets, to redeem the earth from the power of the curse, to save the human family from the ruins of the fall, and to place mankind in that position which God designed them to occupy before this world came into existence, or the morning stars sang together for joy. We believe in and realize these things: we feel them, we appreciate them, and therefore are we thus assembled together.

God has told me to preach the Gospel to every creature, saying, "He that believeth and is baptized shall be saved; and he that believeth not shall be damned." He has told me to do this. (Green, *Testimonies of Our Leaders*, pp. 40-41.)

Personal Experience of John Taylor

The following is told by President Heber J. Grant:

I shall tell you one incident in my life.

A man was cut off from the Church for adultery and asked to be restored. President John Taylor wrote a letter to the brethren that had taken action against the man, in which he said: "I want every man to vote his own convictions, and not to vote to make it unanimous unless it is unanimous."

When the matter was presented and voted upon, the vote stood half for and half against restoration.

Later he came up again, and a majority were in favor of his being baptized.

Finally, all of the men that were at the trial, except one, voted to let him be baptized. President John Taylor sent for me and told me I was the only man that stood in the way of this man's being baptized, and he said: "How will you feel when you meet the Lord, if this man is permitted to come up and say he repented although his sins were as scarlet, and you refused to let him be baptized?"

I said: "I will look the Lord squarely in the eye, and I will tell Him that any man that can destroy the virtue of a girl and then lie and claim that she was maligning him and blackmailing him, will never get back into this Church with my vote. You said in your letter to vote our convictions, and I will vote them and stay with them unless you want me to change."

He said: "Stay with your convictions, my boy."

I walked to my home, only one block away. I picked

up the Doctrine and Covenants. I was reading it prayerfully and humbly, and marking passages. Instead of its
opening at the bookmark, it opened at the passage:

> Wherefore, I say unto you, that ye ought to forgive one
> another; for he that forgiveth not his brother his trespasses standeth
> condemned before the Lord; for there remaineth in him the greater
> sin.
>
> I, the Lord, will forgive whom I will forgive, but of you it is
> required to forgive all men. (D&C 64:9-10.)

I shut up the book and rushed back to the President, and I said, "I give my consent."

Brother Taylor had a habit, when something pleased
him, of shaking himself and laughing, and he said: "My
gracious, Heber, this is remarkable; what has happened?"
And I told him. He said: "Heber, when you left here a
few minutes ago did you not think: what if he had de-
filed my wife or daughter? And when you thought that,
did you not feel as if you would like to just knock the
life out of that man?"

I said, "I certainly did."

"How do you feel now?"

"Well, really and truly Brother Taylor, I hope the
poor old sinner can be forgiven."

"You feel a whole lot better, don't you?"

I said, "I certainly do."

He added: "I put that clause in that letter for you
and my son. You have learned a lesson as a young man.
You have learned a good lesson, that this gospel is one
of forgiveness of sin, of awful sin, if there is true repentance; and it brings peace into your heart when you
forgive the sinner. It brings peace when you love the
man that you hated, provided the man turns to doing
right. You have learned a lesson in your youth. Never
forget it." And I never have. (Quoted in *Conference Report*, October 1941, pp. 148-49.)

Quotations from John Taylor

AMERICA
It was through and by the power of God, that the fathers of this country framed the Declaration of Independence, and also that great palladium of human rights, the Constitution of the United States. There is nothing of a bigoted-narrow-contracted feeling about that instrument; it is broad and comprehensive.

APOSTASY
When you hear a man talk against the authorities of this Church and kingdom, you may know he is sliding down hill.

BOOK OF MORMON
The gospel in the Book of Mormon and the gospel in the Bible both agree; the doctrines in both books are one. This historical part differs only; the one gives the history of an Asiatic, the other of an American people.

CHURCH
I do not believe in a religion that cannot have all my affections, but in a religion for which I can both live and die.

EDUCATION
We want . . . to be alive in the cause of education. We are commanded of the Lord to obtain knowledge, both by study and by faith, seeking it out of the best books. And it becomes us to teach our children, and afford them instructions in every branch of education calculated to promote their welfare, leaving those false aquirements which tend to infidelity, and to lead away the mind and affection from the things of God. We want to compile the intelligence and literacy of this people in book form, as well as in teaching, preaching; adopting all the good and useful books we can obtain; make them. And instead of doing as many of the world do, take the works of God to try to prove that there is no God, we want to prove by God's works that he does exist, that he lives and rules and holds us, as it were, in the hollow of his hand.

FAITH
Faith without works being dead, it is evident that living faith and that which is acceptable to God, is that which not only believes in God, but acts upon that belief. It is not only the cause of action, but includes both cause and action. Or in other words it is belief or faith made perfect by works.

FALL OF MAN
The gospel, when introduced and preached to Adam after the fall, through atonement of Jesus Christ, placed him in a position not only to have victory over death, but to have within his reach and to possess the perpetuity, not only of earthly, but of heavenly life; not only of earthly, but of heavenly dominion; and through the law of that gospel enabled him (and not him alone, but all his posterity) to obtain, not only his first estate, but a higher exaltation on earth and in the heavens, than he could have enjoyed if he had not fallen; the powers and blessings associated with the atonement being altogether in advance of and superior to any enjoyment or privileges that he could have had in his first estate.

FREE ENTERPRISE
One great principle which has existed among men from the beginning of creation until now, is a desire, planted within them by the Almighty, to possess property, lands, houses, farms, etc. . . . As I said before, this principle is correct, only it wants controlling according to the revelations of God.

GOD
I would rather have God for my friend than all other influences and powers.

GOSPEL
What does the gospel show us? It shows us who our Father is; it shows us our relationship to him, and to our earthly father; it shows us our duty towards our children, our duty towards our wives, and wives their duty towards their husbands; it enters into all the ramifications of human existence.

GOVERNMENT
We believe that all legislative assemblies should confine themselves to constitutional principles; and that all such laws should be implicitly obeyed by every American. . . .

We believe that the president, governors, judges, and government officers ought to be respected, honored, and sustained in their stations; but that they ought to use their positions and power, not for political emolument, or party purposes, but for the administration of justice, and equity, and for the well being and happiness of the people.

We believe that legislators ought to be chosen on account of their intelligence, honor, integrity, and virtue, and not because they belong to some particular party clique. . . .

We believe that although there is much to lament, and room for very great improvement, both in our executive, judiciary, and legislative departments, that we have the most liberal, free, and enlightened government in the world.

HOME
Let others who fear not God take their course; but it is for us to train our children up in the fear of God. God will hold us responsible for this trust. Hear it, you elders of Israel and you fathers and you mothers! . . . We want to get together to train our children up in the fear of God, to teach them correct principles ourselves, and place them in possession of such things as will lead them in the paths of life.

JUDGMENT
We may deceive one another in some circumstances, as counterfeit coin passes for that which is considered true and valuable among men. But God searches the hearts and tries the reins of the children of men. He knows our thoughts and comprehends our desires and feelings; He knows our acts and the motives which prompt us to perform them. He is acquainted with all the doings and operations of the human family, and all the secret thoughts and acts of the children of men are open and naked before Him, and for them He will bring them to judgment.

LAST DAYS
The judgments will begin at the house of God. We have to pass through some of these things, but will only be a very little compared with the terrible destruction, the misery and suffering that will overtake the world who are doomed to suffer the wrath of God. It behooves us, as the Saints of God, to stand firm and faithful in the observance of His laws, that we may be worthy of His preserving care and blessing.

LAW

All things are under the influence, control and government of law, just as much as the planetary system with which we are connected is governed by law. It makes no difference what a few of us may do, or how the world may act, the sun rises and sets regularly, the earth revolves upon its axis, and so it is with all the planetary systems. There is no confusion, no disorder in any of the movements of the heavenly bodies. They are governed by a science and intelligence that is beyond the reach of men in mortality. Yet they move strictly according to certain laws by which all of them have been, are, and will be governed. And these laws are under the surveillance and control of the great Law-giver, who manages, controls, and directs all these worlds. If it were not the case, they would move through space in wild confusion, and system would rush against system, and worlds upon worlds would be destroyed, together with their inhabitants. But they are governed by a superhuman power, by a Spirit and Intelligence that dwells in the bosom of the Gods.

LIBERTY

We have a right to liberty that was a right that God gave to all men; and if there has been oppression, fraud or tyranny in the earth, it has been the result of the wickedness and corruptions of men and has always been opposed to God and the principles of truth, righteousness, virtue, and all principles that are calculated to elevate mankind.

MAN

If we take man, he is said to have been made in the image of God, for the simple reason that he is a son of God, and being his son, he is, of course, his offspring, an emanation from God, in whose likeness, we are told, he is made. He did not originate from a chaotic mass of matter, moving or inert, but came forth possessing, in an embryonic state, all the faculties and powers of a God. And when he shall be perfected, and have progressed to maturity, he will be like his Father—a God, being indeed his offspring. As the horse, the ox, the sheep, and every living creature, including man, propagates its own species and perpetuates its own kind, so does God perpetuate his.

MORTALITY

We realize that we are here not to do our will but the will of the Father who sent us. We are here to introduce those eternal principles that exist in the bosom of the Almighty; we are here to build up the Church and Kingdom of God upon the earth, and to form a nucleus through which and by which the God of heaven can work, operate, lead, dictate, and control the affairs of all men.

OBEDIENCE
If you do not magnify your callings, God will hold you responsible for those whom you might have saved had you done your duty.

PEACE
Peace is a desirable thing; it is the gift of God, and the greatest gift that God can bestow upon mortals. What is more desirable than peace? Peace in nations, peace in cities, peace in families.

POLITICS
As we have progressed the mist has been removed, and in relation to these matters, the Elders of Israel being to understand that they have something to do with the world politically as well as religiously, that it is as much their duty to study correct political principles as well as religious, and to seek to know and comprehend the social and political interests of man, and to learn and be able to teach that which would be best calculated to promote the interests of the world.

PRIESTHOOD
What is the priesthood? . . . It is the rule and government of God, whether on earth, or in the heavens; and it is the only legitimate power, the only authority, that is acknowledged by him to rule and regulate the affairs of his kingdom.

Wilford Woodruff, Fourth President (1807-1898)

WILFORD WOODRUFF

Fourth President of the Church

Born: March 1, 1807, Farmington, Connecticut

Died: September 2, 1898, San Francisco, California
(age 91)

President of the Church: April 7, 1889, to September
2, 1898 (9½ years)

Physical Characteristics: Five feet eight inches tall, 170
pounds, blue eyes, medium complexion, beard,
stocky build

Areas of Distinction: Prophet, missionary, pioneer,
miller, farmer, historian, legislator

*Family: Son of Aphek and Beulah Woodruff. Married
Phoebe Whittemore Carter, April 13, 1837 (she died
November 10, 1885), 9 children; married Mary Ann
Jackson, April 15, 1846 (died October 25, 1894), 1
child; married Emma Smith March 13, 1853 (died
March 4, 1912), 8 children; married Sarah Brown,
March 13, 1853 (died May 9, 1909), 8 children;
married Sarah Delight Stocking, July 31, 1857 (died
May 28, 1907), 7 children.

---

*Source: Cowley, *Wilford Woodruff,* pp. 689-692.

Profile of Wilford Woodruff

Noted for keeping careful records of his life and the events of the Church, Wilford Woodruff wrote the following paragraph in his journal:

From the beginning of my ministry in 1834 until the close of 1895 I have traveled in all 172,369 miles; held 7,655 meetings; preached 3,526 discourses; organized 51 branches of the Church and 77 preaching places; my journeys cover England, Scotland, Wales, and 23 states and 5 territories of the Union. My life abounds in incidents which to me surely indicate the direct interposition of God whom I firmly believe has guided my every step. On 27 distinct occasions I have been saved from dangers which threatened my life. I am the father of 17 sons and 16 daughters. I have a posterity of 100 grandchildren and 12 great grandchildren. (Cowley, *Wilford Woodruff*, p. vi.)

He came from a family background of industrious people. His progenitors were among the early settlers of New England. They took part in the American revolution and passed on their love of freedom. Wilford Woodruff's father was a miller, and Wilford assisted him in that trade.

Wilford Woodruff did not join any church until he was twenty-six years old, because he could not find one that harmonized in doctrine and organization with the church of Christ in the New Testament. In 1833, he heard two Latter-day Saint missionaries preaching and immediately received a testimony of their message.

An extremely active child, Wilford must have caused his parents considerable concern. These are examples of some of his accidents: (1) At the age of three he fell into a caldron of scalding water. (2) From a great beam inside a barn he fell on his face on the bare floor of the barn. (3) He made a misstep and fell to the bottom of the stairs, breaking one of his arms. (4) He was chased by a bull and almost gored. (5) He fell from a porch across some timber and broke his other arm. (6) He broke his leg at a saw-

Wilford Woodruff, about 1853

mill. (7) He was kicked in the stomach by an ox. (8) A wagon turned over with him in it. (9) He fell fifteen feet from a broken tree limb to the ground, landing on his back. (10) He nearly drowned in a river. (11) One winter he almost froze to death. (12) He split his instep open with an ax. (13) He was bitten by a mad dog. (14) He was almost killed in a horse accident.

Wilford Woodruff frequently testified that two powers had been at work with him all his life, one to destroy him, the other to protect him and enable him to complete his mission in life. His numerous accidents probably would have killed an ordinary person, but he believed the Lord was protecting him. He commented that he had broken nearly every bone in his body except those of his spine and neck.

He became one of the great missionaries of the Church, serving several missions to England and various parts of the United States and bringing many people into the Church. During his mission to England, he baptized hundreds; entire congregations and villages accepted the message of the gospel. Nothing quite like it has been recorded elsewhere in the history of the Church.

President Woodruff loved to work hard. He labored with his hands as well as his head. It is said that men much younger than himself were not equals in the performance of heavy labor. Hard work was such a part of his life that when he was ninety years old, one of his grandchildren excelled him very little in hoeing some vegetables in the garden. He said with apparent humiliation, "Well, it is the first time in my life that one of my children has ever outdone me in hoeing."

Dr. Joseph M. Tanner gives the following sketch of Wilford Woodruff:

"To the law and to the testimony; and if they speak not according to this word, it is because there is no light in them." If the whole religious life of Wilford Woodruff could be summed up in a single sentence, it would be in that Scriptural statement by which the truth of God's purposes was made evident. The Scripture was his safe guide in every walk of life. To him it was a living fountain. . . . He was a devout student of the Bible, and that book ac-

The Wilford Woodruff home

counts not alone for the spiritual quality of his life, but for the peculiar workings of his mind. There was nothing in life that he could not measure in terms of Holy Writ.

. . . To Wilford Woodruff God was a companion, a kind and loving father, a protector, a guide. . . . He regarded himself as a child of God to whom and with whom he had a right to speak.

. . . Nothing satisfied his spiritual cravings short of an actual communication he was looking, hoping, praying. When it came, it was as clear to his understanding as the rays of light at noonday sun. However, he put it to the test; he measured it in the light of Scripture; tested it by individual experiences, and it was in perfect harmony with his spiritual and intellectual being; and when once he put his hand to the plow, he never looked back.

. . . It is difficult in such a man to draw a line between his spiritual and his physical life. Certain it is, he made no distinction. Everything that touched divine purpose in the name of God; if he dug ditches and tilled the earth, it was equally in obedience to a divine command. He was just as devout with the scythe or the sickle as he was with the hymn book or in the pulpit.

. . . He was a man of medium height, of a robust nature, heavy set, and of unbounded nervous energy. . . . He loved to work. . . . To him it was a blessing, a privilege, an opportunity. . . . He could turn from one occupation to another without the least apparent effort. He would toil assiduously in the harvest field, and with scarcely a moment's notice be ready to receive the dignitaries of the nation that might happen to visit Salt Lake City while he was thus engaged. To sweat, was a divine command as much so as to pray; and in his life he exemplified in the highest degree that simple Christian life that makes for the physical, mental, and moral well-being of man. He believed sincerely in the moral supremacy of manual toil. He loved it and enjoyed it.

. . . No man ever did more in the Church to exalt work and put upon it the impress of divine command than Wilford Woodruff; and he was as unostentatious in physical toil as he was in every other occupation which he honestly and faithfully pursued.

. . . With him, however, friends were not selected because of their station in life; they were among all classes, the humblest as well as the highest. . . .

. . . Elder Woodruff was throughout all his life an ideal neighbor. His interest in those about him was one of helpfulness.

. . . By nature he was an unsuspicious man and that made his life free from the jealousies, envies, and misgivings so destructive of human happiness. That nature made him an optimist. He went about life not only looking for the good, but with ability to see it.

. . . He was not a man of marked prejudices, and there is no evidence that he ever pursued with malice those in whom he had lost confidence.

. . . In the details of administration, he was not very particular how things were done, provided they could be accomplished without friction and in a spirit which conformed to the principles of the gospel. He was never insistent, nor persistent in having his own way in his association with his fellowmen. . . . Instances are revealed in his journals where he took a strong stand when questions of right and wrong were at stake; and he manifested the fire of righteous zeal whenever any question arose not in harmony with his conception of God's message to the children of men.

. . . Whenever he spoke words of reproof, it was because he conceived it his duty to do so, not because it was his nature to criticize or to find fault.

. . . His family life was devoid of every show of ostentation. He enjoyed the companionship of the youngest child, and kept in touch with the sorrows and joys of family life. . . . He loved his wives and children, and in their midst was free, easy, and approachable. His discipline never carried with it any severity. In his home he found relaxation and rest from the strenuous life he led. His children loved him. They were free to reason and persuade. . . . His own example called for an industrious and obedient life in his home. It was easy for his children to understand what they should do by what they saw him do. . . . They would learn their duties by doing them. (Cowley, *Wilford Woodruff*, pp. 642-51.)

FOUR GENERATIONS
OF THE FAMILY OF
PRESIDENT WILFORD WOODRUFF.

Four generations of the Wilford Woodruff family

In 1889, at the time Wilford was called to preside over the Church, many of the leaders were in hiding.

The Edmunds Law had taken the Saints' voting, jury, and local rule rights and had made it illegal to live in polygamy. The Edmunds-Tucker Law now took away all Church property. The Church was even forced to pay rent for the use of the temple block, and President Woodruff could not come out of hiding to address the Saints in general conference.

GEORGE Q. CANNON
1889-1898

WILFORD WOODRUFF
1889-1898

JOSEPH F. SMITH
1889-1898

THE FIRST PRESIDENCY
1889-1898

The First Presidency, 1889-98: President Wilford Woodruff (center) and counselors George Q. Cannon and Joseph F. Smith

A beginning solution to the persecution problem came in 1890 when President Woodruff received the revelation suspending plural marriage. In September 1890 the Manifesto was announced to the world, and in October it was ratified in general conference, making it binding on the Saints. In the following years of President Woodruff's administration, the attitude of the world toward the Church improved steadily.

At the funeral services of President Woodruff, this

eloquent tribute was paid to him by President George Q. Cannon:

> In the passing of President Woodruff, a man has gone from our midst whose character was probably as angelical as any person who has ever lived upon the earth. . . .
>
> He did no man an injury, nor was he too proud even in his Apostolic calling to toil as other men toiled. . . . He was of a sweet disposition and possessed a character so lovely as to draw unto him friends in every walk of life. . . . He was gentle as a woman and his purity was like unto that of the angels themselves. . . .
>
> For years he lived on his 20-acre farm and took pleasure in beautifying his surroundings and wresting from the earth the elements to sustain life. . . .
>
> He was a heavenly being. It was heaven to be in his company. (Nibley, *The Presidents of the Church*, pp. 134-35.)

He was honest, unassuming, faithful, and industrious, and in the days of Joseph Smith he was called "Wilford the Faithful." Deserving of such a title, he maintained it to the end.

Interesting Facts and Contributions
of Wilford Woodruff

1. He kept a complete journal of his life, which has been invaluable to interpreters of Mormonism.

2. He assisted in the removal of the Saints from Illinois and was in the first company of pioneers to the Salt Lake Valley. It was from his carriage that Brigham Young first saw the valley.

3. "From the year 1834 to the close of 1895 he traveled 172,369 miles, held 7,655 meetings, attended 75 semi-annual conferences, 344 quarterly conferences; preached 3,526 discourses, established 77 preaching places in the missionary field; organized 51 branches of the Church; received 18,977 letters; wrote 11,519 letters; assisted in the confirmation into the Church of 8,952 persons, and in addition to his work in the St. George Temple, labored 603 days in the Endowment House in Salt Lake City. He traveled through England, Scotland, Wales, six islands of the sea, and 23 states and 5 territories of the United States." (Jenson, *LDS Biographical Encyclopedia*, vol. 1, p. 26.)

4. A great missionary, he baptized hundreds of persons into the Church in England in a period of eight months.

5. In 1850 he was elected a member of the senate of the Provisional State of Deseret. He served several terms in the territorial legislature.

6. In 1855 he became president of the Salt Lake City Horticulture Society. He was noted for his achievements in scientific horticulture and irrigation.

7. In 1856 he became Assistant Church Historian; in 1833 he became Church Historian.

8. The signers of the Declaration of Independence appeared to President Woodruff and asked that temple work be done for them.

9. During his administration fast day in the Church was changed from Thursday to Sunday.

10. He presented a "political address" that provided that men who are called to spend all their time in the ministry should not neglect their spiritual duties to seek political office without being properly released for that purpose.

11. He issued the Manifesto, a document that discontinued the practice of plural marriage.

12. He made the first voice recording as President.

13. He did much to encourage the cause of Church education.

Significant Dates and Events in Lifetime of Wilford Woodruff

Church Membership   1887: 192,000 (est.)   1898: 228,032
1898—Stakes: 40   Missions: 20   Temples: 4

U.S. Population, 1898: 73 million (est.)

World Population, 1898: 1.5 billion (est.)

U.S. Presidents (1887-98): Grover Cleveland, Benjamin Harrison, William McKinley

1807	Born in Farmington, Hartford County, Connecticut, March 1.
1821	Began work, learning trade of miller.
1830	Informed by Robert Mason of the restoration of the gospel.
1832	Read of Momonism in a newspaper article.
1833	Baptized in icy waters by Zera Pulsipher, December 31.
1834	Arrived in Kirtland; met Joseph Smith and made his home with him. Participated in march of Zion's Camp (age 26).
1834-36	Served mission to Southern States.
1837	Married Phoebe Carter. Received patriarchal blessing from Joseph Smith, Sr., April 15.
1837-48	Served mission to Eastern States and Fox Islands.
1839	Ordained an apostle by Brigham Young at Far West, Missouri, April 26 (age 32).
1839-41	Served mission to Great Britain.
1840	Arrived in Ledbury, Herefordshire, on March 4 and baptized about 600 persons in the next 38 days.
1841	With Heber C. Kimball, secured copyright to Book of Mormon at Stationer's Hall, London, in the name of Joseph Smith, Jr., February 8. Appointed a member of the

Nauvoo City Council, October 5. Viewed Urim and Thummim at Joseph Smith's home, Nauvoo, December 26.

1842   Business manager of *Times and Seasons*, January. Hauled stone for Nauvoo Temple, January.

1843   Served mission to Eastern States to solicit money for building Nauvoo Temple.

1844   Served mission to Eastern States.

1844-46   Presided over European Mission.

1846   Aided in the Saints' exodus westward.

1847   Entered Salt Lake Valley with Brigham Young.

1848-50   Presided over Church in Eastern States.

1850   Left New York with company for the West, April 9.

1851   Appointed to territorial legislature, served one term in lower house and twenty sessions in upper house.

1856   Appointed Assistant Church Historian.

1858-77   President of Deseret Agricultural and Manufacturing Society (which position later became president of Utah State Fair Board).

1867   Participated in reestablishment of the School of the Prophets in Salt Lake City.

1871   Pioneered in Rich County, Utah.

1877   Appointed president of St. George Temple, January 1. Baptized for the signers of the American Declaration of Independence, St. George Temple, August 21.

1879   Did missionary work among the Indians while in hiding because of plural marriage persecutions.

1880   Received revelation concerning the duties of the apostles and elders of Israel, which was submitted to the Twelve on April 4; accepted by that body as the word of God. Was sustained as President of the Council of the Twelve, October 6. Wrote a prefatory prayer confirming his revelation of January 26, 1880, which received the approval of President John Taylor, December 28 (age 73).

1881   Became president of the YMMIA.

1883   Was sustained as Church Historian and general Church recorder.

1884   Attended dedication of the Logan Temple and afterwards toured Idaho.

1885   Attended dedication of Brigham Young College, Logan.

1885-87 Went into self-imposed exile (Edmunds Act) with headquarters at St. George.

1887   Became leader of the Church as President of the Council of the Twelve (apostolic presidency). Watched funeral procession of President John Taylor from veiled windows of Historian's Office, July 17.

1887-96 *The following became states: North Dakota, South Dakota, Washington, Wyoming, Idaho, Utah.*

1887-98 Missions opened: Samoan, Society Islands, California, Eastern States, Montana, Colorado, Northwestern, Australian, New Zealand, Swiss, German.

1888   Manti Temple was dedicated by President Lorenzo Snow, May 21. General Church Board of Education was organized to establish and direct work of Church schools.

1889   Sustained as President of the Church, April 7, with George Q. Cannon and Joseph F. Smith as counselors in the First Presidency. Issued significant manifesto on church-state relationships, December 12 (age 82).

    Eiffel Tower was built in Paris, France. Territory of Oklahoma was opened to settlement. First Pan-American Conference was held. Brazil proclaimed itsef a republic.

1890   Manifesto was issued, discontinuing the practice of plural marriage, September 24.

1891   First LDS missionaries arrived at Tongan Islands. LDS College opened in Salt Lake City, October 8.

    Great earthquake in Japan.

1892   *Robert E. Peary proved Greenland to be an island.*

1893   President Woodruff dedicated the Salt Lake Temple, April 6. Tabernacle Choir sang at the Chicago World's Fair. A world parliament of religions was held at the World's Fair, to which the Church was not invited, and refused to listen to B. H. Roberts, representing the Church.

    A great panic was brought on by fear that the government would be forced off the gold standard.

1894   The Genealogical Society was established, November 13.

President Grover Cleveland, by proclamation, restored all political and civil rights to those who had been disfranchised by antipolygamy legislation. Sino-Japanese War began.

1896   Fast day was changed from Thursday to the first Sunday of the month, December 6. A monument was erected at the intersection of Main and South Temple streets in Salt Lake City in honor of Brigham Young. Congress passed a resolution restoring the escheated property of the Church.

Utah became a state. The first commercial projection of motion pictures. Henry Ford's first car appeared. Gold was discovered in Alaska.

1897   Wilford Woodruff dedicated Brigham Young Monument; ordained his son, Abraham Owen Woodruff, an apostle.

Earthquake in India was felt 900 miles away.

1898   Wilford Woodruff delivered his last public address at a July 24 celebration at Pioneer Square. He departed for the Pacific Coast, hoping to benefit his health, in July; died in San Francisco September 2 (age 91). First LDS baptisms in Jerusalem were held at Mary's Well.

Spanish-American War. Marie and Pierre Curie announced two elements they named polonium and radium.

1887-98   *Significant inventions: diesel engine (Germany); Stanley Steamer (U.S.); rayon (France); zipper (U.S.); adding machine (U.S.); X-ray (Germany); Kodak camera (U.S.); movie projector (U.S.); wireless telegraph (U.S.); automatic pistol (U.S.); photographic roll film (U.S.); safety razor (U.S.); modern submarine (U.S.).*

The First Presidency

During Wilford Woodruff's Administration

First Counselor	President	Second Counselor
George Q. Cannon	Wilford Woodruff	Joseph F. Smith
(1860)	(1839)	(1867)
1889-98	1889-98	1889-98

Council of the Twelve—April to October 1889

Lorenzo Snow (1849)	George Teasdale (1882)
Franklin D. Richards (1849)	Heber J. Grant (1882)
Brigham Young, Jr. (1868)	John W. Taylor (1884)
Moses Thatcher (1879)	Marriner W. Merrill (1889)
Francis M. Lyman (1880)	Anthon H. Lund (1889)
John Henry Smith (1880)	Abraham H. Cannon (1889)

Died

Added

1888—Erastus Snow	Matthias F. Cowley (1897)
1896—Abraham H. Cannon	Abraham O. Woodruff (1897)

Dropped from the Council

1896—Moses Thatcher

September 1898

Lorenzo Snow (1849)	Heber J. Grant (1882)
Franklin D. Richards (1849)	John W. Taylor (1884)
Brigham Young, Jr. (1868)	Marriner W. Merrill (1889)
Francis M. Lyman (1880)	Anthon H. Lund (1889)
John Henry Smith (1880)	Matthias F. Cowley (1897)
George Teasdale (1882)	Abraham O. Woodruff (1897)

Note: Dates in parentheses indicate date ordained member of the Council of the Twelve.

Testimony of Wilford Woodruff

I have been acquainted long enough with this work to know its truth; I have had sufficient experience in it to see and to know that the hand of God is in it, and that it is controlled and guided by the spirit of the Almighty and the revelations of Heaven; to know that from the commencement of it, it has been the design of the God of Heaven to establish His Kingdom upon the earth, to be thrown down no more forever.

Those who have been acquainted with the Prophet Joseph, who laid the foundation of this Church and Kingdom, who was an instrument in the hand of God in bringing to light the Gospel in this last dispensation, know well that every feeling of his soul, every sentiment of his mind, and every act of his life proved that he was determined to maintain the principle of truth even to the sacrificing of his life. His soul swelled wide as eternity for the welfare of the human family.

The Gospel has gone forth in our day in its true glory, power, order and light, as it always did when God had a people among men that He acknowledged. That same organization and Gospel that Christ died for, and the apostles spilled their blood to vindicate, is again established in this generation. How did it come? By the ministering of an Holy Angel of God out of heaven, who held converse with man and revealed unto him the darkness that enveloped the world, and unfolded unto him the gross darkness that surrounded the nations, those scenes that should take place in this generation, and would follow each other in quick succession, even unto the coming of the Messiah.

The Angel taught Joseph Smith those principles which are necessary for the salvation of the world; and the Lord gave him commandments and sealed upon him the Priesthood, and gave him power to administer the ordinances of the house of the Lord. He told him the Gospel was not among men and that there was not a true organization of His kingdom in the world, that the people had turned away from His true order, changed the ordinances and broken the everlasting covenant, and inherited lies and things wherein there was no profit.

He told him the time had come to lay the foundation for the establishment of the Kingdom of God among men for the last time, preparatory to the winding up scene. Joseph was strengthened by the Spirit and power of God, and was enabled to listen to the teachings of the Angel. He told him he should be made an instrument in the hands of the Lord, if he kept His commandments, in doing a good work upon the earth; that his name should be held in honor by the honest in heart, and in dishonor throughout the nations by the wicked. He told him he should be an instrument in laying the foundation of a work that should gather tens of thousands of the children of men, in the generation in which he lived, from every nation under heaven, who should hear the sound of it through his instrumentality. He told him the nations were wrapped in wickedness and abominations, and that the judgments of God were ready to be poured out upon them in their fullness; that the angels were holding the vials of His wrath in readiness; but the decree is, that they shall not be poured out until the nations are warned, that they may be left without an excuse. (Green, *Testimonies of Our Leaders*, pp. 42-43.)

Personal Experience of Wilford Woodruff

My wife Phoebe was attacked on the twenty-third of November by a severe headache, which terminated in brain fever. She grew more and more distressed daily as we continued our journey. It was a terrible ordeal for a woman to travel in a wagon over such rough roads, afflicted as she was. At the same time our child was also very sick.

The first of December was a trying day to my soul. My wife continued to fail, and about four o'clock in the afternoon appeared to be stricken with death. I stopped my team, and it seemed as if she then would breathe her last, lying there in the wagon. Two of the sisters sat beside her, to see if they could do anything for her in her last moments. I stood upon the ground, in deep affliction, and meditated. Then I cried to the Lord, praying that she might live and not be taken from me, and claiming the promises the Lord had made to me through the Prophet and Patriarch. Her spirit revived, and I drove a short distance to a tavern, got her into a room and worked over her and her babe all night, praying to the Lord to preserve their lives.

In the morning, circumstances were such that I was under the necessity of removing them from the inn, as there was so much noise and confusion there that my wife could not endure it. I carried her out to her bed in the wagon and drove two miles, when I alighted at a house and carried my wife and her bed into it, with a determination to tarry there until she recovered her health or passed away. This was on Sunday morning,

December second. After getting my wife and things into the house and providing wood to keep up a fire, I employed my time in taking care of her. It looked as if she had but a short time to live. She called me to her bedside in the evening, and said she felt as if a few moments more would end her existence in this life. She manifested great confidence in the cause we had embraced, and exhorted me to have confidence in God and to keep His commandments. To all appearances she was dying. I laid hands upon her and prayed for her, and she soon revived and slept some during the night.

December 3 found my wife very low. I spent the day in taking care of her, and the day following I returned to Eaton to get some things for her. She seemed to be sinking gradually, and in the evening the spirit apparently left her body, and she was dead. The sisters gathered around, weeping, while I stood looking at her in sorrow. The spirit and power of God began to rest upon me until, for the first time during her sickness, faith filled my soul, although she lay before me as one dead.

I had some oil that was consecrated for my anointing while in Kirtland. I took it and consecrated it again before the Lord, for anointing the sick. I then bowed down before the Lord, prayed for the life of my companion, and in the name of the Lord anointed her body with the oil. I then laid my hands upon her, and in the name of Jesus Christ I rebuked the power of death and of the destroyer, and commanded the same to depart from her and the spirit of life to enter her body. Her spirit returned to her body, and from that hour she was made whole; and we all felt to praise the name of God, and to trust in him and keep his commandments.

While I was undergoing this ordeal (as my wife related afterwards) her spirit left her body, and she saw it lying upon the bed and the sisters there weeping. She looked at them and at me, and upon her babe. While gazing upon this scene, two persons came into the room, carrying a coffin, and told her they had come for her body. One of these messengers said to her that she might have her choice. She might go to rest in the spirit world, or, upon one condition, she could have the privilege of returning to her tabernacle and of continuing her labors upon the earth. The condition was that if she felt she could stand by her husband, and with him pass through all the cares, trials, tribulations, and afflictions of life which he would be called upon to pass through for the gospel's sake unto the end, she might return. When she looked at the situation of her husband and child she said, "Yes I will do it." At the moment that decision was made the power of faith rested upon me, and when I administered to her, her spirit re-entered her tabernacle. (Cowley, *Wilford Woodruff*, pp. 96-98.)

Quotations from Wilford Woodruff

APOSTASY
It will do me no good if I apostatize because I think somebody else does not do right.

BAPTISM
Being baptized into the Church is like learning the alphabet in our mother tongue—it is the very first step. But having received the first principles of the gospel of Christ, let us go on to perfection.

CHILDREN
Our children should be prepared to build up the kingdom of God. Then qualify them in the ways of childhood for the great duties they will be called upon to perform.

CHRIST
The Savior came and tabernacled in the flesh, and entered unto the duties of the priesthood at thirty years of age. After laboring three and a half years he was crucified and put to death in fulfillment of certain predictions concerning him. He laid down his life as a sacrifice for sin, to redeem the world. When men are called upon to repent of their sins, the call has reference to their own individual sins, not to Adam's transgressions. What is called the original sin was atoned for through the death of Christ irrespective of any action on the part of man, also man's individual sin was atoned for by the same sacrifice, but on condition of his obedience to the gospel plan of salvation when proclaimed in his hearing.

CHURCH
I have had sufficient experience in this work to know that the hand of God is in it; that it is controlled and guided by his Spirit and by revelation from heaven. It is the design of God to establish his kingdom upon earth to be thrown down no more.

DISPENSATIONS
We live in a dispensation and generation in which the kingdom has been built up, and it will be permanently established, never more to be thrown down.

DEATH

All men who go into the spirit world, and who bear the Holy Priesthood, will continue their labors. Their work will follow them. Their work will not cease when they lay their tabernacles down here in the tomb.

ETERNAL PROGRESSION

If there was a point where man in his progression could not proceed any further, the very idea would throw a gloom over every intelligent and reflecting mind. God himself is still increasing and progressing in knowledge, power, and dominion, and will do so, worlds without end. It is just so with us.

EXALTATION

Is there anything that will pay you to lose the principles of salvation, to lose a part in the first resurrection with the privilege of standing in the morning of the resurrection clothed with glory, immortality, and eternal life. . . ? No, there is nothing.

FAITH

If a person goes without food for twenty-four hours, we all know that that individual will become very hungry; and it is precisely so with those who hunger for the principles of eternal life. While we enjoy the Spirit of the Lord, we shall find that there is enough and abundance to feed every human soul.

FASTING

I can fast, and so can any other man; and if it makes my head ache by keeping the commandments of God, let it ache.

HOME

Our children should not be neglected; they should receive a proper education in both spiritual and temporal things. That is the best legacy any parents can leave to their children. We should teach them to pray, and instill into their minds while young every correct principle. Ninety-nine out of every hundred children who are taught by their parents the principles of honesty and integrity, truth and virtue, will observe them through life. Such principles will exalt any people or nation who make them the rule of their conduct. . . . Our children should be prepared to build up the kingdom of God. Then qualify them in the days of childhood for the great duties they will be called upon to perform. . . .

LAW

All who embrace the principles of the gospel of Christ will be saved by them. He that abides a law will be preserved by it. Any man who abides the law of the gospel will be saved and receive exaltation and glory by it.

MOTHER
I consider that the mother has a greater influence over her posterity than any other person can have.

PRAYER
Whenever you are in doubt about any duty or work which you have to perform never proceed to do anything until you go and labor in prayer and get the Holy Spirit. Wherever the Spirit dictates you to go or to do, that will be right; and, by following its dictates, you will come out right.

RESURRECTION
While I was upon my knees praying, my room was filled with light. I looked up and a messenger stood by my side. I arose, and this personage told me he had come to instruct me. He presented before me a panorama . . . he showed me the resurrection of the dead— what is termed the first and second resurrection . . . vast fields of graves were before me, and the Spirit of God rested upon the earth like a shower of gentle rain, and when that fell upon the graves they were opened, and an immense host of human beings came forth.

REVELATION
Yes, we have revelation. The Church of God could not live twenty-four hours without revelation.

SECOND COMING OF CHRIST
He will never come until the Jews are gathered home and have rebuilt their temple and city and the Gentiles have gone up there to battle against them. He will never come until his Saints have built up Zion and have fulfilled the revelations which have been spoken concerning it. He will never come until the Gentiles throughout the whole Christian world have been warned by the inspired elders of Israel.

SPIRIT WORLD
I will say that this nation and all nations, together with presidents, kings, emperors, judges, and all men, righteous and wicked, have got to get into the spirit world and stand before the bar of God. They have got to give an account of the deeds done in the body.

TEMPLES
What will be the condition of these saviors upon Mount Zion? These Saints of the Lord will hold the keys of salvation to their father's house to the endless ages of eternity.

TITHING

I want the brethren to understand this one thing, that our tithing, our labor, our works are not for the exaltation of the Almighty, but they are for us.

Lorenzo Snow, Fifth President (1814-1901)

LORENZO SNOW

Fifth President of the Church

Born: April 3, 1814, Mantua, Ohio

Died: October 10, 1901, Salt Lake City, Utah (age 87)

President of the Church: September 13, 1898, to
October 10, 1901 (3 years)

Physical Characteristics: Five feet six inches tall, 140
pounds, slender build, gray eyes, full beard, white
hair, small but rugged in appearance

Areas of Distinction: Prophet, writer, educator,
missionary, pioneer, legislator, colonizer

*Family: Son of Oliver and Rosetta Pettibone Snow.
Married Charlotte Squires, 1845 (died Sept. 25,
1850); married Mary Adaline Goddard, 1845 (died
Dec. 28, 1898), three children; married Sarah Ann
Prichard, 1845 (died, no date); married Eleanor
Houtz, 1845 (died Sept. 13, 1896); married Harriet
Amelia Squires, Jan. 17, 1846 (died May 12, 1890),
five children; married Caroline Horton, Oct. 9,
1853 (died Feb. 21, 1857), three children; married
Mary Elizabeth Houtz** (died Mar. 31, 1906); married
Phoebe Amelia Woodruff** (died Feb. 15, 1897);
married Sarah Minnie Jensen, June 12, 1871 (died
Jan. 2, 1908), five children. Total number of
children not available.

*Genealogical Society
**Marriage date not available

Profile of Lorenzo Snow

In 1836 Lorenzo Snow, an undergraduate at Oberlin College, became thoroughly disillusioned regarding religion. He is quoted as saying, "If there is nothing better than is to be found here in Oberlin College, goodbye to all religions." A visit to his sister Eliza, who had joined The Church of Jesus Christ of Latter-day Saints, brought him in contact with Joseph Smith and other members. His decision to join the Church in June 1836 led to an intense desire for a full testimony of the truth of the gospel. Consequently, he sought a secluded wooded area to pray. He remembered the experience thus:

> I had no sooner opened my lips in an effort to pray, than I heard a sound, just above my head, like the rustling of silken robes, and immediately the Spirit of God descended upon me, completely enveloping my whole person, filling me, from the crown of my head to the soles of my feet, and O, the joy and happiness I felt. . . . I then received a perfect knowledge that God lives, that Jesus Christ is the son of God, of the restoration of the holy Priesthood, and the fulness of the Gospel. (Snow, *Biography and Family Record of Lorenzo Snow*, pp. 7-8.)

A short time later, Elder Joseph Smith, Patriarch to the Church and father of the Prophet, gave Lorenzo Snow a remarkable blessing. Among its promises were these:

> Thou hast a great work to perform. . . . God has called thee to the ministry. Thou must preach the gospel . . . to the inhabitants

Lorenzo Snow, 1853

of the earth. Thou shalt become a mighty man. Thou shalt have . . .
power to rend the [veil] and see Jesus Christ at the right hand of
the Father. . . . there shall not be a mightier man on earth than thou,
thy faith shall increase and grow stronger till it shall become like
Peter's. Thou shall restore the sick; the diseased shall send to thee
their aprons and handkerchiefs and by thy touch their owners shall
be made whole. The dead shall rise and come forth at thy bidding. . . .
Thou shalt have long life . . . yet not be old; age shall not come
upon thee; the vigor of thy mind shall not be abated and the vigor
of thy body shall be preserved. . . . No power shall be able to take
thy life as long as thy life shall be useful to the children of men.
(*Improvement Era*, June 1919, p. 655.)

This remarkable prophecy, given to a young man
just twenty-two years of age, was explicitly fulfilled.

Lorenzo Snow did perform a great work. He preached the reemphasized law of tithing, helping to save the Church from financial ruin and to lay the foundation for its present strength and growth. In a temporal sense, certainly there was no mightier man in the world, especially during his presidency over the Church.

But his administrative talents were no greater than his spiritual ones. He healed the sick in the particular way his patriarchal blessing had specified. Lucille Snow Tracy, his daughter, remembers sick people sending handkerchiefs to her father, and his retiring to his closet, kneeling in prayer, and blessing the senders that they might return to health and strength.

He also brought the dead back to life. One incident happened while he was speaking in the Brigham City Tabernacle. He was handed a note stating that a young girl, Ella Jensen, had just died, and asking that he arrange the funeral program. He left immediately, taking with him Rudger Clawson, president of Box Elder Stake. It was more than two hours after the girl's death that the two men arrived at the house. Jacob Jensen, the girl's father, remembered what happened:

> After standing at Ella's bedside for a minute or two, President Snow asked if we had any consecrated oil in the house. I was greatly surprised, but told him yes and got it for him. He handed the bottle of oil to Brother Clawson and asked him to anoint Ella. He then confirmed the anointing.
>
> During the administration I was particularly impressed with some of the words which he used and can well remember them now. He said: "Dear Ella, I command you, in the name of the Lord Jesus Christ, to come back and live, your mission is not ended. You shall yet live to perform a great mission."
>
> He said she should yet live to rear a large family and be a comfort to her parents and friends.
>
> . . .After President Snow had finished the blessing, he turned to my wife and me and said: "Now do not mourn or grieve any more. It will be all right. Brother Clawson and I are busy and must go, we cannot stay, but you just be patient and wait, and do not mourn, because it will be all right."

About an hour went by and friends, hearing the news of Ella's death came to offer condolences. The father continued his account:

. . .We were sitting there watching by the bedside, her mother and myself, when all at once she opened her eyes. She looked about the room, saw us sitting there, but she looked for someone else, and the first thing she said was: "Where is he? Where is he?" We asked, "Who? Where is who?" "Why, Brother Snow," she replied. "He called me back. . . . Why did he call me back? I was so happy and did not want to come back." (*Improvement Era*, September 1929, pp. 881-86.)

GEORGE Q. CANNON
1898-1901

LORENZO SNOW
1898-1901

JOSEPH F. SMITH
1898-1901

THE FIRST PRESIDENCY
1898-1901

The First Presidency, 1898-1901: President Lorenzo Snow (center) and counselors George Q. Cannon and Joseph F. Smith

This girl, who then gave a thrilling account of her experience in the three hours after death, lived to become the mother of eight children.

Another remarkable incident happened while Brother Snow was on a mission to the Sandwich (Hawaiian) Islands when he himself was virtually raised from the dead. A small surf boat carrying the missionaries to the mainland was overturned, and some time elapsed before Elder Snow's body was recovered. When he was found, though his body was stiff and lifeless, he was miraculously restored to life and health.

Lorenzo Snow, one of a family of talented converts, was called to be an apostle in 1849 at the age of thirty-four. In the same year he was sent to Europe to extend the missionary work of the Church, and he helped establish new missions in Italy, Switzerland, and Malta and directed the opening of a mission in India.

During the community building period in Utah, his leadership was further manifest in the successful organization and management of the Brigham City Mercantile and Manufacturing Association, which became a pattern for similar home-industry enterprises among the settlements of the Saints.

He lived for a time in Brigham City (1873-80), where he helped the people start a woolen mill, a tannery, a shoe factory, a hat factory, and a cheese factory. He also started a tailor shop, a furniture shop, a wagon shop, a blacksmith, a tin shop, and many other types of shops. He taught the people to work together. Herds of sheep and cattle were soon owned communally. The townspeople planted trees, built dams, dug irrigation ditches, and planted crops. The people had little money, so the men were paid for their work in scrip, which could be exchanged for food, clothing, building materials, and furniture, as well as to pay for the services of masons, carpenters, blacksmiths, admission to concerts, or newspaper subscriptions.

When President Wilford Woodruff died September 2, 1898, Lorenzo Snow, in his humility, went to the temple to seek the Lord's help. He fasted and prayed for three days and nights, seeking the Lord's answer concerning what he should do. The Lord Jesus Christ appeared to him and told him he was to organize the presidency of the Church at once.

On September 13, 1898, eleven days after the death of Wilford Woodruff, President Snow succeeded to the presidency. Although he was eighty-four years old, he took up his responsibilities with great faith and remarkable vigor, and accomplished two important goals in his three-year administration. He helped free the Church from debt through the revival of spiritual and temporal unity of its members, and he gave missionary work a new impetus and vitality in America and abroad.

Many nonmembers of the Church recognized President Snow's greatness. So distinguished did this good man become and so impressive was his character and personality that a lecturer and writer, the Rev. Doctor Prentis from South Carolina, said of him:

> I had expected to find intellect, intellectuality, benevolence, dignity, composure and strength depicted upon the face of the President of the Church of Jesus Christ of Latter-day Saints; but when I was introduced to President Lorenzo Snow for a second I was startled to see the holiest face but one I had ever been privileged to look upon. His face was a poem of peace, his presence a benediction of peace. In the tranquil depths of his eyes were the "home of silent Prayer" and the abode of spiritual strength. As he talked of the more sure word of prophecy and the certainty of the hope which was his, and the abiding faith which had conquered the trials and difficulties of a tragic life . . . I watched the play of emotions and studied with fascinated attention, the subtle shades of expression which spoke so plainly the workings of his soul; and the strangest feeling stole over me, that I stood on holy ground; that this man did not act from the commonplace motives of policy, interest or expediency, but he acted from a far off center. . . . The picture of that slight, venerable form hallowed with the aura of an ineffable peace will haunt my heart like the vision of a celestial picture thrown upon the camera . . . of my dreaming soul. (Romney, *The Life of Lorenzo Snow*, pp. 14-15.)

Another nonmember characterized him thus:

> President Snow is a cultured man, in mind and soul and body. His language is choice, diplomatic, friendly, scholarly. His mannerism shows the studied grace of schools. The tenor of his spirit is as

gentle as a child. You are introduced to him. You are pleased with
him. You converse with him, you like him. You visit with him
long, you love him. And yet, he is a "Mormon!"

So wrote the Reverend W. D. Cornell in an article
that appeared in the *Commonwealth* in 1899.

President Snow was a genial and kind man, yet unflinching in his sense of duty and the cause of truth. He
once declared that he would sooner die a thousand deaths
than surrender his faith; those who heard him believed
him.

But over all, his distinguished trait was his absolute simplicity,
not a lack of knowledge, but an inherent love of truth and distaste
for untruth and indirection. No newspaper interviewer ever received
anything but a direct answer of unmistakable meaning from him. . . .

In addition to his high spiritual endowment Lorenzo Snow was
a keen, capable business executive who pulled the Church out of
the depths of financial poverty, restored its credit, stimulated the
Saints to pay their tithing and started the Church on the road to
economic prosperity. . . .

Of all men that we have known, Lorenzo Snow, in his last
days, looked most like a Prophet. When you met him, you felt
that you were in the presence of one who had stepped out of a
finer world; one who was fit to mingle with the elect in the holiest
places. He lived very close to the Lord. (Hinckley, *The Faith of Our
Pioneer Fathers*, pp. 54-55.)

The *Deseret News* of October 11, 1901, commented:

The news of the death of President Lorenzo Snow has been
received with sorrow from all classes of the community. It occasioned
a severe shock to the Latter-day Saints, and great regret among
people who knew him but were not believers in the faith of which
he was so prominent a representative. Even the strenuous opponents
of the Church speak of him in terms of respect for his eminent
abilities, kindly disposition and firm and upright character.

Interesting Facts and Contributions
of Lorenzo Snow

1. He was the last President to know Joseph Smith personally as a friend.
2. He served as President for only three years.
3. He saw the Savior in the Salt Lake Temple.
4. His reaction to plural marriage illustrates his loyalty to the teachings of the Church. When Joseph Smith explained its principles to him, he decided to marry although he was at the time a bachelor.
5. He was arrested for practicing plural marriage. His case was especially important, since it became the test case for the legality of the so-called segregation ruling. He served eleven months in prison. Later the Supreme Court of the United States reversed the Utah court's ruling that the "segregation ruling" was unconstitutional.
6. In 1852 he was elected to the territorial legislature, where he served for thirty years. For ten years he was president of the upper house.
7. In 1853 he led fifty families to Brigham City, which became his residence for forty years. Later he established the United Order there. He will long be remembered for his efforts to make a success of the United Order.
8. He was a promoter and manager of many financial and business enterprises.
9. He improved the financial status of the Church and started the Church on the road to economic prosperity.
10. There was increased missionary activity during his term of office.

11. A great champion of education, he was the first of the Presidents of the Church to have some college education. In 1888 he became a member of the General Church Board of Education.

12. He was the first president of the Salt Lake Temple.

13. He served as general president of both the YMMIA and the Deseret Sunday School Union.

14. He brought about a change in Church policy with regard to the apostles working directly with the Saints. He felt it was time for the Twelve to travel and become witnesses of Christ throughout the world rather than work in Zion only.

15. One of his greatest contributions to the Church's theology is his aphorism: "As man is, God once was; as God is, man may be." This principle was later called the doctrine of eternal progression.

16. He served five missions: Southern States, Great Britain, Italy-Switzerland, Hawaii, Europe-Holland.

Significant Dates and Events in Lifetime of
Lorenzo Snow

Church Membership, 1898: 228,032   1901: 278,645

1901—Stakes: 50   Missions: 21   Temples: 4

U.S. Population, 1901: 77.5 million (est.)

World Population, 1901: 1.6 billion (est.)

U.S. Presidents, 1898-1901: William McKinley, Theodore Roosevelt

1814   Born at Mantua, Ohio, April 3.

1831   His mother and sister, Leonora, joined the Church. Lorenzo heard the Prophet Joseph Smith speak at Hiram, Ohio.

1835   His military career ended and he was awarded a lieutenant's commission; entered Oberlin College. Eliza R. Snow, sister of Lorenzo, joined the Church.

1836   Baptized on June 23 by John Boynton of the Council of the Twelve. Attended the School of the Prophets in Kirtland.

1837   Served a mission in Ohio.

1838-39   Moved to Far West; served a mission to southern Missouri, Illinois, Kentucky, and Ohio.

1840-43   Served a mission to Great Britain, and presented a copy of the Book of Mormon to Queen Victoria.

1843   Schoolteacher at Lima, Illinois. Led a company of 250 Saints to Nauvoo.

1844   Learned of martyrdom of Joseph Smith while on an electioneering mission for the Prophet in Ohio.

1845   Married Charlotte Squires and Mary Adaline Goodard; Sarah Ann Richards and Harriet Amelia Squires.

1846-48   Crossed the plains. Presided over Mt. Pisgah, grain settlement in Ohio. Became very ill and almost died.

1848   Arrived in Salt Lake Valley.

1849   Was ordained an apostle on February 12 by Heber C. Kimball (age 34). Helped organize Perpetual Emigration Fund.

1849-52   Served mission to Europe (Italy, England, Switzerland, Malta).

1850   Organized Church in Italy; sent elders to Malta and to Bombay, India.

1852   Organized Polysophical Society, organization for mutual development in many fields of thought.

1853   Called to preside over colonization of Brigham City.

1854   Participated in organization of Philosophical Society, later called Universal Scientific Society.

1856   Became president of Box Elder Stake.

1864   Served short-term mission to Hawaii.

1864-66   Labored among the Saints, especially in Brigham City.

1865   Organized Brigham City Cooperative Association.

1872-73   President of Utah Territorial Legislative Council. Toured Europe and Asia Minor and participated in dedication of Palestine for the gathering of the Jews.

1873   Was sustained as counselor to President Brigham Young, April 4.

1874   Was sustained as assistant counselor, May 9.

1885   Served short-term mission to Indian Israel in northwestern United States.

1886-87   Served eleven-month prison term on plural marriage charge.

1888   Dedicated Manti Temple.

1889   Became President of the Council of the Twelve (age 75).

1893   Became President of the Salt Lake Temple.

1897   *The Improvement Era* began publication, sponsored by the YMMIA.

1898   Was sustained as President of the Church September 13, at age 84, with George Q. Cannon and Joseph F. Smith as counselors. Church bonds were issued because of financial difficulties, since Church had been disincorporated. Brigham

Young College was dedicated at Logan, Utah, December 24.
New Zealand Mission was opened. Nationwide opposition
to the Church came because Brigham H. Roberts was elected
to Congress; he was denied his seat after months of hearings
because he had practiced plural marriage.

Hawaii, Puerto Rico, and the Philippines became American territories.

1898-1901 Missions opened: Mexican, Japanese.

1899   At a solemn assembly of principal officers of the priesthood,
           held on July 2, a resolution was adopted by 623 leaders
           who pledged to observe the law of tithing and teach the
           Saints to do the same.

           *The British and Dutch began fighting the Boer War, which led
           to British control of South Africa.*

1899-1901 Members in foreign lands were encouraged to build
           Zion in their countries and not immigrate to Utah.

1900   Fiftieth anniversary of the introduction of the gospel into
           Scandinavia was observed.

           *First voice radio transmission was demonstrated. An underground
           explosion at Scofield, Utah, killed 200 miners. A hurricane and
           tidal wave wrecked Galveston, Texas, killing an estimated 7,000
           people, the greatest loss of life in any storm in American history.*

1901   Lorenzo Snow died at Salt Lake City, October 10 (age 87).

           *President William McKinley was assassinated September 14. First
           wireless telegraph message was sent across the Atlantic.*

1898-1901 *Significant inventions: electric steel (France); gas turbine (U.S.);
           photographc paper (U.S.); tractor (U.S.); wireless telephone (U.S.).*

The First Presidency
During Lorenzo Snow's Administration

First Counselor	President	Second Counselor
George Q. Cannon	Lorenzo Snow	Joseph F. Smith
(1860)	(1849)	(1867)
1898-1901	1898-1901	1898-1901

Council of the Twelve—October 1898

Franklin D. Richards (1849)   John W. Taylor (1884)
Brigham Young, Jr. (1868)   Marriner W. Merrill (1889)
Francis M. Lyman (1880)   Anthon H. Lund (1889)
John Henry Smith (1880)   Matthias F. Cowley (1897)
George Teasdale (1882)   Abraham O. Woodruff (1897)
Heber J. Grant (1882)   Rudger Clawson (1898)

Died   **Added**

1899—Franklin D. Richards   Reed Smoot (1900)

April 1900

Brigham Young, Jr. (1868)   Marriner W. Merrill (1889)
Francis M. Lyman (1880)   Anthon H. Lund (1889)
John Henry Smith (1880)   Matthias F. Cowley (1897)
George Teasdale (1882)   Abraham O. Woodruff (1897)
Heber J. Grant (1882)   Rudger Clawson (1898)
John W. Taylor (1884)   Reed Smoot (1900)

Note: Dates in parentheses indicate date ordained a member of the Council of the Twelve.

Testimony of Lorenzo Snow

I testify before this assembly, as I have testified before the people throughout the different states of the union, and throughout England, Ireland, Scotland, Wales, Italy, Switzerland and France, that God Almighty, through my obedience to the Gospel of Jesus, has revealed to me tangibly that this is the work of God, that this is His Gospel, and that this is His Kingdom which Daniel prophesied should be set up in the last days. I prophesy that any man who will be humble before the Lord—any man who will, with child-like simplicity, be baptized for the remission of his sins, shall receive the Holy Ghost, which shall lead him into all truth, and show him things to come; he shall receive a knowledge from God that His Kingdom has been established in these latter days, and that it shall never be thrown down, or be left to another people.

In saying this, I say no more than every man could say, and has said, who had a dispensation of the Gospel. I would not have traveled over the face of the earth as I have for the last thirty-five years unless God had revealed this unto me. I have already said nothing but absolute duty ever prompted me to travel and preach this Gospel; but I received a dispensation from the Most High, and I could say, and do say now, as the Apostle Paul said, "I received not this Gospel from man, but I received it by revelation from God." (Green, *Testimonies of Our Leaders*, p. 45.)

Personal Experience of Lorenzo Snow

For some time President Woodruff's health had been failing. Nearly every evening President Lorenzo Snow visited him at his home. This particular evening the doctors said that President Woodruff could not live much longer, that he was becoming weaker every day. President Snow was greatly worried.

My father went to his room in the Salt Lake Temple, dressed in his robes of the priesthood, knelt at the sacred altar in the Holy of Holies in the house of the Lord, and there plead to the Lord to spare President Woodruff's life, that President Woodruff might outlive him, and that the great responsibility of Church leadership would not fall upon his shoulders. Yet he promised the Lord that he would devotedly perform any duty required at his hands. At this time he was in his eighty-sixth year.

Soon after this President Woodruff was taken to California, where he died Friday morning at 6:40 o'clock, September 2, 1898. President George Q. Cannon at once wired the information to the President's office in Salt Lake City. The telegram was delivered to him on the street in Brigham. He read it to President Rudger Clawson, then president of Box Elder Stake, who was with him, went to the telegraph office, and replied that he would leave on the train about 5:30 that evening. He reached Salt Lake City about 7:15, proceeded to the President's office, gave some instructions, and then went to his private room in the Salt Lake Temple.

President Snow put on his holy temple robes, repaired again to the same sacred altar, offered up the signs of the Priesthood, and poured out his heart to the Lord. He reminded the Lord how he plead for President Woodruff's life to be spared, that President Woodruff's days would be lengthened beyond his own, that he might never be called upon to bear the heavy burdens and responsibilities of the Church. "Nevertheless," he said, "Thy will be done. I have not sought this responsibility, but if it be Thy will, I now present myself before Thee for Thy guidance and instruction. I ask that Thou show me what Thou wouldst have me do."

After finishing his prayer he expected a reply, some special manifestation from the Lord. So he waited—and waited—and waited. There was no reply, no voice, no visitation, no manifestation. He left the altar and the room in great disappointment. Passing through the Celestial room and out into the large corridor, a glorious manifestation was given President Snow, which I relate in the words of his granddaughter, Allie Young Pond:

One evening while I was visiting Grandpa Snow in his room in the Salt Lake Temple, I remained until the door keepers had gone and the night-watchmen had not yet come in, so grandpa said he would take me to the main front entrance and let me out that way. He got his bunch of keys from his dresser. After we left his room, and while we were still in the large corridor leading into the celestial room, I was walking several steps ahead of grandpa when he stopped and said: "Wait a moment, Allie, I want to tell you something. It was right here that the Lord Jesus Christ appeared to me at the time of the death of President Woodruff. He instructed me to go right ahead and reorganize the First Presidency of the Church at once and not wait as had been done after the death of the previous presidents, and that I was to succeed President Woodruff."

Then grandpa came a step nearer and held out his left hand and said: "He stood right here, about three feet above the floor. It looked as though he stood on a plate of solid gold."

Grandpa told me what a glorious personage the Savior is and described his hands, feet, countenance and beautiful white robes, all of which were of such a glory of whiteness and brightness that he could hardly gaze upon him.

Then he came another step nearer and put his right hand on

my head and said: "Now granddaughter, I want you to remember that this is the testimony of your grandfather, that he told you with his own lips that he actually saw the Savior, here in the temple, and talked with him face to face." (Leroi C. Snow, "An Experience of My Father's," *Improvement Era*, September 1933, p. 677.)

Quotations from Lorenzo Snow

BROTHERHOOD
There is nothing more elevating to ourselves and pleasing to God than those things that pertain to the accomplishment of a brotherhood.

CHRIST
Jesus, while traveling here on earth, fulfilling his mission, told the people he did not perform the miracles he wrought in their midst by his own power, nor by his own wisdom; but he was there in order to accomplish the will of his Father. He came not to seek the glory of men, and the honor of men; but to seek the honor and glory of his Father that sent him. Said he, "I am come in my Father's name, and ye receive me not, if another shall come in his own name, him ye will receive." Now, the peculiarity of his mission, and that which distinguished it from other missions, was this: he came not to seek the glory and honor of men, but to seek the honor and glory of his Father, and to accomplish the work of his Father who sent him. Herein lay the secret of his prosperity; and herein lies the secret of the prosperity of every individual who works upon the same principle.

CHURCH
God established the Church of Jesus Christ of Latter-day Saints, by direct revelation; this is a fact, clearly and distinctively revealed to thousands. The so-called "Mormon" people, in these valleys, are the acknowledged people of God, and are here, not by their own choice, but by immediate command of God. The work and management is the Lord's—not the people's—they do His bidding, and He, alone, is responsible for the result.

EXALTATION
The reward of righteousness is exaltation.

GODHOOD
As man is, God once was; as God is, man may be.

HEAVEN
A person never can enjoy heaven until he learns how . . . to act upon its principles.

HOLY GHOST
Some suppose they must obtain religion before they are baptized; but the Savior and apostles teach us to be baptized in order to get religion. Be baptized, says Peter, for the remission of sins, and ye shall receive the Holy Ghost. To obtain the gift of the Holy Ghost is to obtain religion. Faith and repentance were to go before baptism; but remission of sins, and gift of the Holy Ghost, were to follow this ordinance.

MARRIAGE
When two Latter-day Saints are united together in marriage, promises are made to them concerning their offspring that reach from eternity to eternity. They are promised that they shall have the power and the right to govern and control and administer salvation and exaltation and glory to their offspring worlds without end. And what offspring they do not have here, undoubtedly there will be opportunities to have them hereafter. What else could man wish? A man and a woman in the other life, having celestial bodies, free from sickness and disease, glorified and beautified beyond description, standing in the midst of their posterity, governing and controlling them, administering life, exaltation and glory, worlds without end.

PREEXISTENCE
We have learned that we existed with God in eternity before we came into this life, and that we kept our estate. Had we not kept what is called our first estate and observed the laws that governed there, you and I would not be here today. We are here because we are worthy to be here, and that arises, to a great extent at least, from the fact that we kept our first estate.

PRIESTHOOD
The priesthood or authority in which we stand is the medium or channel through which our Heavenly Father has purposed to communicate light, intelligence, gifts, powers, and spiritual and temporal salvation unto the present generation.

TITHING
It is God's truth that the time has now come when he will not look favorably upon negligence of this principle. I plead with you in the name of the Lord, and I pray that every man, woman, and child who have means shall pay one-tenth of their income as a tithing.

Joseph F. Smith, Sixth President (1838-1918)

JOSEPH F. SMITH

Sixth President of the Church

Born: November 13, 1838, Far West, Missouri

Died: November 19, 1918, Salt Lake City, Utah (age 80)

President of the Church: October 17, 1901, to November 19, 1918 (17 years)

Physical Characteristics: Five feet eleven inches tall, 180-185 pounds; full beard, gray hair, brown eyes, prominent nose; stately and distinguished appearance; wore glasses

Areas of Distinction: Prophet, writer, historian, pioneer, missionary, legislator, farmer

*Family: Son of Hyrum and Mary Fielding Smith. Married Levira Annett Clark Smith April 5, 1859 (she died December 18, 1888), no children; married Julina Lambson May 5, 1866 (died January 10, 1936), 13 children; married Sarah Ellen Richards, March 1, 1868 (died March 22, 1915), 11 children; married Edna Lambson, January 1, 1871 (died February 23, 1926), 10 children; married Alice Ann Kimball December 6, 1883 (died December 19, 1946), 7 children; married Mary Taylor Schwartz January 13, 1884 (died Dec. 5, 1956), 7 children.

---

*Source: *Life of Joseph F. Smith,* pp. 487-490.

Profile of Joseph F. Smith

The period of Church history during which Joseph F. Smith was born was stormy. Violence, persecutions, plunderings, and imprisonments without trial or conviction were common occurrences in the lives of his father, Hyrum Smith, and the Prophet Joseph.

A few days prior to Joseph F.'s birth, his father, together with the Prophet and some other leaders of the Church, was betrayed into the hands of an armed mob. George M. Hinkle, a disgruntled Church member and an officer in the Missouri militia, was responsible for the treachery. He intended to commit murder but Hyrum's and Joseph's lives were spared when General Alexander W. Doniphan opposed Hinkle's plans. Instead, the prisoners were transferred to jail and incarcerated for several months in a filthy dungeon.

In the meantime, Hyrum's wife, Mary Fielding Smith, labored through the last remaining days of her confinement. Twelve days after her husband was taken prisoner, she gave birth to her son Joseph, on November 13, 1838. When he was just a few days old, mobbers entered the home and ransacked it; then they overturned the bedding on which the infant lay and attempted to smother him; his life appeared to be gone when he was discovered. Fortunately he was revived in time.

From 1838 to 1844 the bitter persecution continued.

Church leaders were constantly in danger, many were thrown into prison, and others were put to death. The culmination of these violent years came on June 27, 1844, less than six years after Joseph's birth, when his father and his uncle, Joseph the Prophet, were martyred in Carthage Jail.

Sorrow and tragedy seemed to be Joseph F. Smith's lot from the very beginning, but as Charles Spurgeon, the great English clergyman, said, "Many owe the grandeur of their lives to their tremendous difficulties." Certainly Joseph F. Smith had his share of adversity. Undoubtedly this affected the grandeur of his life.

He passed through the trying scenes of Missouri and Illinois, drove an ox team across the plains from the Missouri River, and finally entered the Salt Lake Valley with his mother on September 23, 1848. Four years later, when Joseph was fourteen years old, Mary Fielding Smith died. Many years later he would remark: "The strongest anchor in my life, which helped me to hold to every principle, was the love of my dear mother."

As a young boy he learned well the importance of honesty, responsibility, and hard work. One day when he was about nine years of age, he was entrusted with a herd of cattle. Suddenly a small band of Indians rode up, hoping to steal and drive off the cattle. Joseph didn't run for safety but stayed with the cattle. Two of the Indians, one on each side of the boy, took him by the arms and lifted him out of the saddle. Suddenly, seeing men working in the fields, they dropped the boy and rode quickly away, thus preserving his life.

On May 27, 1854, this mature young man of fifteen left for a mission to Hawaii. His missionary experiences there were remarkable, and the natives to whom he taught the gospel never forgot the boy missionary. Many years later when he returned to the islands, persons who still remembered came to greet him with tears of joy and gratitude. In the midst of the great celebration, a blind

Joseph F. Smith at age 19

woman came tottering over, calling, "Iosepa, Iosepa." In her hand were a few choice bananas. With tears streaming down his cheeks, Joseph F. Smith, now the President of the Church, took her in his arms and accepted her loving offering. This humble native woman had nursed the young missionary when he was ill on the island fifty years before.

One of the most severe anti-Mormon campaigns ever conducted was unleashed against the Church during the administration of President Smith. And when principles of truth were at stake he was a fighter. He had known persecution all of his life, and he excelled in competition. Joseph Fielding Smith later said of his father, "President Smith was physically strong, with muscles like steel and with endurance far beyond most other men." This was true whether it be physical or moral strength.

President and Mrs. Joseph F. Smith

In 1901 Thomas Kearns, a rich mining engineer and member of the U.S. Senate who was seeking reelection, sought the support of President Smith and the Church. President Smith informed him that the Church was not in politics. Feeling rebuffed, Mr. Kearns, through his control of the Salt Lake *Tribune*, vigorously attacked both the Church and President Smith. He, along with others, organized the "American Party," and during its years of existence from 1901-11 a malicious campaign of falsehood was carried out, caricaturing and villifying President Smith in a shameful manner. In his humble and forgiving way, President Smith replied to these vicious, daily attacks in these words:

> There are those who speak only evil of the Latter-day Saints. There are those—and they abound largely in our midst—who will shut their eyes to every virtue and to every good thing connected with the latter-day work, and will pour out floods of falsehood and misrepresentation against the people of God. I forgive them for this. I leave them in the hand of the just Judge. (Smith, *Essentials in Church History*, p. 512.)

A teacher of Christ-like principles, these are some of the things he taught:

"Love and honor your parents and do all you can to make them happy."

"Be kind to your brothers and sisters."

"Respect your neighbors."

"Be generous and forgiving even to your enemies."

"Be liberal to the poor."

"Be considerate of the weak and aged."

"Make no promises you cannot keep, and when you make a promise, keep it."

"Avoid quarrels and shun quarrelsome people; be a peacemaker."

He had great faith in the importance of virtue in the lives of members of his family. He said:

> I have learned that there are a great many things which are far worse than death. With my present feelings and views and the understanding that I have of life and death, I would far rather follow every child I have to the grave in their innocence and purity, than to see them grow up to man and womanhood and degrade themselves by the pernicious practices of the world, forget the

Joseph F. Smith, 1874

gospel, forget God and the plan of life and salvation, and turn away from the only hope of eternal reward and exaltation in the world to come. (*Journal of Discourses*, vol. 4, pp. 75-76.)

Elder Edward H. Anderson provides us with a description and evaluation of Joseph F. Smith:

President Smith has been constantly in the service of the public, and by his straightforward course has won the love, confidence and esteem of the whole community. He is a friend of the people, is easily approached, a wise counselor, a man of broad views, and, contrary to first impressions, is a man whose sympathies are easily aroused. He is a reflex of the best character of the Mormon people—inured to hardships, patient in trial, God-fearing, self-sacri-

The Joseph F. Smith home in Salt Lake City

ficing, full of love for the human race, powerful in moral, mental and physical strength. President Smith has an imposing physical appearance. He is tall, erect, well-knit and symmetrical in build. He has a prominent nose and features. When speaking, he throws his full, clear, brown eyes wide open on the listener, who may readily perceive from their penetrating glimpse the wonderful mental power of the tall forehead above. His large head is crowned with an abundant growth of hair, in his early years dark, but now, like his full beard, tinged with a liberal sprinkling of gray. In conversation, one is forcibly impressed with the sudden changes in appearance of his countenance, under the different influences of his mind; now intensely pleasant, with an enthusiastic and childlike interest in immediate subjects and surroundings; now absent, the mobility of his features set in that earnest, almost stern, majesty of expression so characteristic of his portraits—so indicative of the severity of the conditions and environments of his early life. As a public speaker, his leading trait is an intense earnestness. He impresses the hearer with his message more from the sincerity of its delivery, and the honest earnestness of his manner, than from any learned exhibition of oratory or studied display of logic. He touches the hearts of the people with the simple eloquence of one who is himself convinced of the truths presented. He is a pillar of strength in the Church, thoroughly imbued with the truths of the gospel and the divine origin of this work. His whole life and testimony are an inspiration to the young. (Jenson, *LDS Biographical Encyclopedia*, pp. 73-74.)

Following Joseph F. Smith's death, Charles W. Nibley, a lifelong friend and associate, said:

As a preacher of righteousness who could compare with him? He was the greatest that I ever heard—strong, powerful, clear, appealing. It was marvelous how the words of living light and fire flowed from him.

JOHN R. WINDER
1901-1910

JOSEPH F. SMITH
1901-1918

ANTHON H. LUND
1901-1910

THE FIRST PRESIDENCY
1901-1910

The First Presidency, 1901-10: President Joseph F. Smith (center) and counselors John R. Winder and Anthon H. Lund

I have visited at his home when one of his children was down sick. I have seen him come home from his work at night tired, as he naturally would be, and yet he would walk the floor for hours with that little one in his arms . . . loving it, encouraging it in every way. . . .

Never was man more moral and chaste and virtuous to the last fiber of his being than he. Against all forms or thoughts of licentiousness, he was set, and as immovable as a mountain. (Smith, *Gospel Doctrine*, p. 522-24.)

Joseph F. Smith lived as he taught. He preached sermons in the way he lived as well as in the words he spoke. His love and kindness illustrated what God is like. He stood as an example of what God can do with an individual who submits to His will.

Interesting Facts and Contributions of
Joseph F. Smith

1. He was only a boy of eight when he drove his mother's ox team across Iowa. He drove two yoke of oxen more than a thousand miles across the plains when he was ten years old.

2. His whole childhood was spent during the period of the violent and bitter conflict between Mormons and non-Mormons in Missouri and Illinois.

3. He was acquainted with Joseph Smith in his childhood and was the last President of the Church who was acquainted with the Prophet.

4. He was called to a mission in Hawaii at the age of fifteen. He served five missions: three to Hawaii and one each in Great Britain and Europe.

5. He was ordained an apostle at the young age of twenty-seven.

6. He served as counselor to four Presidents: Brigham Young, John Taylor, Wilford Woodruff, and Lorenzo Snow—a total of thirty-eight years in the First Presidency.

7. In the early sixties he became active in politics. He served on the municipal council of Salt Lake City, and for seven consecutive terms (1865-74) was a member of the lower house of the territorial legislature. In 1880 and again in 1882 he sat in the upper house; during the second term he was president of that house. In 1882 he also presided over the constitutional convention of Utah, but he was legally disqualified under the Edmunds Law because of his plural marriages.

8. It had been prophesied by Lorenzo Snow in 1864 that Joseph F. Smith would someday be President;

Wilford Woodruff also prophesied that he would someday be President.

9. He went into voluntary exile for seven years so he would not be arrested, for he had knowledge of records of marriages performed by the Church. He was unable to appear in public until he was granted pardon by the President of the United States in 1891.

10. He was the first President to visit Europe as President.

11. He and his counselors inaugurated the home evening program in 1915.

12. In his sermons and writings he placed great emphasis on sexual purity and temple marriage.

13. In 1901 a bureau of information was established under his direction on Temple Square in Salt Lake City to help create a positive image for the Church. He also laid the groundwork for a building program to convert historical spots of Church history into tourist attractions and information centers.

14. The seminary program was started during his administration.

15. His book *Gospel Doctrine*, used as a course of study for Melchizedek Priesthood classes, is one of the most popular and widely used books in the Church.

16. "His chief contribution was the strengthening of the Church organization itself, and through his kindly spirit of compromise, the fostering of more friendly relations with non-Mormons both in Utah and outside." (*Dictionary of American Biography*, vol. 17, p. 314.)

Significant Dates and Events in Lifetime of
Joseph F. Smith

Church Membership, 1901: 278,645   1918: 495,962

1918—Stakes: 75   Missions: 22   Temples: 4

U.S. Population, 1918: 103 million (est.)

World Population, 1918: 1.7 billion (est.)

U.S. Presidents, 1901-18: Theodore Roosevelt, William Taft, Woodrow Wilson

1838	Joseph F. Smith was born in Far West, Missouri, November 13.
1846-48	Drove an ox-team across the plains from Nauvoo to Salt Lake Valley (age 8-10).
1848-52	Worked as a herds boy.
1852	Became an orphan at the death of his mother, Mary Fielding Smith.
1854-57	Served mission to Hawaii (age 15).
1857	Served in Echo Canyon campaign of Utah War.
1859	Married Levira Annett Clark Smith.
1860-63	Served mission to Great Britain.
1864	Employed in Church Historian's Office. Served special mission to Hawaii.
1865-74	Served as member of territorial house of representatives.
1866	Married Julina Lambson. Was ordained an apostle by Brigham Young July 1 at Salt Lake City. Was named counselor in First Presidency (age 27).
1867	Was sustained as member of Council of the Twelve. Went to Provo to help build up that city and Utah County; served one term on Provo City council.

1868   Married Sarah Ellen Richards.

1871   Married Edna Lambson.

1874-75   Served as president of European Mission.

1876   Presided over settlements in Davis County, Utah.

1877   Served second term as president of European Mission.

1878   Served short-term mission to eastern United States.

1880   Named second counselor to John Taylor in First Presidency (age 42).

1880-84   Served in upper branch of Utah legislature.

1883   Married Alice Ann Kimball.

1884-91   Went into voluntary exile because of polygamy persecution; served among Saints in southwest United States, Mexico, Hawaii, Canada, eastern United States.

1889   Was named second counselor to Wilford Woodruff in the First Presidency.

1893   Served in constitutional convention for Utah.

1898   Was named second counselor to President Lorenzo Snow in the First Presidency.

1901   Was sustained as President of the Church, November 10, at a special conference (age 63); John R. Winder and Anthon H. Lund were sustained as counselors. Ordained his son, Hyrum Mack Smith, an apostle, October 24.

1901-18   Missions opened: Swiss and German, Japan, Middle States, Swedish, Danish-Norwegian, French, Tongan.

1902   *The Children's Friend*, published by the Primary, began publication. Church began a program to improve the world image of the Church with a bureau of information on Temple Square in Salt Lake City and purchase of Church historical places. It began to tell its own story to millions of visitors at visitors' centers.

          Martinique, West Indies: Mt. Pelee erupted and wiped out the city of St. Pierre, killed 40,000.

1903   Dedicatory prayer was offered in Moscow, dedicating that land for the preaching of the gospel. Reed Smoot, member of the Council of the Twelve, was elected to the United States Senate, starting a bitter political attack on the Church because it was thought he believed in principle of polygamy. (Only after protracted hearings was Smoot permitted to hold the position.) The mass media acquainted thousands concerning the Church.

Orville Wright piloted the first airplane flight. The Iroquois Theater fire in Chicago killed 602 persons. "The Great Train Robbery," first movie with a story line, was released.

1904   Joseph F. Smith issued an official statement reaffirming the Church's position of forbidding plural marriages. The American Party, an anti-Mormon political organization, began a campaign against the Church, charging it with domination of local politics.

1905   Joseph F. Smith dedicated the Joseph Smith Monument at Sharon, Vermont, birthplace of the Prophet.

An earthquake in Kangra, India, killed 20,000. Albert Einstein, a 26-year-old physicist, published his theory of relativity. Japan defeated Russia in the Russo-Japanese War.

1906   Joseph F. Smith toured the missions in Europe, the first President to visit Europe while serving as President. Church was cleared entirely of debt.

San Francisco earthquake and subsequent fire killed 700. Earthquake in Valparaiso, Chile, killed 1,500. Federal Food and Drug Act was established to protect the public against impure foods.

1907   *Oklahoma became a state.*

1908   A general committee was formed to prepare uniform study courses for priesthood quorums.

First Model T Ford went on the market. Earthquake in Messina, Italy, killed 85,000, destroyed the city.

1909   *Admiral Robert E. Peary discovered the North Pole.*

1910   Joseph F. Smith ordained his son Joseph Fielding Smith an apostle, April 7.

Union of South Africa was founded. The Mexican Revolution began.

1911   *Boy Scout movement was begun. A flood in Eastern China killed 100,000. Explorer Roald Amundsen discovered the South Pole.*

1912   The Church's seminary program began. Church members living in Mexico were robbed and persecuted and forced to seek refuge in America.

Arizona and New Mexico became states. The ship Titanic sank after colliding with an iceberg. The Republic of China was established.

1913   The Seagull Monument was erected on Temple Square.

The 16th Amendment to the U.S. Constitution empowered Congress to levy income taxes.

1913-18   Persecution of the Church throughout the United States subsided, and a period of prosperity and toleration began. Many meetinghouses and tabernacles were erected, as well as the LDS Hospital in Salt Lake City, Bishop's Building, and Church Office Building.

1914   *The first scheduled airline flight was made in America. The Panama Canal opened. World War I began in Europe, fulfilling the prophecy given to Joseph Smith in 1832.*

1915   The *Relief Society Magazine* began publication.

1915   *The first telephone line linking New York and San Francisco began operating. The transcontinental telephone line was completed.*

1917   President Smith made his last public trip to visit the Saints; journeyed to Southern Utah.

The Russian Revolution began and the Bolsheviks seized power.

1918   Joseph F. Smith received vision on salvation of the dead and the visit of the Savior to the world of spirits after his crucifixion; vision was subsequently published after first being submitted to the First Presidency and other General Authorities. He died in Salt Lake City November 19 at age 80; no public funeral could be held because of a nationwide influenza epidemic.

1901-18   *Significant inventions: helicopter (France); air conditioning (U.S.); electrocardiograph (Netherlands); airplane (U.S.); cellophane (Switzerland); tank (England); tractor (U.S.); radio vacuum tube (U.S.).*

The First Presidency
During Joseph F. Smith's Administration

First Counselor	President	Second Counselor
*John R. Winder 1901-10	Joseph F. Smith (1866) 1901-18	Anthon H. Lund (1889) 1901-10
Anthon H. Lund (1889) 1910-18		John Henry Smith (1880) 1910-11
		Charles W. Penrose (1904) 1911-18

Council of the Twelve—November 1901

Brigham Young, Jr. (1868)
Francis M. Lyman (1880)
John Henry Smith (1880)
George Teasdale (1882)
Heber J. Grant (1882)
John W. Taylor (1884)

Marriner W. Merrill (1889)
Matthias F. Cowley (1889)
Abraham O. Woodruff (1897)
Rudger Clawson (1898)
Reed Smoot (1900)
Hyrum Mack Smith (1901)

Died

1903—Brigham Young, Jr.
1904—Abraham O. Woodruff
1906—Marriner W. Merrill
1907—George Teasdale
1916—Francis M. Lyman
1918—Hyrum Mack Smith

Added

George Albert Smith (1903)
Charles W. Penrose (1904)
George F. Richards (1906)
Orson F. Whitney (1906)
David O. McKay (1906)
Anthony W. Ivins (1907)
Joseph Fielding Smith (1910)
James E. Talmage (1911)
Stephen L Richards (1917)
Richard R. Lyman (1918)

Excommunicated

1911—John W. Taylor

Resigned from the Council

1905—Matthias F. Cowley

---

*Never ordained an apostle.
Note: Dates in parentheses indicate date ordained a member of the Council of the Twelve.

October 1918

Heber J. Grant (1882)	David O. McKay (1906)
Rudger Clawson (1898)	Anthony W. Ivins (1907)
Reed Smoot (1900)	Joseph Fielding Smith (1910)
George Albert Smith (1903)	James E. Talmage (1911)
George F. Richards (1906)	Stephen L Richards (1917)
Orson F. Whitney (1906)	Richard R. Lyman (1918)

Testimony of Joseph F. Smith

I bear my testimony to you, that I have received an assurance which has taken possession of my whole being. It has sunk deep into my heart; it fills every fibre of my soul; so that I say before this people, and would be pleased to have the privilege of saying it before the whole world, that God has revealed unto me that Jesus is the Christ, the Son of the living God, the Redeemer of the world; that Joseph Smith is, was, and always will be a prophet of God, ordained and chosen to stand at the head of the dispensation of the fulness of times, the keys of which were given to him, and he will hold them until the winding-up scene—keys which will unlock the door into the kingdom of God to every man who is worthy to enter, and which will close that door against every soul that will not obey the law of God. I know, as I live, that this is true, and I bear my testimony to its truth. If [these] were the last words I should ever say on earth, I would glory before God my Father that I possess this knowledge in my soul, which I declare unto you as I would the simplest truths of heaven. I know that this is the kingdom of God, and that God is at the helm. He presides over His people. He presides over the President of this Church and has done from the Prophet Joseph down to the Prophet Lorenzo; and He will continue to preside over the leaders of this Church until the winding-up scene. He will not suffer it to be given to another people, nor to be left to men. He will hold the reins in his own hands: for He has stretched out His arms to do His work, and He will do it, and have the honor of it. . . .

I bear testimony to you and to the world, that Joseph Smith was raised up by the power of God to lay the foundations of this great Latter-day work; to reveal the fulness of the Gospel to the world in this dispensation; to restore the Priesthood of God to the world, by which men may act in the name of the Father, and of the Son, and of the Holy Ghost, and it will be accepted of God; it will be by His authority. I bear testimony to it; I know that it is true.

I bear my testimony to the divine authority of those who have succeeded the Prophet Joseph Smith in the presidency of this Church. They were men of God. I knew them; I was intimately associated with them; and as one man may know another, through the intimate knowledge that he possesses of him, so I can bear testimony to the integrity, to the honor, to the purity of life, to the intelligence, and to the divinity of the mission and calling of Brigham, of John, of Wilford, and of Lorenzo. They were inspired of God to fill the mission to which they were called, and I know it. I thank God for that testimony and for the spirit that prompts me and impels me towards these men, toward their mission, toward this people, toward my God and my Redeemer. I thank the Lord for it, and I pray earnestly that it may never depart from me. (Green, *Testimonies of Our Leaders*, pp. 47-49.)

Personal Experience of Joseph F. Smith

It was on the seventh day of August, 1906, that President Smith and party arrived in Rotterdam, having come from the boat at Antwerp two days before. There was living in that city a boy of eleven years of age, John Roothoff by name, who had suffered greatly for a number of years with his eyes. His mother was a faithful member of the Church, as also was the boy, who was slowly losing his sight and was unable to attend school. The boy said to his mother: "The Prophet has the most power of any missionary on earth. If you will take me with you to the meeting and he will look into my eyes, I believe they will be healed."

According to his desire he was permitted to accompany his mother to the meeting. At the close of the meeting, as was the custom, President Smith moved towards the door and began to shake hands and speak encouragingly to the people as they passed from the hall. As John Roothoff approached him, led by his mother and his eyes bandaged, President Smith took him by the hand and spoke to him kindly. He then raised the bandage slightly and looked sympathetically into the inflamed eyes, at the same time saying something in English which the boy did not understand. However he was satisfied. President Smith had acted according to the boy's faith, and according to his faith it came to pass. When he arrived home, he cried out with great joy: "Mama, my eyes are well; I cannot feel any more pain. I can see fine now, and far too." (Smith, *Life of Joseph F. Smith*, p. 397.)

Quotations from Joseph F. Smith

ALCOHOL
There is no valid or convincing argument, economic, social, financial, moral or religious, against wiping out the liquor traffic. On the contrary, every strong point favors the use of our franchise for the establishment of temperance, the abolishment of the saloon, and the absolute prohibition of the sale of liquor.

BIRTH CONTROL
I think it is a crying evil, that there should exist a sentiment, or a feeling among any members of the Church to curtail the birth of their children. I think that is a crime wherever it occurs, where husband and wife are in possession of health and vigor and are free from impurities that would be entailed upon their posterity. I believe that where people undertake to curtail or prevent the birth of their children that they are going to reap disappointment by and by. I have no hesitancy in saying that I believe that is one of the greatest crimes of the world today, this evil practice.

BROTHERHOOD
In speaking of nationalities, we all understand or should that in the Church . . . there is neither Scandinavian, nor Swiss, nor German, nor Russian, nor British, nor any other nationality. We have become brothers in the household of faith.

CHRIST
I accept Jesus of Nazareth as the Only Begotten Son of God in the flesh. This is a great principle, though it seems hard for some people to understand it—those who believe in the foolish notion that God is a "vapor" if you please, ether, electricity, "energy" or anything else you might call him or it, and that he fills the immensity of space, is everywhere present at the same time, etc. etc.

CHURCH
Drunkards, whore-mongers, liars, thieves, those that betray the confidence of their fellowmen, those who are unworthy of credence, unworthy of love and confidence—all such, when their character

becomes known, are disfellowshipped from the Church, and are not permitted to have a standing in it, if we know it. . . . When a man abandons the truth, virtue, his love for the gospel and for the people of God, and becomes an open, avowed enemy, it becomes the duty of the Church, and the Church would be recreant to its duty if it did not sever him from the communion, cut him off, and let him go where he pleases.

EVIL
There are at least three dangers that threaten the Church within, and the authorities need to awaken to the fact that the people should be warned against them. As I see these, they are the flattery of prominent men in the world, false educational ideas, and sexual impurity.

FALL
Adam fell that a world of waiting spirits who had kept their first estate, and were therefore worthy of promotion, might be "added upon" by being given mortal bodies in their second estate, through which, if found faithful, they were to have "glory added upon their heads for ever and ever."

GOD
It is a commandment of the Lord that we shall remember God morning and evening and, as the Book of Mormon tells us, "at all times." We should carry with us the spirit of prayer throughout every duty that we have to perform in life. Why should we? One of the simple reasons that appeals to my mind with great force is that man is so utterly dependent upon God!

GODHEAD
Let it be remembered that Christ was with the Father from the beginning, that the gospel of truth and light existed from the beginning and is from everlasting to everlasting. The Father, Son, and Holy Ghost, as one God, are the fountain of truth. From this fountain all the ancient learned philosophers have received their inspiration and wisdom—from it they have received their knowledge. If we find truth in broken fragments through the ages, it may be set down as an incontrovertible fact that it originated at the fountain and was given to philosophers, inventors, patriots, reformers, and prophets by the inspiration of God. It came from him through his Son Jesus Christ and the Holy Ghost, in the first place, and from no other source. It is eternal.

HOME
It is the duty of parents to teach their children the principles of the

gospel, and to be sober-minded and industrious in their youth. They should be impressed from the cradle to the time they leave the parental roof to make homes and assume the duties of life for themselves, that there is a seed time and harvest, and as man sows, so shall he reap. . . . above all else, let us train our children in the principles of the gospel of our Savior, that they may become familiar with the truth and walk in the light which it sheds forth to all those who will receive it. "He that seeketh me early," the Lord has said, "shall find me, and shall not be forsaken." It behooves us, therefore, to commence in early life to travel in the strait and narrow path which leads to eternal salvation.

IMMORALITY

We are not here to practice immorality of any kind. Above all things, sexual immorality is most heinous in the sight of God. It is on a par with murder itself, and God Almighty fixed the penalty of the murderer at death: "Whoso sheddeth man's blood, by man shall his blood be shed." Furthermore, he said that whosoever committed adultery should be put to death. Therefore, we raise our voices against sexual immorality, and against all manner of obscenity.

MAN

Man is the child of God, formed in the divine image and endowed with divine attributes, and even as the infant son of our earthly father and mother is capable in due time of becoming a man, so the undeveloped offspring of celestial parentage is capable, by experience through ages of eons, of evolving into a God.

NEIGHBOR

Love your neighbor as yourself? How are you to do it? If your neighbor is in danger, protect him to the utmost of your power. If you see your neighbor's property in danger of injury, protect his property as you would your own, as far as it lies in your power. If your neighbor's boy or girl is going astray, go directly to your neighbor, in the spirit of love, and help him to reclaim his child.

OBEDIENCE

Religion is not believing in the commandments only; it is in doing them.

PATRIARCHAL ORDER

There is no higher authority in matters relating to the family organization, and especially when the organization is presided over by one holding the higher Priesthood, than that of the father. The authority is time honored, and among the people of God in all dispensations it has been highly respected and often emphasized by the teachings of the prophets who were inspired of God. The patriarchal order is of divine origin and will continue throughout time and eternity. There is, then, a particular reason why men, women and children should understand this order and this authority in the households of the people of God, and seek to make it what God intended it to be, a qualification and preparation for the highest exaltation of his children. In the home the presiding authority is always vested in the father, and in all home affairs and family matters there is no other authority paramount.

PATRIOTISM

A truly patriotic spirit in the individual begets a public interest and sympathy which should be commensurate with our nation's greatness. To be a true citizen of a great country takes nothing from, but adds to, individual greatness. While a great and good people necessarily add greatness and goodness to national life, the nation's greatness reacts upon its citizens and adds honor to them, and insures their welfare and happiness. . . . Our national welfare should always be a theme deeply rooted in our minds and exemplified in our individual lives, and the desire for our nation's good should be stronger than political party adherence. The nation's welfare means the welfare of every one of its citizens. . . . To be a worthy and a prosperous nation, it must possess those qualities which belong to individual virtues. The attitude of our country toward other nations should always be honest and above suspicion, and every good citizen should be jealous of our nation's reputation both at home and abroad. National patriotism is, therefore, something more than mere expression of willingness to fight, if need be.

PRIESTHOOD

There is no office growing out of the priesthood that is or can be greater than the priesthood itself. It is from the priesthood that the office derives its authority and power. No office gives authority to the priesthood. No office adds to the power of the priesthood. But all offices in the Church derive their power, their virtue, their authority from the priesthood.

RELIGIOUS HOBBIES

Religious hobbies are dangerous in the Church of Christ. They are dangerous because they give undue prominence to certain principles or ideas to the detriment and dwarfing of others just as important, just as binding, just as saving as the favored doctrines or commandments. . . . We have noticed this difficulty: that saints with hobbies are prone to judge and condemn their brethren and sisters who are not zealous in the one particular direction of their pet theory, as they are. The man with the Word of Wisdom only in his brain, is apt to find unmeasured fault with every other member of the Church who entertains liberal ideas as to the importance of other doctrines of the gospel.

SABBATH

It is the duty of Latter-day Saints to honor the Sabbath day to keep it holy, just as the Lord has commanded us to do. Go to the house of prayer. Listen to instruction. Bear your testimony to the truth. Drink of the fountain of knowledge and of instruction, as it may be opened for us from those who are inspired to give us instruction. When we go home, get the family together. Let us sing a few songs. Let us read a chapter or two in the Bible, or in the Book of Mormon, or in the book of Doctrine and Covenants. Let us discuss the principles of the gospel which pertain to advancement in the school of divine knowledge, and in this way occupy one day in seven.

SELF-DISCIPLINE

How humiliating it must be to a thoughtful man to feel that he is a slave to his appetites, or to an overweening and pernicious habit, desire or passion. We believe in strict temperance. We believe in abstinence from all injurious practices and from the use of all harmful things.

SERVICE

Our motto is not simply "Live and let live," but "Live and help to live." We should help to make the lives of others happy and progressive. The kindly word fitly spoken should be followed by timely action.

SIN

We are responsible for our own sins, and we will be held responsible for our deliverance from them, for they lead to the second death.

SPIRITUAL GIFTS

The devil himself can appear like an angel of light. False prophets and false teachers have arisen in the world. There is perhaps no gift of the Spirit of God more easily imitated by the devil than the gift of tongues. Where two men or women exercise the gift by the inspiration of the Spirit of God, there are a dozen perhaps who do it by the inspiration of the devil.

SPIRITUALITY

Spend ten minutes in reading a chapter from the words of the Lord before you go to your daily toil. Feed your spiritual selves at home, as well as in public places.

TITHING

The law of tithing is a test by which the people as individuals shall be proved. Any man who fails to observe this principle shall be known as a man who is indifferent to the welfare of Zion, who neglects his duty as a member of the Church, and who does nothing toward the accomplishment of the temporal advancement of the kingdom of God. He contributes nothing, either toward the building of temples or maintaining them; he does nothing toward spreading the gospel to the nations of the earth, and he neglects to do that which would entitle him to receive the blessings and ordinances of the gospel.

WOMAN

I cannot tolerate the young lady who appears well in society at the expense of the comfort of her mother at home. Do not fear to divide the burdens and to do all in your power to brighten the lot of your mother and you will find blessings that are never found in the path of selfishness. Maintain your dignity, integrity and virtue at the sacrifice of life and you will be esteemed as the noblest type of womanhood.

Heber J. Grant, Seventh President (1856-1945)

HEBER J. GRANT

Seventh President of the Church

Born: November 22, 1856, Salt Lake City, Utah

Died: May 14, 1945, Salt Lake City, Utah (age 88)

President of the Church: November 23, 1918, to May 14, 1945 (26½ years)

Physical Characteristics: Six feet tall, weighed 175-180 pounds, slender build, protruding nose, receding forehead, gray eyes, wore glasses, dark to gray hair

Areas of Distinction: Prophet, banker, business executive, missionary, humanitarian

*Family: Son of Jedediah and Rachel Ivins Grant. Married Lucy Stringham November 1, 1877 (died January 3, 1893), six children; married Hulda Augusta Winters, May 26, 1884 (died June 2, 1951), one child; married Emily J. Harris Wells, May 27, 1884 (died May 25, 1908), five children.

---

*Source: Genealogical Society

Profile of Heber J. Grant

"That which we persist in doing becomes easy to do, not that the nature of the task has changed, but that our capacity to do has increased." These words by Ralph Waldo Emerson served as one of the mottos by which Heber J. Grant lived. His life was an example of what can be accomplished through persistence.

His father was the first mayor of Salt Lake City and also served with Brigham Young in the First Presidency. He died from pneumonia at the age of forty-one, a little over a week after the birth of Heber J. Grant. Heber's mother was a self-reliant, courageous woman of sturdy pioneer stock. She was Heber's greatest teacher. He loved her dearly and worked hard to help her. By the time he was twenty-one years old, he had earned enough to build a home for her. In tribute to his mother President Grant said: "I live today as one whose mother was all to me. She set an example of love and of honor second to none. Her life was a sermon that rings through my soul to this day. One of the main reasons I am President of the Church today is that I have followed the advice and counsel and the burning testimony of the divinity of God, which came to me from my mother."

When he was a young man, he declined an offered appointment to the U.S. Naval Academy at Annapolis, Maryland, and made up his mind to be a businessman.

Heber J. Grant as a young man

He had unusual business acumen and an active imagination.

Heber J. Grant liked to make money. He knew how to do it. He enjoyed doing it. But he was never selfish with his wealth, and he always paid his obligations to the Lord first. Sometimes he paid tithing on money he had not yet earned because he felt he needed an extra blessing. He said that the Lord never disappointed him.

He engaged in a number of ventures at various times, including banking, a woolen mill, lumber, sugar and refining factories, insurance, ranching, cattle raising, vinegar manufacturing, the newspaper business, a brokerage, soap making, bee culture, merchandizing, and an implement business.

Heber M. Wells, a boyhood associate and later the first governor of the State of Utah, said of him:

He has probably been instrumental in establishing and furthering the cause of more successful intermountain industries than any other man of his time. His personal credit, his unquestioned integrity, his super-salesmanship brought capital to the aid of the Church, the community and private enterprises. In times of panic and in times of plenty, Heber J. Grant has been able to raise a few dollars or millions where other men have failed to raise any amount. (Hinckley, *Highlights in the Life of a Great Leader,* p. 51.)

Heber J. Grant and his mother

President and Mrs. Heber J. Grant and their family in England, March 26, 1914

Heber J. Grant had numerous experiences where his financial genius helped the Church. He saved two Church banks during the disastrous, prolonged panic of 1891-93. He made a trip to New York City in 1891 to sell $100,000 worth of ZCMI notes owned by one of the banks. The New York Stock Exchange was then lending money at one-half of 1 percent a day, 182.5 percent a year. The ZCMI notes bore 6 percent interest.

President Wilford Woodruff had blessed Heber J. Grant that he would get all the money he needed, but directors of the Deseret National Bank laughed at the idea of his being able to cash ZCMI notes in the East at 6 percent per annum. He stopped off in Omaha and then in Chicago and tried to cash some of the notes but was turned down. When he arrived in New York, he had not sold one of his notes, but from then on he was divinely guided, and he successfully borrowed $336,000 in all. He stopped in Chicago and Omaha on his way home, and the bankers were astonished and wondered how he had accomplished such an impossible mission.

The Heber J. Grant home in Salt Lake City

Apostle Grant is pre-eminently a business man, and would doubtless have devoted his days to financial affairs exclusively, if the call to the Apostleship had not changed the trend of his life from its natural course, and awakened in him that less prominent but nevertheless strongly rooted religious feeling that possesses his soul. He entered the business world as a messenger boy in an insurance office. From thence he arose step by step by determined effort and close attention to duty. His efforts to learn banking led to his securing the position of assistant cashier in Zion's Savings Bank and Trust Co., during the absence on a mission of Cashier

B. H. Schettler. This position led him to desire the presidency of a bank, which desire was gratified by his becoming the president of the State Bank of Utah, at its organization in 1890, which position he resigned to fill a mission to Japan whither he was called to open the gospel door, leaving Salt Lake City July 24, 1901. (Jenson, *LDS Biographical Encyclopedia*, p. 148.)

President Grant had a great sense of humor that he employed throughout his life. For example, a nonmember friend of his once said, "How can you afford to spend hundreds of dollars every year in giving books away to your friends?"

He replied, "Oh, I get a great deal of pleasure out of it, and in addition I sometimes give pleasure to four or five hundred others. Sometimes I give away in a year a thousand or two thousand pamphlets that cost only ten cents each, and it is my cigar money. I am sure it does not cost me any more than you spend to gratify your own appetite in smoking cigars."

The friend said, "Well, you have knocked me out in the first round and with the first blow."

Heber J. Grant made his first trip to Chicago in 1883 at the age of twenty-six. At that time many people had strange ideas about Mormons. He attended a nice dinner at the Palmer House, after which he followed the example of a friend and left his hat on. One of the ladies turned to Brother Grant and said: "Now, now, really, Mr. Grant, I don't wish to give offense, but would you mind removing your hat?"

"Not at all, madam," he told her. "I am only twenty-six years old and the horns do not come out on the Mormons until they are thirty-two. You will have to wait six more years."

He reported that the woman blushed and said: "Oh, I have heard that Mormons have horns."

He said: "I suppose you had. But they do not come out, dear madam, until we are thirty-two years old. I am sorry that I shall have to disappoint you."

Preston Nibley wrote:

President Grant outside the Church Office Building

Perhaps the most outstanding contribution President Grant made to the Church during the years of his presidency was his ability to meet and mingle with the prominent and influential people of the nation; to break down opposition; to remove prejudice and to make and win friends for the Latter-day Saints. He was a great and outstanding missionary. (Nibley, *The Presidents of the Church*, p. 253.)

Joseph Anderson, Assistant to the Council of the Twelve, served as secretary to President Grant. He made this comment about him:

Hard-headed business men, men who in their every day life and also in their social contacts, are accustomed to encounter attempts at deception, perversions of fact, and evasions of truths, find in President Grant, and greatly admire him for it, a man of simple faith, one whose word can be relied upon implicitly, a man who is willing to tell in detail the intimate facts of his life, not given to exaggeration, not withholding that which the most curious might wish to know. A distinguishing feature of his character is his frankness. He is honest in his faith and testimony; he never deceives, nor has he any desire to do so.

He is truly the greatest ambassador of friendship and good will to the professional and business man that the Church ever had. No one can begin to estimate the amount of good he has done for the Church in the matter of allaying prejudice in the minds of influential people.

Whether in the presence of the chairman of the board of a three billion dollar banking institution, the president of a great railroad or insurance company, the head of a noted institution of learnin or whether in the home of the lowliest wage earner or tiller of the soil, President Grant is at perfect ease. (*Improvement Era*, November 1941, p. 691.)

ANTHONY W. IVINS
1925-1931

HEBER J. GRANT
1918-

CHARLES W. NIBLEY
1925-1931

THE FIRST PRESIDENCY
1925-1931

The First Presidency, 1925-31: President Heber J. Grant (center) and counselors Anthony W. Ivins and Charles W. Nibley

In 1941 Elder John A. Widtsoe of the Council of the Twelve wrote the following:

As a successful financier he has shared with others the opportunities that he created or discovered. Poor or rich, in season or out of season, he has given to the needy, fed the hungry, blessed the sorrowful, and spoken kindly of his fellow men. He remains susceptible to every call made upon him, from the widow's cry for succor to the desire of a ward that he travel far to dedicate a meeting house. At fourscore years he has not learned to say "no" when asked for help. That is a divine characteristic. . . . He is a man possessed of a determined will for righteousness, progressive, fearless in the cause of truth, generous in thought and action, loving in friendship, true, wise, and forgiving. Throughout his nature runs the love of beauty, truth, and intelligence, culminating in a mighty spiritual character. He is a friend of God, and his divine Father has been his friend. (*Improvement Era*, July 1941, p. 30.)

Interesting Facts and Contributions
of Heber J. Grant

1. He was the first President of the Church born in the western states. He had not experienced the earlier persecution that had been experienced by other Presidents.

2. His administration of twenty-seven years was second to the longest of a President of the Church.

3. At the age of twenty-three he became secretary to the general presidency of the YMMIA.

He received the inspiration that he would be called to the Council of the Twelve. Also, Eliza R. Snow prophesied in tongues that he would be an apostle.

5. He was only twenty-five years old when he was ordained an apostle. He was the youngest man ordained of all the men who became President.

6. He was a man who accomplished a great deal through continued determination. Though he was a poor baseball player, singer, and penman, through constant effort he developed himself in all of these areas and many others.

7. As a young man, public speaking was very difficult for him, but later in life he became an effective and inspiring speaker.

8. He played baseball for various teams. One of these teams won the championship of the territory.

9. He was a financial genius and was well acquainted with influential people and financial and industrial institutions.

10. He helped many people in many ways. He gave away thousands of dollars, clearing mortgages from homes of widows, seeing after other financial matters and that many people had proper medical attention.

11. During his administration he encouraged the youth of the Church to seek a good education. In 1926 the institute of religion program of the Church was started, providing for religious education on the college level.

12. He opened the Japanese Mission as mission president.

13. He fostered the building of temples.

14. He was the first President to give gospel messages over the radio.

15. Nationwide attention was given to the Church and to President Grant when the welfare program was introduced. People were impressed by the Church's ability to look after its own members.

16. He served with four Presidents: President John Taylor, President Wilford Woodruff, President Lorenzo Snow, and President Joseph F. Smith.

17. He saved two Church banks during the U.S. panic.

Significant Dates and Events in Lifetime of
Heber J. Grant

Church Membership, 1918: 495,962   1945: 979,454

1945—Stakes: 155   Missions: 38   Temples: 7

U.S. Population, 1945: 141 million (est.)

World Population, 1945: 2.3 billion (est.)

U.S. Presidents, 1918-45: Woodrow Wilson, Warren G. Harding, Calvin Coolidge, Herbert C. Hoover, Franklin Delano Roosevelt, Harry S Truman

1856	Born in Salt Lake City, November 22. His father, Jedediah M. Grant, second counselor to Brigham Young and first mayor of Salt Lake City, died one week later.
1860s	Played baseball on several championship teams.
1871	Employed as bank clerk and started career in business world.
1875	Bookkeeper and policy clerk for Wells Fargo and Company. Was called to presidency of first ward YMMIA.
1876	Banker with Zion's Savings Bank & Trust Company.
1877	Married Lucy Stringham. President Brigham Young died.
1880	Secretary to the general YMMIA presidency. Called as president of Tooele Stake. Formed a syndicate and bought $350,000 of ZCMI stock.
1882	Called to be an apostle, October 13 (age 25); ordained by George Q. Cannon, October 16.
1883-84	Served a mission to the Indians.
1884	Married Augusta Winters and Emily Harris Wells. Entered into partnership with his brother, Joshua F. Grant, and George T. Odell to deal in wagons, machinery, agricultural implements.

1886-95   Engaged in establishing life insurance company, other business enterprises, culminating in Heber J. Grant Insurance Company in 1895.

1890   President of State Bank of Utah.

1891-93   Saved two Church banks during prolonged panic.

1896   When Utah became a state, Heber J. Grant was considered as a candidate for governor but withdrew nomination.

1897   Became member of general presidency of YMMIA, business manager of *The Improvement Era* (of which he was a founder).

1901-03   Organized and presided over Japanese Mission.

1904-06   Served as president of the British and European missions.

1906   Had interview with King Oscar of Sweden.

1916   Was sustained as President of the Council of the Twelve.

1918   Was set apart as President of the Church, November 23 (age 62). Named as counselors in the First Presidency were Anthon H. Lund and Charles W. Penrose.

           18th Amendment to U.S. Constitution prohibited the manufacture, possession, and sale of liquor. First airmail route was established.

1918-45   Missions opened: Canadian, Danish, Norwegian, Armenian, French, German Austrian, North Central States, South American, East Central States, Czechoslovak, Texas, Brazilian, Argentine, Spanish American, Japanese, New England, Swiss-Austrian, West German, East German, Western Canadian, Northern California, Navajo-Zuni.

1919   The Hawaii Temple was dedicated, November 27. Church membership reached half a million.

           Two British fliers made the first nonstop trans-Atlantic flight.

1920   One-hundredth anniversary of the First Vision was observed. The Church began withdrawing from all high school work in favor of public schools; some of Church's academies were turned over to the state for use as junior colleges.

           The first commercial radio broadcasts were made. The 20th Amendment to the U.S. Constitution gave women the right to vote. The League of Nations was established.

1922   Heber J. Grant was one of the main speakers as the Church
           began broadcasting on radio on KZN (later KSL).

1923   Alberta Temple was dedicated, July 27. Radio broadcasting
           of general conference sessions began.

           An earthquake in Yokohama, Japan, killed 95,000.

1926   The Church purchased the Hill Cumorah and the Whitmer
           farm in upstate New York, September 25. Institute of
           religion program in colleges was instituted. The Genealogi-
           cal Society established a research department to aid mem-
           bers in collecting and compiling records of their kindred
           dead.

1927   Arizona Temple at Mesa was dedicated, October 23. Mor-
           mon Battalion monument was dedicated in Salt Lake City.

           *"The Jazz Singer," first feature-length film with spoken dialogue,
           was released. Charles Lindberg flew nonstop from New York to
           Paris.*

1929   Tabernacle Choir began broadcasting on radio, June 15.

           *Stock market crash on October 29 started the Great Depression
           of the 1930s.*

1930   The centennial of the Church's organization was observed.

1930s   Utah had its economic limitations. Thousands of members
           gathered in other states and the Church grew. Musical
           groups and athletics were missionary helps in Europe, South
           America and South Africa.

1931   *Church News* section of the *Deseret News* began publication.

1931-34   Church turned over Weber College, Dixie College, and
           Snow College to state of Utah to continue as public junior
           colleges. Gila Junior College was turned over to the state
           of Arizona. LDS University in Salt Lake City was discon-
           tinued as such, but a portion of the school survived as the
           LDS Business College.

1933   *The 21st Amendment to the U.S. Constitution ended prohibition.
           The New Deal of the Roosevelt Administration began with the
           "hundred days," as Congress passed emergency laws to end the
           depression.*

1935   Hill Cumorah Monument was dedicated in New York.

           Social Security Act was passed by Congress.

1936   The Church Welfare Plan was established. Winter Quarters Monument was dedicated near Omaha, Nebraska.

1937   President Grant visited the missions in Europe; participated in the centennial celebration of the introduction of the gospel in Great Britain. The first performance of the present version of the Hill Cumorah Pageant at Palmyra, New York, was given.

The 800-foot-long dirigible "Hindenberg" crashed, killing 35.

1938   LDS Deseret Industries was founded in Salt Lake City.

1939   The Genealogical Society started microfilming. Missionaries were withdrawn from nations in Europe because of Germany's open hostilities against Poland.

World War II began with the German invasion of Poland.

1940   President Grant's health was impaired because of a partial paralysis, but his mind was clear and alert. A Churchwide hymn singing program was fostered that had great effect in revitalizing the singing of hymns in Church services.

1941   The First Presidency added Assistants to the Council of the Twelve as General Authorities, April 6.

Japan attacked U.S. Navy at Pearl Harbor, Hawaii, December 7. U.S. declared war against Japan, December 8.

1942   *First nuclear chain reaction was achieved at the University of Chicago.*

1943   *Italy surrendered to the Allies.*

1944   President Grant spoke in general conference for the last time, October.

1945   President Grant died in Salt Lake City, May 14 (age 88).

Germany surrendered to the Allies, May 9.

1918-45   *Significant inventions: ethyl gasoline (U.S.); nylon (U.S.); liquid rocket fuel (U.S.); radar (Scotland); cyclotron (U.S.); jet aircraft engine (Great Britain); cotton picking machine (U.S.); quick-frozen foods (U.S.); sound motion pictures (U.S.); Cinemascope (France); Cinerama (U.S.); iron lung (U.S.); atomic bomb (U.S.); automatic digital computer (U.S.); atomic reactor (U.S.); television (U.S.).*

The First Presidency
During Heber J. Grant's Administration

First Counselor	President	Second Counselor
Anthon H. Lund	Heber J. Grant	Charles W. Penrose
(1889)	(1882)	(1904)
1918-21	1918-45	1918-21
Charles W. Penrose		Anthony W. Ivins
(1904)		(1907)
1921-25		1921-25
Anthony W. Ivins		*Charles W. Nibley
(1907)		1925-31
1925-34		
		J. Reuben Clark, Jr.
J. Reuben Clark, Jr.		(1934)
(1934)		1933-34**
1934-45		
		David O. McKay
		(1906)
		1934-45

Council of the Twelve—June 1919

Rudger Clawson (1898)
Reed Smoot (1900)
George Albert Smith (1903)
George F. Richards (1906)
Orson F. Whitney (1906)
David O. McKay (1906)

Anthony W. Ivins (1907)
Joseph Fielding Smith (1910)
James E. Talmage (1911)
Stephen L Richards (1917)
Richard R. Lyman (1918)
Melvin J. Ballard (1919)

Died

1931—Orson F. Whitney
1933—James E. Talmage
1934—Anthony W. Ivins
1936—Alonzo A. Hinckley
1939—Melvin J. Ballard
1941—Reed Smoot
1943—Sylvester Q. Cannon
1943—Rudger Clawson

Added

John A. Widtsoe (1921)
Joseph F. Merrill (1931)
Charles A. Callis (1933)
Alonzo A. Hinckley (1934)
Albert E. Bowen (1937)
Sylvester Q. Cannon (1938)
Harold B. Lee (1941)
Spencer W. Kimball (1943)
Ezra Taft Benson (1943)
Mark E. Petersen (1944)

*Never ordained an apostle.

**The delay in filling the vacancy was due to the fact that Elder Clark had been serving as U. S. Ambassador to Mexico.

Note: Dates in parentheses indicate date ordained member of the Council of the Twelve.

Excommunicated
> 1943—Richard R. Lyman
> > (baptized again—1954)

April 1945

George Albert Smith (1903)	Charles A. Callis (1933)
George F. Richards (1906)	Albert E. Bowen (1937)
Joseph Fielding Smith (1910)	Harold B. Lee (1941)
Stephen L Richards (1917)	Spencer W. Kimball (1943)
John A. Widtsoe (1921)	Ezra Taft Benson (1943)
Joseph F. Merrill (1931)	Mark E. Petersen (1944)

Testimony of Heber J. Grant

I know that God lives, I know that Jesus is the Christ, I know that Joseph Smith was a Prophet of God, I know that the Gospel tree is alive, that it is growing, that the fruits of the Gospel growing upon the tree are good. I have reached out my hand, I have plucked the fruits of the Gospel, I have eaten of them and they are sweet, yea, above all that is sweet. That is the inspiration that comes to every Latter-day Saint who realizes the force of this Gospel that we have espoused. It is the Gospel of Jesus Christ. It is the plan of life and salvation. God lives; Jesus is the Christ, and He is the chief corner stone of this great work—He is directing it, and He will continue to direct it. He chose His prophet, and He gave him instructions and authority to establish this work; and the power and the influence of Joseph Smith are now being felt as the Angel promised. His name is known for good or for evil all over the world; but it is not known for evil except by those who malign him. Those who know him, those who know of his teachings, know that his life was pure and that his teachings were, in very deed, God's law.

We have the plan of life and salvation; we have the ordinances of the Gospel not only for the living but for the dead. We have all that is necessary, not only for our own salvation, but that we may be in very deed "Saviors upon Mount Zion," and enter into the temples of our God and save our ancestors who have died without a knowledge of the Gospel. . . .

I want to bear witness that no man or woman ever lived, who kept the commandments of God and lived according to the teachings of the Gospel of Jesus Christ, whose example was not worthy of the imitation of all men and all women, in any land, and in any clime. This Gospel of Jesus Christ, which I have embraced, is in very deed the plan of life and salvation. It is in very deed the Gospel revealed again to the earth. It is the same Gospel that was proclaimed by our Lord and Master, Jesus Christ; and He gave His life in testimony of the same. And the lives of our Prophet and Patriarch were given as a witness to the divinity of the work in which we are engaged. For a hundred years this Gospel has been proclaimed to the world without money, without price. Freely we have received, and freely we have given to the world. (Green, *Testimonies of Our Leaders*, pp. 50-51.)

Personal Experience of Heber J. Grant

My wife Lucy was very sick for nearly three years prior to her death. At one time I was in the hospital with her for six months. When she was dying, I called my children into the bedroom and told them their mamma was dying. My daughter Lutie said she did not want her mamma to die and insisted that I lay hands upon her and heal her, saying that she had often seen her mother, when sick in the hospital in San Francisco, suffering intensely, go to sleep immediately and have a peaceful night's rest when I had blessed her. I explained to my children that we all had to die some time, and that I felt that their mamma's time had come.

The children went out of the room, and I knelt down by the bed of my dying wife and told the Lord that I acknowledged his hand in life or in death, in joy or in sorrow, in prosperity or adversity; that I did not complain because my wife was dying, but that I lacked the strength to see my wife die and have her death affect the faith of my children in the ordinances of the gospel. I therefore pleaded with him to give to my daughter Lutie a testimony that it was his will that her mother should die.

Within a few short hours, my wife breathed her last. Then I called the children into the bedroom and announced that their mamma was dead. My little boy Heber commenced weeping bitterly, and Lutie put her arms around him and kissed him, and told him not to cry, that the voice of the Lord had said to her, "In the death of your mamma the will of the Lord will be."

Lutie knew nothing of my prayers, and this manifestation to her was a direct answer to my supplication to the Lord, and for it I have never ceased to be grateful. (Heber J. Grant, "When Great Sorrows Are Our Portion," *Improvement Era*, June 1912, pp. 726-27.)

Quotations from Heber J. Grant

BLESSINGS
Each blessing that you and I enjoy comes from God. We are under obligation to him for every breath of life, and he gives us everything we have.

BROTHERHOOD
No matter in what land we may dwell the gospel of the Lord Jesus Christ makes us brothers and sisters, interested in each other, eager to understand and know each other.

CHRIST
We all know that no one ever lived upon the earth that excited the same influence upon the destinies of the world as did our Lord and Savior Jesus Christ; and yet He was born in obscurity, cradled in a manger. He chose for his apostles poor, unlettered fishermen. More than nineteen hundred years have passed and gone since His crucifixion, and yet all over the world, in spite of all strife and chaos, there is still burning in the hearts of millions of people a testimony of the divinity of the work that He accomplished.

DEBT
If there is any one thing that will bring peace, and contentment into the human heart, and into the family, it is to live within our means. And if there is any one thing that is grinding and discouraging and disheartening, it is to have debts and obligations that one cannot meet.

FASTING
Every living soul among the Latter-day Saints that fasts two meals once a month will be benefited spiritually and be built up in the faith of the Lord Jesus Christ.

GIVING
The Lord loves a generous giver. No man living upon the earth can pay donations for the poor, can pay for building meetinghouses and temples . . . can take of his means and send his boys and girls

to proclaim this gospel, without removing selfishness from his soul.

GOD

We believe absolutely that we are made in the image of God. We believe that Jesus Christ was actually the son of his Father, as I am the son of my father, and we believe they are personages. Why? Because Joseph Smith saw God, and God introduced Jesus Christ to him.

GOSPEL

Every Latter-day Saint who is loyal to the principles of the Gospel is not seeking wealth; he is not asking himself the question, "What have I," and "What can I gain?" The true Latter-day Saint is asking, "What can I do to better myself, to encourage those with whom I am associated and to uplift the children of God?" That is the inspiration that comes to every Latter-day Saint who realizes the force of this Gospel that we have espoused.

GOVERNMENT

I counsel you, I urge you, I plead with you, never, so far as you have voice or influence, permit any departure from the principles of governments on which this nation was founded, or any disregard of the freedoms which, by the inspiration of God our Father, were written into the Constitution of the United States.

MISSIONARY WORK

I want to emphasize that we as a people have one supreme thing to do and that is to call upon the world to repent of all sin, to come to God. And it is our duty above all others to go forth and proclaim the gospel of the Lord Jesus Christ, the restoration again to the earth of the plan of life and salvation. . . . We have in very deed the pearl of great price. We have that which is of more value than all the wealth and scientific information which the world possesses.

MOTHER

There seems to be a power which the mother possesses in shaping the life of the child that is far superior, in my judgment, to the power of the father, and this almost without exception. I have talked with a great many highly educated men and women who have usually been willing to credit the mothers for their success in life more than the fathers. As the daily vocations in life take father away from home, they do not have the opportunity to get as close to the hearts of their children as do the mothers. After all it is by love, genuine love of our fellows, that we accomplish the most. A mother's love seems to be the most perfect and the most sincere, the strongest of any love we know anything about. I, for one, rejoice in it because of its wonderful example to me.

PROGRESSION
It is by the performance of the plain, simple, everyday duties that devolve upon us that we will grow in the spirit of God.

TESTIMONY
I can no more give a man a testimony of this gospel that I can eat for him. I can tell him how to get it. I can tell him of the blessings of God to me. But each and every man must live the gospel if he expects to obtain an individual testimony of the divinity of this work.

TITHING
I bear witness—and I know that the witness I bear is true—that the men and women who have been absolutely honest with God, who have paid their one-tenth . . . God has given them wisdom whereby they have been able to utilize the remaining nine-tenths, and it has been of greater value to them, and they have accomplished more with it than they would if they had not been honest with the Lord.

TRUTH
I have heard that a lie can travel around the world while truth is getting out of bed, but nevertheless, truth eventually overtakes the lie and steps on it.

WEALTH
The great criterion of success in the world is that men can make money, but I want to say to you Latter-day Saints that to do this is not true success. . . . What is the matter? Why, the appetite for money grows upon a man, increases and strengthens unless he is careful, just as much as the appetite for whiskey, and it gets possession of him, and he loves the money instead of loving it only for the good that he can do with it. He does not estimate properly the value of things.

WELFARE
Our primary purpose was to set up, in so far as it might be possible, a system under which the curse of idleness would be done away with, the evils of a dole abolished, and independence, industry, thrift, and self-respect be once more established amongst our people. The aim of the Church is to help the people to help themselves. Work is to be re-enthroned as the ruling principle of the lives of our Church membership.

WORD OF WISDOM

There is absolutely no benefit to any human being derived from breaking the Word of Wisdom, but there is everything for his benefit, morally, intellectually, physically, and spiritually, in obeying it.

WORK

Work is what keeps people young. . . . We should have an ambition, we should have a desire to work to the full extent of our ability. Working eight or nine hours a day has never injured me, and I do not believe it will injure anyone else. Work is pleasing to the Lord.

George Albert Smith, Eighth President (1870-1951)

GEORGE ALBERT SMITH

Eighth President of the Church

Born: April 4, 1870, Salt Lake City, Utah

Died: April 4, 1951, Salt Lake City, Utah (age 81)

President of the Church: May 21, 1945, to April 4, 1951
(6 years)

Physical Characteristics: Six feet tall, weighed about 160
pounds, slender build, wore a beard, gray hair,
hazel eyes, glasses, had a thin face with a kindly
expression

Areas of Distinction: Prophet, business executive,
Scouter, writer, civic and government official,
missionary, humanitarian

Family: Son of John Henry and Sarah Farr Smith.
Married Lucy Emily Woodruff, May 25, 1892
(died November 5, 1937), three children.

Profile of George Albert Smith

Will Rogers, the American humorist, once said, "I never met a man I didn't like."

This and much more was true of George Albert Smith. In character he stood out among men. He was a prophet of God and a great humanitarian. He was a leader by both precept and example. The following illustrates the kind of man President Smith was: Having been informed that his prized Indian blanket had been stolen from his car, he avowed, "I wished that individual had come and asked for it. I would have given it to him gladly, rather than have him become a thief."

Every man is remembered in one way or another. George Albert Smith is remembered for his love and kindness. Since these qualities are co-eternal with God, so must be the life of the man whose years were committed to the living of these divine standards. President Smith's influence will live forever in the many hearts and souls that have been lifted to greater heights because of him. Scores of people, Church members and nonmembers alike, saw the gospel of Christ in action when they viewed him. He made the gospel real and vivid. A man of compassion, he gave freely of his spirit and means to missionaries, the depressed, the sick, the needy. Those who knew him could never recall a vulgar expression nor an unclean word coming from his lips.

George Albert Smith was born just across the street from Temple Square on April 4, 1870, when the Saints had been in the Salt Lake Valley just twenty-three years. His was a noble pedigree. His forebears can be traced to the very beginnings of America, and they were a great influence for good in his life. His great-grandfather was John Smith, brother of Joseph Smith, Sr., and uncle of the Prophet Joseph. John's son, the first George Albert Smith, became an apostle at twenty-two; it was he for whom George Albert Smith was named.

At the age of fourteen, George Albert Smith was given a patriarchal blessing in which he was told: ". . . thou shalt become a mighty prophet in the midst of the sons of Zion. And the angels of the Lord shall administer unto you, and the choice blessings of the heavens shall rest upon you."

The purpose of life on earth is to gain a testimony of the gospel of Jesus Christ, to live it, and to share it with others. George Albert Smith set out early in life to accomplish these goals and never to depart from them.

Believing that the correct name of The Church of Jesus Christ of Latter-day Saints should always be used instead of the various nicknames that had been applied, President Smith asked publishers and other to use it in full. In seeking the cooperation of close associates in bringing this about, he pointed out that there is neither a Mormon Church nor an LDS Church nor a Church of the Latter-day Saints.

President Smith was a man of many interests and hobbies. He was particularly interested in honoring the Mormon pioneers and others who had contributed to the exploration and development of the West.

He was a family man, a devoted husband and father who loved his time spent with his wife and three children. His wife, Lucy Emily Woodruff Smith, was a wonderful companion and made many trips with President Smith to distant lands. Her death in 1937 saddened him greatly.

George Albert Smith, at about age 40

For a man of such pronounced spirituality, President Smith had a remarkably wide and varied experience in secular and civic affairs. He presided over agricultural and industrial congresses. He was active in banking and other industrial enterprises.

Though handicapped in his vision as a young man as the result of excessive heat and sunglare while with a surveying party that laid out the Denver and Rio Grande Railroad at Green River, Utah, he never ceased to be involved with progress and people. He was a friend of youth, for to him they were the men of tomorrow. He was active in leadership of the Boy Scouts and other programs for the benefit of youth.

In 1934, at the national convention of the Boy Scouts of America, he received the Silver Buffalo, the highest award in Scouting in the United States. The award, made for outstanding and meritorious service to boyhood, included the following citation:

George Albert Smith: Business executive, religious leader, former President of the International Irrigation Congress and International Dry Farm Congress. Federal Receiver of Public Moneys and Special Disbursing Agent for the State of Utah. Member of the Quorum of Twelve Apostles of The Church of Jesus Christ of Latter-day Saints and General Superintendent of the Young Men's Mutual Improvement Association of that Church. Organizer and President of the Utah Pioneer Trails and Landmarks Association. Member of the National Executive Board of the Boy Scouts of America. Program Divisional Committee, Committee on Relationships,

President Smith was an avid Scouter

and of its Region Twelve Executive Committee, and identified with its local activities continually almost since its organization. He has been indefatigable in serving the cause of Scouting, and to his enthusiasm for its program must be largely traced the fact that Utah stands above all other states in the percentage of boys who are Scouts.

George Albert Smith was sustained as President of the Church by a solemn assembly at general conference in October 1945. On that occasion he said:

I wonder if anyone here feels as weak and as humble as the man who stands before you. I have been coming to this house since my infancy. I have seen all the Presidents of the Church since that time, sustained by the congregations here, as their names have been presented from this stand. I have seen the Church continue to grow in numbers, and have realized throughout all my years that the Church of Jesus Christ is what its name implies. We who are members of this Church are indeed fortunate to have found the light and to have accepted the truth. . . .

And so today, my brethren, standing here in humility before you, I would like to express to you my gratitude that you have seen fit to promise that you will help the humble man who has been called to preside over this Church as he strives to carry on by the inspiration of the Almighty. For this promise I am grateful, and I thank you that you have offered to do the same thing with regard to the two men who stand by my side as counselors, loyal and true and devoted Latter-day Saints, who have done everything to make my responsibility easier for me to carry. You voted to sustain the Quorum of the Twelve, the quorum that I belonged to for so many years that I felt like a stranger, almost, when I walked out of it to occupy the position as President of the Church.

The years 1945-51 were challenging for the world and for the Church. This was a period for reopening missions, calling more missionaries, rebuilding lives and homes after a devastating world war, and rededication to the Lord. These challenges were directed by the "friend and peacemaker," George Albert Smith.

On February 28, 1950, at the centennial celebration of the University of Utah, an honorary degree was given to President Smith, one of the university's distinguished alumni. Dean O. Meredith Wilson stated in his speech the reasons for conferring this honor:

Mr. President:

May I present George Albert Smith, three times president of societies for developing scientific farming, sixteen years president of the Society for the Aid of the Sightless, founder and president of the Utah Pioneer Trails and Landmarks Association, Director of the Oregon Trails Memorial Association, twenty years an executive of the Boy Scout organization and recipient of the silver beaver and silver buffalo awards, for a generation a leader in and now president of the Church of Jesus Christ of Latter-day Saints, who has traveled over a million miles in the interest of peace.

He has helped to build a living economy, devoted years to the handicapped, kept alive a devotion to the ideals and achievements of the Pioneers, and invested his best efforts in the leadership of tomorrow. A prophet to the members of his Church, a counselor and friend to all, being a servant of all men, he is, in truth, a man of God. For this lifetime of devoted service to the welfare of all his fellow men, I recommend that he be awarded the degree of Doctor of Humanities, honoris causa.

"Keep the commandments of the Lord: then carry on." That was the simple, direct formula for life from President Smith. He died peacefully April 4, 1951, on his eighty-first birthday. Of one thing there is no doubt: George Albert Smith brought to the world a better understanding and attitude toward the Church that was a real contrast to the time when he was a missionary and experienced being shot at by misinformed and bitter people. He was a "man for all seasons," the seasons being peace, brotherhood, love, and kindness. President Harry S Truman said, "I looked upon him as one of our country's great moral leaders."

One of the speakers at his funeral, a non-Church member, gave the following eulogy:

He was a man without guile, a religious man, and a spiritual leader, not only in his own Church—in any group. Even alone with him you had a feeling of this man's spirituality. . . . He loved to talk about the brotherhood of man, his genuine love of all mankind,

The First Presidency: President George Albert Smith (center) and counselors J. Reuben Clark, Jr., and David O. McKay

which after all is the true charity of Christ, deeper than any doctrinal differences, that gift from above that makes for richer, fuller understanding of man's feeling toward man. (*Improvement Era*, June 1951, p. 405.)

President David O. McKay said of him: "He lived as nearly as it is humanly possible for a man to live a Christ-like life."

What was the secret that won President George Albert Smith love and respect of all—from the humble tradesman to the country's chief executives? Where was his strength. He loved everyone. He had a creed and lived it. This is what he believed:

I would be a friend to the friendless and find joy in ministering to the needs of the poor.

I would visit the sick and afflicted and inspire in them a desire for faith to be healed.

I would teach the truth to the understanding and blessing of all mankind.

I would seek out the erring one and try to win him back to a righteous and a happy life.

I would not seek to force people to live up to my ideals, but rather love them into doing the thing that is right.

I would live with the masses and help to solve their problems that their earth life may be happy.

I would avoid the publicity of high positions and discourage the flattery of thoughtless friends.

I would not knowingly wound the feelings of any, not even one who may have wronged me, but would seek to do him good and make him my friend.

I would overcome the tendency to selfishness and jealousy and rejoice in the successes of all the children of my Heavenly Father.

I would not be an enemy to any living soul.

Knowing that the Redeemer of mankind has offered to the world the only plan that will fully develop us and make us really happy here and hereafter I feel it not only a duty but also a blessed privilege to disseminate this truth. (*Improvement Era*, March 1932, p. 295.)

Interesting Facts and Contributions
of George Albert Smith

1. He was an apostle for forty-two years, though his administration as President was short—just six years.

2. John Henry Smith and his son George Albert Smith are the only father and son who have been apostles in the Council of the Twelve at the same time (father, 1880-1910; son, 1903-45).

3. He was the third generation of his family to serve in the First Presidency.

4. He was active in civic and political affairs. He was the first member of the Church to be appointed to a federal office in the state of Utah.

5. He was the first mission president sent to Europe after World War I. Through this experience, he was aware of the problems that war creates, especially in Europe.

6. He traveled thousands of miles over historical trails. Through his efforts with "trail" groups organized to preserve important historical trails and landmarks, many places of Mormon history were marked for posterity.

7. An outstanding Scouter, he helped Church and national programs. He was involved with Scouting for almost forty years.

8. He was a special friend to the Indians. He visited their reservations and homes. He had friends from many tribes. He was an honorary chief among many tribes, and in high places in Washington he pleaded their cause.

9. He was a natural missionary. Wherever he traveled he sought out meetings with important leaders and people, expressing the true mission of the Church, correcting mis-

conceptions, and leaving a spirit of friendship that was to bless the Church in the future.

10. He had a great interest in aviation and loved flying. He took his first flight in 1920 over the English Channel. He was one of the pioneers in aviation in the West and became a director of Western Air Express, now Western Air Lines.

11. He helped to enlarge and expand the *Improvement Era*.

12. He was president of the Society for the Aid of the Sightless for sixteen years.

13. He was a humanitarian who gave generously to countless persons who were in need.

14. He had a keen sense of humor that was reflected from many experiences of life and lightened the burdens of life.

15. He was the first Church President to appear on a telecast of general conference, in 1949.

16. He personally knew six presidents of the United States. Many United States senators, congressmen, and governors were counted among his personal friends.

17. He was the first President to visit Mexico.

Significant Dates and Events in Lifetime of George Albert Smith

Church Population, 1945: 979,454   1951: 1,147,157
1951—Stakes: 191   Missions: 43   Temples: 8
U.S. Population, 1951: 153 million (est.)
World Population, 1951: 2.6 billion (est.)
U.S. President, 1945-51: Harry S Truman

1870   Born in Salt Lake City, April 4

1874-75   His father, John Henry Smith, served a mission in Great Britain

1882-83   Attended Brigham Young Academy.

1883   Began working in ZCMI clothing factory; employed by Grant-Odell Co.

1884   Received his patriarchal blessing, which foretold his future calling to the Council of the Twelve (age 14).

1887-88   Attended the University of Utah.

1888-91   Was salesman for ZCMI.

1891   Served mission to Southern Utah in interests of YMMIA.

1892   Married Lucy Emily Woodruff.

1892-94   Served mission to Southern States (age 22).

1898   Was appointed receiver for the U.S. Land Office and special disbursing agent for Utah by President McKinley.

1903   Was ordained an apostle by President Joseph F. Smith, October 8 (age 33).

1904   Was called to the YMMIA general board.

1909-12   Illness prevented him from being active in the Council of the Twelve.

1910   His father was named second counselor in the First Presidency.

1912   Investigated and approved adoption of the Scouting program in the Church.

1916   Was elected president of International Irrigation Congress.

1917   Was elected president of the International Dry Farm Congress.

1919   When Salt Lake Boy Scout Council was organized, he became a member of the executive board (he served more than 30 years).

1919-21 Served as president of the European Mission.

1921   Was appointed general president of YMMIA.

1922   Was elected vice-president of the National Society of the Sons of the American Revolution. Participated in first radio broadcast in Salt Lake City over Station KZN (later KSL), May 6.

1930   Organized the Utah Pioneer Trails and Landmarks Association.

1931   Was elected a member of the National Executive Board of Boy Scouts of America.

1932   Received the Silver Beaver award.

1934   Received the Silver Buffalo, highest award in Scouting.

1938   Made an extensive six-month tour of missions in the South Pacific, the first General Authority to visit these missions since 1917.

1941   Visited the Hopi and Navajo Indians in Arizona.

1943   Was set apart as President of the Council of the Twelve, July 1 (age 73).

1945   Visited President Truman in connection with sending supplies to Saints in war-torn Europe.

1945   Was sustained as President of the Church, May 21, at age 75, with J. Reuben Clark, Jr., and David O. McKay as counselors in the First Presidency. Dedicated the Idaho Falls Temple, September 23. Directed that relief goods be sent to Saints in Europe at conclusion of World War II.

U.S. dropped atomic bombs on Hiroshima and Nagasaki, August 6, 9. Japan surrendered to the Allies, September 2. The United Nations was organized.

1946   Began an automobile journey over the Mormon Trail to Nauvoo. Visited the Indians in Wyoming, Idaho, Utah, New Mexico. Visited Saints in Mexico, as well as President of Mexico—first President of the Church to visit there. Elder Ezra Taft Benson of the Council of the Twelve was sent to Europe to assist in rehabilitating members and to organize and set in order the missions and branches. Missionary work was resumed, particularly in countries outside the United States.

1947   Entertained governors of 43 states and three territories at governor's convention in Salt Lake City, July 15. Dedicated the "This Is the Place" monument at the mouth of Emigration Canyon in Salt Lake City, July 24, at centennial of pioneers' entrance into Salt Lake Valley. Church membership reached one million.

1948   *Commercial television began. The Marshall Plan gave aid to war-torn countries. An American airplane exceeded the speed of sound.*

1949   *A U.S. rocket reached outer space. An earthquake in Ecuador killed 6,000. The United States and its allies set up the North Atlantic Treaty Organization (NATO).*

1950   Dedicated the BYU Science Building. Received an honorary doctor of humanities degree from the University of Utah. Dedicated the Brigham Young statue at the U.S. Capitol in Washington, D.C. Attended the centennial celebration of missionary work in Hawaii. Delivered the last sermon of his life, December 11. In Prague, Czechoslovakia, one of the most stirring incidents in Church missionary history came to a dramatic close when two missionaries were released from Communist prison.

         The Korean War started. Some 30,000 persons were killed in an earthquake in Assam, India.

1951   President George Albert Smith died in Salt Lake City on April 4, his eighty-first birthday.

First nationwide television began. First jet passenger plane trip was flown.

1945-51   Significant inventions; transistor (U.S.); supersonic airplane (U.S.); Polaroid camera (U.S.); atomic bomb (U.S.).

The First Presidency
During George Albert Smith's Administration

First Counselor	President	Second Counselor
J. Reuben Clark, Jr.	George Albert Smith	David O. McKay
(1934)	(1903)	(1906)
1945-51	1945-51	1945-51

Council of the Twelve—October 1945

George F. Richards (1906)   Albert E. Bowen (1937)
Joseph Fielding Smith (1910)   Harold B. Lee (1941)
Stephen L Richards (1917)   Spencer W. Kimball (1943)
John A. Widtsoe (1921)   Ezra Taft Benson (1943)
Joseph F. Merrill (1931)   Mark E. Petersen (1944)
Charles A. Callis (1933)   Matthew Cowley (1945)

Died   Added

1947—Charles A. Callis   Henry D. Moyle (1947)
1950—George F. Richards   Delbert L. Stapley (1950)

April 1951

Joseph Fielding Smith (1910)   Spencer W. Kimball (1943)
Stephen L Richards (1917)   Ezra Taft Benson (1943)
John A. Widtsoe (1921)   Mark E. Petersen (1944)
Joseph F. Merrill (1931)   Matthew Cowley (1945)
Albert E. Bowen (1937)   Henry D. Moyle (1947)
Harold B. Lee (1941)   Delbert L. Stapley (1950)

Note: Dates in parentheses indicate date ordained member of Council of the Twelve.

Testimony of George Albert Smith

I witness to you, that I know today better than I ever knew before that God lives; that Jesus is the Christ; that Joseph Smith was a prophet of the Living God; and that the Church that he organized under the direction of our Heavenly Father, The Church of Jesus Christ of Latter-day Saints, the Church that was driven into the wilderness —is operating under the power and authority of the same priesthood that was conferred by Peter, James, and John upon Joseph Smith and Oliver Cowdery. I know this, as I know that I live, and I realize that to bear this testimony to you is a very serious matter and that I shall be held accountable by my Heavenly Father for this and all other things that I have taught in his name. (*Improvement Era*, April 1950, pp. 263-64.)

Personal Experience of George Albert Smith

A number of years ago I was seriously ill; in fact, I think everyone gave me up but my wife. With my family I went to St. George, Utah, to see if it would improve my health. We went as far as we could by train, and then continued the journey in a wagon, in the bottom of which a bed had been made for me.

In St. George we arranged for a tent for my health and comfort, with a built-in floor raised about a foot above the ground and could roll up the south width of the tent to make the sunshine and fresh air available. I became so weak as to be scarcely able to move. It was a slow and exhausting effort for me even to turn over in bed.

One day, under these conditions, I lost consciousness of my surroundings and thought I had passed to the other side. I found myself standing with my back to a large beautiful lake, facing a great forest of trees. There was no one in sight, and there was no boat upon the lake or any other visible means to indicate how I might have arrived there. I realized, or seemed to realize, that I had finished my work in mortality and had gone home. I began to look around, to see if I could not find someone. There was no evidence of anyone living there, just those great, beautiful trees in front of me and the wonderful lake behind me.

I began to explore, and soon I found a trail through the woods which seemed to have been used very little, and which was almost obscured by grass. I followed this trail, and after I had walked for some time and had traveled a considerable distance through the forest, I saw a man coming towards me. I became aware that he was a very large man, and I hurried my steps to reach him, because I recognized him as my grandfather. In mortality he weighed over three hundred pounds, so you may know he was a large man. I remember how happy I was to see him coming. I had been given his name and had always been proud of it.

When Grandfather came within a few feet of me, he stopped. His stopping was an invitation for me to stop. Then—and this I would like the boys and girls and young people never to forget—he looked at me very earnestly and said:

"I would like to know what you have done with my name."

Everything I had ever done passed before me as though it were a flying picture on a screen—everything I had done. Quickly this vivid retrospect came down to the very time I was standing there. My whole life had passed before me. I smiled and looked at my grandfather and said:

"I have never done anything with your name of which you need be ashamed."

He stepped forward and took me in his arms, and as he did so, I became conscious again of my earthly surroundings. My pillow was as wet as though water had been poured on it—wet with tears of gratitude that I could answer unashamed.

I have thought of this many times, and I want to tell you that I have been trying, more than ever since that time, to take care of that name. So I want to say to the boys and girls, to the young men and women, to the youth of the Church and of all the world: Honor your fathers and your mothers. Honor the names that you bear, because some day you will have the privilege and obligation of reporting to them (and to your Father in heaven) what you have done with their name. (Smith, *Sharing the Gospel*, pp. 110-12.)

Quotations from George Albert Smith

BOOK OF MORMON

No man can honestly read the Book of Mormon and then say that this boy Prophet wrote it himself, and the most persistent search has failed to reveal that he stole the book. There is too much in the book to have been written by a boy whom his hostile critics brand as an ignoramus. And it should be said here, he had no opportunity for consulting either the little-known sources, which hostile critics have disinterred in trying to destroy him, or the more widely-known sources of which he probably had no knowledge whatever because they were inaccessible to him. No man of his age could have had in his mind, no matter how much he had studied, merely the allusions contained in the Book of Mormon to the holy scriptures, and all that we have of his that came from him when speaking or writing normally, gives not even a suggestion of his power to compose or to utter those great gems of majestic literature which are so plentifully found in the Book of Mormon and the Doctrine and Covenants.

BROTHERHOOD

I plead with you, my brothers and sisters, let us be generous with one another. Let us be as patient with one another as we would like others to be with us. Let us see the virtues of our neighbor and our friends, and speak of these virtues, not find fault and criticize. If we will do that, we will radiate sunshine, and those who know us best will love us.

CHRIST

The Redeemer of mankind possessed more than ordinary intelligence. He was indeed the Son of God, the Only Begotten of God in the flesh. He was sent into the world to remove from the minds of men the delusions that had confounded them for many generations. He came to call men to repentance, to turn them from the error of their way. He went among them representing God, the eternal Father, proclaiming that he was in the image of the Father, and those who had seen him had seen the Father, and told them that

He had been sent to do the will of his Father. He called on all men to turn from error that had crept in among them, to repent of their sins and go down into the waters of baptism.

CONSTITUTION
Sustain the Constitution of the United States. The Lord himself has said that he raised up the very men who prepared it, to the end that it might be an example to all the world. Do you believe it? If you do, then sustain it, and don't let your voice be among those that shall deride and break down the government that is so important for us.

EVIL
We are living in a time when men are running to and fro in the earth, seeking almost everything but the word of God, and surely they are finding what they seek.

EXAMPLE
Now, brothers and sisters, don't scold one another, don't quarrel, don't feel disagreeable toward those who do not understand the gospel; just set them a proper example and live such lives that everyone will be glad to know you. If we can live that way, our children can easily honor us. The Lord commanded us to honor our father and mother and promised certain blessings if we do. I want to say that it is difficult for some of them to do so when they see their parents behaving the way they do. Let us be worthy to be honored. Set your homes in order and have therein a spirit of joy with your companions, friends and neighbors that wherever you go the world will be brighter and happier because of your lives.

FATHER
Fathers, I do not care how much property you have, what honor you may attain to—it is immaterial to me whether your names are written in the records of history because of your accomplishments, or of mere monetary things. The greatest blessings are your boys and your girls. I fear that we may neglect our opportunities with these young people and spend more time with material things than we should, and I repeat, so that not any of us will forget it, that the most precious gifts given to us are our . . . wives and our children, with whom we may have companionship throughout eternity.

HAPPINESS
It ought not to be difficult for us to keep the commandments of the Lord, because keeping them leads to happiness. It ought not to be difficult for husbands and wives to love one another and be true

to one another, because doing so is a source of happiness. It ought not to be difficult for boys and girls to love their parents and honor them, because that is another source of happiness. Always being truthful is a source of happiness. Being honest with our neighbors is a source of happiness. Keeping the Word of Wisdom is a source of happiness. Paying him our tithes and our offerings is a source of blessing and happiness. I might go on and enumerate many other things, but I may sum it all by saying: All the happiness that is worthy of the name, all the real happiness there is in this world, comes from living in accordance with the commandments of God—whether men know it or not.

HOME

One way in which we can keep them [children] closer to us is for us to meet together oftener in our homes. The Church has asked that there be set aside at least one home night each week for all the family to meet together and to enjoy each other's company, to enjoy the simple pleasures of the family fireside, and to discuss with each other those things which are of great and lasting worth.

LAST DAYS

We are living in the latter days, in the time when the Lord said that the world would be afflicted by pestilence and earthquakes, that the sea should heave itself beyond its bounds, that there should be thunderings and lightnings, and wars and rumors of wars. Surely the scriptures are being fulfilled, but before the earth shall be cleansed and purified and prepared for the second coming of our Lord, his Gospel must be proclaimed to all the nations of the earth. His sons and daughters must carry the message of life and salvation that means everything to those who are in darkness.

LOVE

I say there is need in all Israel today—there is need for this man addressing you to examine himself—there is need for everyone of us to look about ourselves and see wherein we are neglecting our privileges and our duty, for tomorrow it may be too late. Today is the acceptable time of the Lord. Let us set our houses in order. Let us love one another. Let us sustain these men whom God has raised up to preside over us. Let us bless them, not only by our lips, but by assisting in every possible way to carry this burden that rests so heavily upon their shoulders. Let us honor these presidents of stakes and these bishops of wards; pray for and bless them and help them. Let us love one another that our Heavenly Father may be able to bless us, and he will bless us if we love one another and do good to all his children.

PIONEERS

Unlike most other westward-bound emigrants of the time, these pioneers came not for wealth, but to create homes, where they could worship God unmolested. This area was then generally considered unfit for colonization, and Brigham Young was advised against settling here by those who had seen it. But these people believed that they were led by the hand of providence, and that this would become a land of promise unto them. . . . They had little money but they possessed in large measure characteristics far more valuable in the development of the frontier. Among these was their remarkable capacity for work. They adopted as their emblem the honey bee and the hive, symbols of industry. Pioneering at best was arduous, but in this harsh, strange land it required even greaer effort. There were among them many skilled men and women. These people were not adventurers. They were by inclination stable folk, gathered from many countries and communities, trained in the arts, crafts and professions. Evidence of their skill is in the remarkable buildings which they constructed, as well as in their other accomplishments. Among their most commendable qualities was a spirit of cooperation. Bound by recognized ties of brotherhood and guided by Christian ideals, which were part of their very fibre, they knew how to live and work together without suppressing individualism. Even more important than these characteristics was their faith in the ultimate achievement of their purposes. They believed that with the blessings of Heaven, the soil would become fruitful and their labors would be rewarded. They prayed over the land, and set to work to make their prayers come true. . . . They came here to build a community where they might worship the Lord. He blessed their efforts and from the foundations they laid has risen the great commonwealth we enjoy today.

SACRAMENT

Before partaking of this sacrament, our hearts should be pure; our hands should be clean; we should be divested of all emnity toward our associates; we should be at peace with our fellowmen; and we should have in our hearts a desire to do the will of our Father and to keep all of His commandments. If we do this, partaking of the sacrament will be a blessing to us and will renew our spiritual strength.

SCOUTING

The program of scouting is one that develops honesty, integrity, truthfulness, love, reverence, and what a wonderful training it is for a boy in scouting to continue on until he gets his Eagle badge. I think I am safe in saying that as a result of scouting thousands of lives were saved in this last World War because of the knowledge of men who had been Scouts and knew what to do in case of emergency. It is marvelous what it has meant to us. And think of what it has contributed to our people and our communities—the fine things that these boys have been able to do under the direction of their scoutmasters in being helpful in the various programs that are intended to bless the areas in which they live. This is a sick world. What a difference it would make if everywhere scouting were taught and practiced. There would not be the bitterness and the heartbreak that is found today in so many places.

SCRIPTURES
Read them prayerfully and faithfully, teach them in your homes; call your families around you and inspire in them a faith in the Living God, by reading those things that have been revealed. They are the most precious of all the libraries in all the world.

TEMPTATION
We live in a day when there are many temptations to evil, and each one who submits himself to any of them loses a blessing.

David O. McKay, Ninth President (1873-1970)

DAVID O. McKAY

Ninth President of the Church

Born: September 8, 1873, Huntsville, Utah

Died: January 18, 1970, Salt Lake City, Utah (age 96)

President of the Church: April 9, 1951, to January 18, 1970 (18 years and 9 months)

Physical Characteristics: Six feet 1 inch tall (tallest President), 195-200 pounds, piercing hazel-brown eyes, flowing white hair, stately and distinguished appearance, strong and forceful features

Areas of Distinction: Prophet, educator, farmer, missionary, writer, athlete, humanitarian, public servant

Family: Son of David and Jennette Evans McKay. Married Emma Ray Riggs January 2, 1901 (she died November 14, 1970); seven children.

Profile of David O. McKay

"He has achieved success who has lived well, laughed often, and loved much, who has gained the respect of intelligent men and the love of little children, who has filled his niche and accomplished his task, who has left the world better than he found it." (Robert Louis Stevenson.)

By these terms—and others one might cite—David O. McKay achieved success.

"Lived well. . . ." A son of David and Jennette Evans McKay, Mormon emigrants from Scotland and Wales, David O. McKay was born September 8, 1873, at Huntsville, Utah. One of ten children, he worked at farm chores, delivered mail and newspapers, played piano for the town band and second base for the town baseball team.

Once, in answer to a question about what had been the most important factors in shaping his life and beliefs he replied:

My home life from babyhood to the present time has been the greatest factor in giving me moral and spiritual standards and in shaping the courses of my life. Sincerity, courtesy, consistency in word and deed exemplified in the lives of my parents and others in the two homes have proved a safeguard and guidance. (Schluter, *A Convert's Tribute to David O. McKay*, p. 27.)

While serving a mission to the British Isles before the turn of the century, he became convinced of the truthfulness of the gospel. During a deeply spiritual

David O. McKay as a young man

meeting in Scotland, he later related, a Church official said to him, "If you are faithful, you will yet stand in the leading councils of the Church." Not many years passed before that prophecy was fulfilled.

In adulthood President McKay enjoyed frequent trips to his boyhood farm home in Huntsville. There he could relax and get a different perspective on the problems of the day. "The air is better at Huntsville," he once commented. "That's what keeps me young." He loved animals, especially horses, and even into his nineties he enjoyed riding his favorite, Sonny Boy.

"Laughed often. . . ." A man of many qualities, he was noted for his sense of humor. Norman Vincent Peale tells this story: "I recall a heart-stopping moment when as the aged President McKay mounted the platform to address a group, he tripped on the stairs. There was a gasp from the people. But he stood up and faced the audience with that irrepressible smile. 'It's awful to grow old,' he said ruefully, 'but I prefer it to the alternative.' " (*Improvement Era*, February 1970, p. 24.)

Another example of his ability to sense humor in life situations happened when he was in his early nineties.

One day while climbing a hill to inspect a site for a chapel, two local Church officers reached out to assist him, one on either arm. Part way up the hill President McKay stopped and said, "Brethren, I don't mind helping one of you climb this hill, but I can't carry you both." (Stewart, *Remembering the McKays*, p. 34.)

"Loved much. . . ." He had a deep understanding of human frailties. Kind and wise, he sought answers to problems through prayer. He freely gave of himself to others; in fact, his formula for happiness was: "Keep busy serving others."

He loved meeting people and had a remarkable memory for names and faces. He sometimes stood for hours to personally shake hands with young and old. People didn't forget him when they shook his hand, looked into his eyes, and felt his warmth and inspiration.

Now what is the source of his influence, the secret of his superior leadership? Put this question to his most intimate friends and they will answer—his love for mankind, his humanness. He has a luminous and impressionable mind, a will of the strongest fibre, a great and tender heart. He is a clear and graceful writer, an appealing and convincing speaker, a delightful companion, a chivalrous leader; a lovable man who holds forever your confidence. You trust him—you believe in him. His loyalty is superb. He never forsakes a friend and is big enough to love the sinner while he hates the sin. This gives him a lifting power that comes only to noble souls. He has a really great heart, a deep and abiding sympathy, a passionate love for the souls of men—all qualities which the world stands so much in need of.

Another secret of his success is his sweet and unimpeachable character. He lives above the fog and turmoil of daily circumstances. David O. McKay never did a mean or little thing, he is guilty of no injustice to his fellows, he is free from the indictments of selfishness and trickery. All his days he has lived upon a high moral plateau and has risen to spiritual altitudes which few people reach, inspiring all the while those about him to climb to the same heights. (Bryant S. Hinckley, in *Improvement Era*, May 1932, p. 446.)

President David O. McKay

The marriage of David O. and Emma Ray Riggs (they were married in the Salt Lake Temple January 2, 1901) presented an ideal that married people might try to emulate. One of their sons reported that President McKay always rose when she entered the room. He enjoyed

The McKay home at Huntsville, Utah

opening the car door, offering his arm, holding her coat, and practicing other courtesies. He said of her: "She is the sweetest, most helpful wife that ever inspired a man to noble endeavor. She has been an inspiration, my life-long sweetheart, an angel of God come upon earth."

"Gained respect. . . ." Several years before David O. McKay became President of the Church, Wayne Rogers sat in a New York Stake quarterly conference and recorded his impressions of this great spiritual leader:

> I am always mentally reconstructing not only what he said but also how he looks: A stately figure well over six feet tall and apparently muscular—at any rate enough to be ultra forceful; a well-blocked face, handsomely engraved. . . ; eyes fiercely tender, hardening and softening in rhythmic harmony to the beautiful thoughts that flow from a strong, expressive mouth; straight lips— the melting point of character—gave him an expression . . . that was wonderful.

Here is a man whose every feature, every line, and every expression mirror a life of kindness, a life of devotion, a life of understanding, of service, and of sympathy. . . .

I still possess a haunting apprehension of the depths of his nature that will never be sounded; of the unfathomable well of feeling and sincerity that will never be drained; of the understanding that while penetrating the comprehension of a mere child drives home an unforgettable lesson to the adult. He is a man that, in full maturity, has retained the sweet, sincere simplicity of a child and has combined it with his superior intellect and mellowness of experience to stand forth as a great spiritual leader. (*Improvement Era,* June 1951, p. 400.)

Several presidents of the United States were his personal friends, as were many leading world statesmen. A certain official meeting him for the first time later commented, "If you were to fashion man in the image of God, there is the pattern."

Elder Richard L. Evans of the Council of the Twelve made these observations shortly after President McKay became President:

May we retouch this portrait with a few points of personal impression—the point of his presence in his office in the very early morning hours, and on almost any day long after conventional closing time; his delightful laugh and his quick and keen and always kindly humor; his reading of a bit of "Bobby" Burns, or the telling of a Scotch story in the dialect of his father's father; his steady and appraising gaze, and the light in his eyes and the changes in his ever-expressive face; the broad shoulders and the long, firm stride as he purposefully walks from place to place; the wonderful head of silvered hair; his encouragement, his confidence, and his consideration; and his faith and his firmness.

. . . And with all this surpassing pressure, I have never seen him impatient at interruption in his office; he is always the gracious host, equally gracious to the humble as to the great.

. . . His life has been filled with service these seventy-seven years—and thus has he been richly prepared for his present responsibilities. (*Improvement Era,* June 1951, p. 400.)

"Filled his niche and accomplished his task. . . ." David O. McKay was sustained as President of the Church

The First Presidency: President David O. McKay and counselors Henry D. Moyle and Hugh B. Brown

by a solemn assembly at general conference on April 9, 1951. At that time he stated his feelings about the great responsibility and honor of the office:

When that reality came [death of President George Albert Smith] as I tell you, I was deeply moved. And I am today, and pray that I may, even though inadequately, be able to tell you how weighty this responsibility seems. The Lord has said that the three presiding high priests chosen by the body, appointed and ordained to this office of presidency, are to be "upheld by the confidence, faith, and prayer of the Church." No one can preside over this Church without first being in tune with the head of the Church, our Lord and Savior, Jesus Christ. He is our head. This is his Church. Without his guidance and constant inspiration, we cannot succeed. With his guidance, with his inspiration, we cannot fail. . . . Today you have by your vote placed upon us the greatest responsibility, as well as the greatest honor, that lies within your power to bestow as members of the Church of Jesus Christ of Latter-day Saints. Your doing so increases the duty of the First Presidency to render service to the people. (*Improvement Era*, June 1951, pp. 406-407.)

A teacher by profession and one who lived as he taught, President McKay felt that education was an eternal process. He loved to read. He loved the scriptures, the works of Shakespeare and other literary masters. His writings and sermons reflected his knowledge of thought-provoking ideas and beautiful poetry.

President McKay spent much time speaking and teaching about the importance of home and the family. He stated that "no other success can compensate for failure in the home." He encouraged all members to strengthen their families by holding weekly family home evenings.

Himself a great missionary for the Church throughout the world, he often entreated: "Every member a missionary." He circled the earth, visited far corners, traveled on foot, by horse and buggy, and by jet airliner, and presented his beliefs to people wherever he went. By means of television and radio, his face, voice, and warm personality were known to millions.

The most frequently used expressions used to describe President McKay were: "kind," "a complete gentleman," "a noble individual," "a man of God," "a great teacher," "a great organizer," "the temple builder," "beloved leader."

"Left the world better. . . ." While in his early nineties, President McKay was seriously ill on several occasions, and many thought that there was no hope for his life. But each time he regained his strength, determined to live life to its fullest. Then on a Sunday morning, January 18, 1970, at the age of 96, he passed away.

Major newspapers throughout the world noted his death with his picture and a list of accomplishments. The *New York Times* carried the story on the front page and continued for one full page inside (with three photographs)—space equaled or exceeded only by the passing of the nation's former presidents.

A fitting conclusion, even an epitaph, might be David O. McKay's own words. In 1968 he was asked to describe his greatest accomplishment and his greatest experience. He said: "Making the church a worldwide organization," and "the feeling of such peace and satisfaction and love for all God's children, which comes late in life after more than 80 years of work in the Church and

President David O. McKay on horseback at his home in Huntsville, Utah

travels among people of all lands. My one greatest desire
to them is that they may have peace and happiness in this
world and the world to come." (Schluter, *A Convert's Tribute to David O. McKay*, p. 56.)

Interesting Facts and Contributions
of David O. McKay

1. He served longer than any other person as a General Authority—sixty-four years.

2. He served with three Presidents of the Church: President Joseph F. Smith, President Heber J. Grant, and President George Albert Smith.

3. Besides those General Authorities serving today (1971), President McKay worked with thirty-five apostles. He saw four Patriarchs, six Presiding Bishops, and many members of the First Council of the Seventy come into office.

4. He was a personal friend of several presidents of the United States and leading statesmen from throughout the world. Wherever he traveled he sought out meetings with top government leaders, expressing the true mission of the Church, correcting misconceptions, leaving a spirit of friendship that was to bless the Church many times over.

5. He was the most widely traveled General Authority in history. He traveled more than two million miles as President.

6. In 1900 he became a member of the Weber Stake Sunday School superintendency. In this organization he introduced a new method of teaching and of teacher instruction that was later to affect the entire Church. He established teacher preparation meetings and individual cooperative outlines for the lessons that were prepared. His teaching philosophy was "aim," "illustration," and "application."

7. He fortified the home through his sermons, his writings, and his emphasis on the family home evening and home teaching programs.

8. On his ninetieth birthday (1963), it was noted that at least half of the living members of the Church had known no other President of the Church; 50 percent of the membership of the Church had been baptized since 1951, twelve years before.

9. During his life, temples were built at St. George, Logan, Manti, and Salt Lake City, Utah; Laie, Hawaii; Alberta, Canada; Mesa, Arizona; Idaho Falls, Idaho; Bern, Switzerland; Los Angeles and Oakland, California; Hamilton, New Zealand; and London, England. Eight temples were built or announced during his administration.

10. His leadership and innovative and administrative abilities were everywhere present, even in the vast business responsibilities of the Church. A revised financial structure was established; the President of the Church became the chairman of the boards of all Church businesses; and full-time presidents were named to head businesses that had taken so much of the time of previous Church leaders.

11. During his administration, more than 3,750 Church buildings were constructed, including 2,000 ward and branch chapels. Many major buildings and housing complexes were built at Brigham Young University, and 69 new elementary and high school buildings were constructed in many areas of the South Pacific, Central America, South America, and Mexico.

12. The $10 million David O. McKay Hospital in Ogden, Utah, was built.

13. The number of missions more than doubled, to a total of 88, and the number of missionaries grew from about 2,000 to 13,000 during President McKay's administration. He instituted three language training schools for missionaries and seminars for newly called mission presidents.

14. A schoolteacher himself, he had a lifelong interest in education. During his administration the number of seminary and institute students tripled, to more than 162,000. Seminary programs are now found throughout the world, with formal classes as well as home study programs available. The institute program is now functioning at college and university campuses in the United States and other countries. At Brigham Young University, the enrollment nearly quadrupled, resulting in the university's becoming the largest church-affiliated university in America. The Latter-day Saint Student Association was established to serve the needs of LDS college students.

15. There were 184 stakes when he became President of the Church; the 500th was created on the day of his death, January 18, 1970. During his administration the first stakes were organized outside the United States, including New Zealand, Australia, Holland, England, Germany, Switzerland, Mexico, Samoa, Brazil, Argentina, Guatemala, Uruguay, and Tonga.

16. Many of his sermons were compiled into books, and he was the subject of several other books during his lifetime. These included *Stepping Stones to an Abundant Life, Treasures of Life, Secrets of a Happy Life, True to the Faith, Man May Know for Himself, Highlights in the Life of David O. McKay, Ancient Apostles, Gospel Ideals, Cherished Experiences, Home Memories of President David O. McKay, A Convert's Tribute to David O. McKay,* and *Remembering the McKays.*

17. He served seventeen years as counselor in the First Presidency and almost nineteen years as President, for a total of nearly thirty-six years as a member of the First Presidency. (This was exceeded only by Joseph F. Smith's record of over thirty-eight years.)

18. He served longer as President than six of the previous eight Presidents of the Church. Only two Presidents—Heber J. Grant and Brigham Young—served longer.

19. His administration was a period of worldwide growth of the Church. The era of the jet airplane and rapid communication helped Church leaders keep in touch with members everywhere and expound the gospel. Worldwide coverage of conference sessions provided millions with the opportunity to learn of the Church.

20. He was the first President to visit, as President, South Africa, Asia, South America, Australia, New Zealand, and Central America.

Significant Dates and Events in Lifetime of David O. McKay

Church Membership, 1951: 1,147,157 1970: 2,807,456

1970—Stakes: 499 Missions: 88 Temples: 13

U.S. Population, 1970: 204 million (est.)

World Population, 1970: 3.5 billion (est.)

U.S. Presidents, 1951-70: Harry S Truman, Dwight D. Eisenhower, John F. Kennedy, Lyndon B. Johnson, Richard M. Nixon

1873   Born at Huntsville, Utah, September 8

1881-83 His father served as a missionary in Great Britain

1897   Graduated from University of Utah. Served as president and valedictorian of his class.

1897-99 Served mission to Scotland (age 24-26).

1899   Joined faculty of Weber Stake Academy (now Weber State College) at Ogden, Utah.

1901   Married Emma Ray Riggs.

1902   Served as principal of Weber Academy.

1906   Was ordained an apostle by President Joseph F. Smith, April 9. Served on the Church board of education. Was named second assistant president of the Deseret Sunday School Union (DSSU) (age 32).

1909   Became first assistant president, DSSU.

1918-34 General president, DSSU.

1919-21 Church Commissioner of Education.

1920-21 Made world tour of Church missions, traveling 65,500 miles.

1921   Dedicated China for the preaching of the gospel. Received the gift of the Maori tongue while addressing Saints in New Zealand.

1921-22   Member of the board of regents, University of Utah.

1922-24   President of the European Mission.

1932   Chairman of Utah Council for Child Health and Protection.

1934   Was sustained as second counselor to President Heber J. Grant in the First Presidency, October 6, age 61.

1938-47   Was Chairman of Utah State Centennial Commission.

1940-41   Served on board of trustees of Utah State Agricultural College (now Utah State University).

1942   Was chairman of Utah State Advisory Committee of the American Red Cross and of Utah Council for Child Health and Protection.

1945   Was sustained as second counselor to President George Albert Smith.

1950   Was sustained as President of the Council of the Twelve, September 30. Received an honorary doctor of laws degree from Utah State Agricultural College (now Utah State University).

1951   Was sustained as President of the Church, April 9, with Stephen L Richards and J. Reuben Clark, Jr., as counselors. Received honorary doctorate degrees from Brigham Young University, the University of Utah, and Temple University (Philadelphia) (age 78).

1951-70   Missions opened: Central American, South Australian, Northern Far East, Southern Far East, South African, Northern Mexican, West Spanish-American, New Zealand South, Brazilian South, South German, Andes, Swiss, Austrian, Eupoean, North British, Eastern Atlantic States, Florida, West Mexican, Rarotongo, Alaskan-Canadian, French East, Texas (new), Scottish-Irish, Central British, Central German, West European, South American, Berlin, Chilean, Southwest British, Bavarian, Irish, Korean, Northeast British, North Argentine, North Scottish, Southeast Mexican, Franco-Belgian, Cumorah, Northern Indian, British South, Guatemala-El Salvador, California South, Italian, Andes South, Philippine, Ohio, Texas South, Pacific Northwest, Brazilian North, Colombia-Venezuela, Australian West,

Mexico North Central, Japan, Japan-Okinawa, California Central, California East, Arizona, South Central States, Southeast Asia.

1952   Toured nine missions of Europe. Servicemen's committees were established in stakes, wards, and missions. First telecast of general conference.

Rich uranium deposits were found near Moab, Utah. The U.S. tested a hydrogen bomb on November 1.

1953   Received the Silver Buffalo from Boy Scouts of America. Church School System (colleges, institutes, seminaries) was unified.

Ezra Taft Benson was named to President Eisenhower's Cabinet as Secretary of Agriculture (served eight years). The Korean War ended in truce, July 27.

1954   Toured South Africa, South America, Central America. Dedicated David O. McKay Building on the BYU campus. Received the Cross of the Commander of the Royal Order of the Phoenix from the Greek government.

The Supreme Court ruled that racial segregation in public schools is unconstitutional.

1955   Toured Tahiti, Tonga, New Zealand, Australia. Dedicated the Swiss Temple. First nationwide telecast of general conference sessions. Tabernacle Choir went on tour to Europe.

Polio vaccine was developed. Atomic power plants harnessed atomic energy for peaceful purposes.

1956   Dedicated the Los Angeles Temple. Received the Silver Beaver Scouting award.

1957   The Book of Mormon was recorded in a "talking book" for the blind.

Russia launched the first man-made satellite.

1958   Toured the missions of the South Seas. Dedicated the New Zealand Temple, Church College of New Zealand, London Temple, Church College of Hawaii. Auckland Stake in New Zealand was organized, the first overseas stake.

America launched its first space satellite.

1959   *Alaska and Hawaii became states. The St. Lawrence Seaway was completed by the U.S. and Canada, opening the interior of North America to ocean-going vessels.*

1960 Gave initial message in Churchwide youth fireside series, with about 200,000 persons assembled in 170 gathering places. Aaronic Priesthood monument was dedicated on the banks of the Susquehanna River, June 18. The first stake in Australia and first stake in England were organized.

The Congo received independence from Belgium and was immediately plunged into fierce tribal conflicts. Earthquake in Agadin Morocco, destroyed the city and killed 15,000.

1960-70 During this decade visitors centers and exhibits spread the gospel message to millions; several Assistants to the Council of the Twelve were called; the full Church program became available for the first time in 16 non-English languages.

1961 Presided at first mission presidents seminar, where a uniform method of teaching the gospel was presented. Church correlation program was started. Members of the First Council of the Seventy were ordained to the office of high priest. Swiss Stake was organized. Foreign language training missions were started to train missionaries.

The Peace Corps was started. Yuri Gagarin, Russian Cosmonaut, became the first man in space. The Communists built the Berlin Wall, cutting off escape route of East Germans fleeing to West Berlin.

1962 First short-wave broadcast of a general conference was conducted, with messages beamed in English and Spanish to Europe, Africa, South America, Central America, Mexico. The Tabernacle Choir sang at the Seattle World's Fair. President McKay was honored by business and civic leaders at a dinner in Salt Lake City.

John Glenn was the first American to orbit the earth. War between the United States and Russia was narrowly averted during the Cuban missile crisis. The Supreme Court ruled official prayers and Bible reading in public schools unconstitutional.

1963 President McKay dedicated the new Salt Lake Temple annex. Church membership passed the two-million mark. The Polynesian Cultural Center was built at Laie, Hawaii.

President John F. Kennedy was assassinated at Dallas, Texas.

1964   President McKay was hospitalized with a heart ailment. The Oakland Temple was dedicated. Nauvoo, Illinois, was designated as a National Historical Landmark.

Widespread unrest and violence spread through American cities. The Tonkin Gulf incident brought congressional resolution authorizing retaliation against North Vietnam. The Civil Rights Act provided minority groups equal access to public accommodations, forbade discrimination in employment, unions, etc. U.S. Surgeon General declared smoking harmful to health.

1965   President McKay received honorary doctorate from Weber State College. Two counselors were added in the First Presidency. Family home evenings were inaugurated January 1.

The U.S. started regular bombing of North Vietnam. It was reported that a billion people were now living under Communism. The Vietnam War expanded. Roman Catholic leaders modernized their church.

1966   The largest convocation of Mormon students gathered in the Salt Lake Tabernacle for a special tribute to President McKay, sponsored by the institute of religion at the University of Utah. The Granite Mountain Records Vaults were built, housing genealogical records.

Pollution became a national and international concern.

1967   Regional Representatives of the Council of the Twelve were appointed to conduct leadership training of stake leaders and ward bishoprics. The Salt Lake Temple Annex opened for ordinance work.

The first successful heart transplant was performed in South Africa. Drug abuse became a national and international problem during the late 1960s. Arab-Israeli War erupted.

1968   One counselor was added to the First Presidency. President McKay received the Exemplary Manhood award from BYU students; the Distinguished American award from the National Football Foundation and Hall of Fame.

Senator Robert F. Kennedy and Martin Luther King were assassinated. The United Nations General Assembly adopted a treaty to halt the spread of nuclear weapons. North Korea seized U.S. Navy ship "Pueblo" and held the crew members for several months.

1969 President McKay attended dedicatory ceremonies for the David O. McKay Hospital in Ogden. Construction was started on the new Church Office Building in Salt Lake City. World Conference on Records, sponsored by the Church, was attended by representatives from many states, nations. The Tabernacle Choir sang at inauguration of President Richard M. Nixon.

Two prominent Church members were named to President Nixon's Cabinet: George W. Romney, Secretary of Housing and Urban Development, and David M. Kennedy, Secretary of the Treasury. Neil Armstrong, American astronaut, became the first man to walk on the moon.

1970 President McKay died January 18 in Salt Lake City of congestive heart failure (age 96).

1951-70 *Significant inventions: Heart-lung machine (U.S.); picturephone (U.S.); Hovercraft (England); atomic-powered submarine (U.S.); laser (U.S.); tape cassette (Netherlands); measles and polio vaccines (U.S.); air conditioning for cars (U.S.); laser (U.S.); cryotron (U.S.); nuclear energy electric power plant (USSR); fibre optics (U.S.); maser (U.S.).*

The First Presidency
During David O. McKay's Administration

First Counselor	President	Second Counselor
Stephen L Richards (1917) 1951-59	David O. McKay (1906) 1951-70	J. Reuben Clark, Jr. (1934) 1951-59
J. Reuben Clark, Jr. (1934) 1959-61		Henry D. Moyle (1947) 1959-61
Henry D. Moyle (1947) 1961-63		Hugh B. Brown (1958) 1961-63
Hugh B. Brown (1958) 1963-70		N. Eldon Tanner (1962) 1963-70

Counselors to the First Presidency

Hugh B. Brown (1958)
June-October 1961

Joseph Fielding Smith (1910)
1965-70

Thorpe B. Isaacson*
1965-70

Alvin R. Dyer**
1968-70

Council of the Twelve—April 1951

Joseph Fielding Smith (1910)
John A. Widtsoe (1921)
Joseph F. Merrill (1931)
Albert E. Bowen (1937)
Harold B. Lee (1941)
Spencer W. Kimball (1943)

Ezra Taft Benson (1943)
Mark E. Petersen (1944)
Matthew Cowley (1945)
Henry D. Moyle (1947)
Delbert L. Stapley (1950)

---

*Not ordained an apostle.
**Ordained an apostle but not a member of the Council of the Twelve.

Note: Dates in parentheses indicate date ordained member of the Council of the Twelve.

Died

Added

1952—Joseph F. Merrill
1952—John A. Widtsoe
1953—Albert E. Bowen
1953—Matthew Cowley
1958—Adam S. Bennion
1962—George Q. Morris

Marion G. Romney (1951)
LeGrand Richards (1952)
Adam S. Bennion (1953)
Richard L. Evans (1953)
George Q. Morris (1954)
Hugh B. Brown (1958)
Howard W. Hunter (1959)
Gordon B. Hinckley (1961)
N. Eldon Tanner (1962)
Thomas S. Monson (1963)

October 1969

Joseph Fielding Smith (1910)
Harold B. Lee (1941)
Spencer W. Kimball (1943)
Ezra Taft Benson (1943)
Mark E. Petersen (1944)
Delbert L. Stapley (1950)

Marion G. Romney (1951)
LeGrand Richards (1952)
Richard L. Evans (1953)
Howard W. Hunter (1959)
Gordon B. Hinckley (1961)
Thomas S. Monson (1963)

Testimony of David O. McKay

Just above the pulpit in the meeting house where, as a boy, I attended Sunday services, there hung for many years a large photograph of the late President John Taylor, and under it, in what I thought were gold letters, this phrase, "The Kingdom of God or Nothing." The sentiment impressed me as a mere child years before I understood its real significance. I seemed to realize at that early date that there is no other Church or organization that approaches the perfection or possesses the Divinity that characterizes the Church of Jesus Christ. As a child, I felt this intuitively; in youth, I became thoroughly convinced of it; and to-day I treasure it as a firm conviction of my soul.

Another truth that I have cherished from childhood is that God is a personal Being, and is, indeed, our Father whom we can approach in prayer, and receive answers thereto. I cherish as one of the dearest experiences in life the knowledge that God hears the prayer of faith. It is true that the answer may not come as direct and at the time or in the manner we anticipate; but it comes, and at a time and in a manner best for the interests of him who offers the supplication. On more than one occasion, I have received direct and immediate assurances that my petition was granted. At one time, particularly, the answer came as distinctly as though my Father stood by my side and spoke the words. These experiences are part of my being and must remain so as long as memory and intelligence last. They have taught me that "Heaven is never deaf but when man's heart is dumb."

Just as real and just as close to me seems the Savior of the world. He is God made manifest in the flesh; and I know that "There is no other name given under heaven whereby mankind may be saved."

I have an abiding testimony that the Father and the Son appeared to the Prophet Joseph Smith, and revealed through him the Gospel of Jesus Christ, which is indeed "The power of God unto salvation." I know, too, that a knowledge of the truth of the Gospel may be obtained only through obedience to the principles thereof. In other words, the best way to know the truth of any principle is to live it. Such is the way marked out by the Savior when He said, "If any man will do His will he shall know of the doctrine, whether it be of God or whether I speak of myself."

The divinity of the Church of Jesus Christ of Latter-day Saints is shown in its organization as well as in its teachings. Godhood, Brotherhood, Service—these three guiding principles in the Christ life permeate all our Church activity.

I love the work. I love the brethren who preside over it; for they are faithful and true men, performing their many duties under the inspiration of the Almighty.

In conclusion, I desire to testify to another thing, viz.: The Lord is not only guiding His Church, but overruling the destiny of nations, preparatory to the preaching of the Gospel to every "nation, kindred, tongue and people." (Green, *Testimonies of Our Leaders*, pp. 54-55.)

Personal Experience of David O. McKay

The bustling little town of Huntly, New Zealand, nestles along the broad banks of the lower Waikato River, in a pleasant valley of gently rolling hills lush with grass, trees, and the cool evergreen verdure of this pleasant land. On the west bank of the river once stood the small frame chapel of the Puketapu (Sacred-mount) Branch of the Church, largest congregation and center of the former Waikato District of the New Zealand Mission. Here, one cool autumn day in 1921, occurred one of the greatest spiritual manifestations in the history of the mission.

In that year, the little Maori village was all abustle with activity. The Saints of the district and the local Puketapu Branch were busy making preparations, as hosts, for the coming *hui-tau*—the annual missionwide conference to be held in April. Meeting tents and sleeping tents must be provided; *kumara* (sweet potato), meat, vegetables, and potatoes must be gathered in great quantity; provisions and preparations must be made to house and feed the multitude who would assemble. This was to be no ordinary conference. A prophet of God was to be in attendance. The first General Authority ever to visit New Zealand, Elder David O. McKay of the Quorum of the Twelve, was expected to be present. Anticipation was keen.

A number of revisions had to be made in plans for the conference. Word had been received that the visiting brethren from Zion desired to meet with the Saints there. They would not arrive by the date initially set for the conference, April 6, so the date was changed tentatively to April 15. However, some dock labor troubles had upset boat schedules, and the definite date of arrival was uncertain. Not until the April 13 issue of the mission newspaper was it officially announced—a new conference date had been set. A cablegram from the visitors, Elder McKay and his companion, Hugh J. Cannon, had been received, indicating an arrival date of April 20. Since the Saints were eager to meet a General Authority, the committee agreed (for the third time) to change plans, and the conference was rescheduled for April 23, 24, and 25.

Excitement was at its peak as members and friends gathered at the meeting grounds of the Puketapu Branch. The conference sessions, held in large meeting tents, were filled to overflowing. Out of courtesy, several of the leading Maori brethren were invited to speak. They made only brief remarks, however, saying they had come "to fill their baskets." They were just an empty kit, with no food inside. Long had they desired to feed at the fountainhead of truth, to see a prophet. Now that one had arrived, they said, "Let us listen, and fill our baskets."

Stuart Meha, stalwart mission worker, had been selected to act as interpreter for Elder McKay. He was well qualified, but he felt the heavy burden of this assignment. He knew the people would want to hear every word, every thought.

Then the prophet stood up. How he longed to speak to them in their own tongue. But he would ask that, through the Spirit, they might receive an understanding of the things he would say. His overwhelming love and dynamic personality seemed to bring the audience into full rapport.

And then it happened: as the sermon proceeded it seemed as though the entire congregation understood. Brother Meha, taking notes preparatory to giving the translation, noticed the unusual reaction of the assemblage.

He was startled. Even the older Maori Saints who could not speak English were nodding their heads in full appreciation.

Still uncertain of what had happened, Brother Meha arose to give the translation. But as he spoke in the Maori tongue, one old brother interrupted and said that an important point had been omitted from the translated version. Three times this happened—three times during the translation Brother Meha was interrupted and reminded of a point he had overlooked. Suddenly he realized: These Maori members, though they did not know English, had understood, in detail, the entire sermon! The entire congregation had received the gift of interpretation, and through the manifestation of the Spirit, they obtained a full understanding of the sermon.

The entire conference was an unusual spiritual feast. Never had the little Maori village experienced such an event. For years afterward the Saints would remember and talk of that special conference, and point out the spot where the meetings were held.

One young Maori in particular would never forget, for not only had he seen and heard the prophet's sermon that day; he was also involved in another unusual drama. This was James Elkington, who had been assigned to patrol the village grounds to help maintain order. Outside agitators had attempted to disrupt some of the conference proceedings. Once Brother Elkington had been obliged to ask them to leave, but in another meeting they rushed forward to the rostrum where Brother McKay was speaking. Uncertain of what to do, everyone was temporarily immobilized. But President McKay simply straightened up, looked at the agitator, put forth his hand, and in the quiet dignity of his majestic personality, bade their leader welcome. As soon as the erstwhile troublemaker touched the hand of President McKay, he seemed to wilt like a falling leaf. He ceased to speak, went limp, and quietly withdrew from the meeting, never to return.

Today the slim spire of a sacred temple rises from the green pastures of the Waikato, only a few miles distant from Huntly, a constant reminder and a tower of strength to the Saints in New Zealand. Perhaps it is understandable why the Maori Saints have a special place in their hearts for David O. McKay and why they think of him as their own prophet. (Elwin W. Jensen, "In Puketapu," *Improvement Era*, February 1970, pp. 74-75.)

Quotations from David O. McKay

BROTHERHOOD

He lives most who . . . sees God and goodness in it all, who sees an overruling providence in all the world and recognizes God's children as brothers and sisters, in every one of whom there is something good.

CHARACTER

Every noble impulse, every unselfish expression of love, every brave suffering for the right, every surrender of self to something higher than self; every loyalty to an ideal; every unselfish devotion to principle; every helpfulness to humanity; every act of self-control; every fine courage of the soul, undefeated by pretense or policy, but by being, doing, and living the good for the very good's sake—that is spirituality.

CHASTITY

In the Church there is no double standard of morality. . . . Pure water does not flow from a polluted spring—nor a healthy nation from a diseased parentage.

CHRIST

For 1,000 years and more Jesus Christ has been an inspiration to millions of men and women. His has been the influence that has fired the imagination of poets; the influence that has guided the artists' touch that has given imperishable beauty to the world; the influence that has put new harmony into musicians' souls and sent vibrating through the ages songs of praise and thanksgiving; the power that has supported through centuries the humble laborers whose only comfort through unrequited toil and oppression sprang from the realization that One was standing at the end of life's journey saying: "Come unto me, all ye that labour and are heavy laden, and I will give you rest" (Matt. 11:28); His the influence that has given every good thing to the world today; His the life that was sacrificed to bring peace and goodwill and eternal salvation to all mankind.

CHRISTMAS
The danger which arises in our celebration on Christmas is the possibility of subordinating the real purpose of commemorating the spiritual to be overshadowed by the material. The true spirit of giving happiness to others, the fellowship of good friends, and the satisfying knowledge that Christmas reminds us of Christ's promise of a new and better life must always be uppermost in our minds.

COMMUNISM
The position of this Church on the subject of Communism has never changed. We consider it the greatest satanical threat to peace, prosperity, and the spread of God's work among men that exists on the face of the earth. . . . The entire concept and philosophy of Communism is diametrically opposed to everything for which the Church stands—belief in Deity, belief in the dignity and eternal nature of man, and the application of the gospel to efforts for peace in the world. Communism is militantly atheistic and is committed to the destruction of faith wherever it may be found. . . . Communism debases the individual and makes him the enslaved tool of the state, to which he must look for sustenance and religion. Communism destroys man's God-given free agency. No member of this Church can be true to his faith, nor can any American be loyal to his trust, while lending aid, encouragement, or sympathy to any of these false philosophies; for if he does, they will prove snares to his feet.

EDUCATION
True education is awakening a love for truth, a just sense of duty, opening the eyes of the soul to the great purpose and end of life.

FAMILY
We believe that the home is the center of civilization, and the responsibilities of the home rest upon the parents.

FREE AGENCY
Next to the bestowal of life itself, the right to direct that life is God's greatest gift to man. . . . Freedom of choice is more to be treasured than any possession earth can give. It is inherent in the spirit of man. It is a divine gift to every normal being. Whether born in abject poverty or shackled at birth by inherited riches, everyone has this most precious of all life's endowments—the gift of free agency; man's inherited and inalienable right. Free agency is the impelling source of the soul's progress. It is the purpose of the Lord that man become like him. In order for man to achieve this it was necessary for the Creator first to make him free.

GOALS
Man's success or failure, happiness or misery, depends upon what he seeks and what he chooses.

HOME
Home is the center from which woman rules the world. It is there she teaches her child self-restraint, develops in him the confidence and strength that spring from self-control. It is there the child learns respect for the rights of others. It is in a well-directed home that men and women first develop a consciousness that true happiness lies in conforming one's life to the laws of nature and to the rules of social conduct.

HOME
No other success can compensate for failure in the home.

LOVE
Happiness and peace will come to earth only as the light of love and human compassion enter the souls of men.

LOYALTY
Loyalty, one of the noblest attributes of the soul, means being faithful and true; it means fidelity to duty, fidelity to love, fidelity to a cause or a principle, true to self—always.

MARRIAGE
May youth so prepare themselves to be worthy of that form of marriage consummated in a temple of the Most High. There, as true lovers kneel to plight their troth, each may cherish the assurance:

   1.   That their married course begins in purity—the source of life is unpolluted.

   2.   That their religious views are the same. The difficulty of rearing children properly is aggravated when father and mother have divergent views regarding doctrine and church affiliation.

   3.   That their vows are made with the idea of an eternal union, not to be broken by petty misunderstandings or difficulties.

   4.   That a covenant made in God's presence and sealed by the Holy Priesthood is more binding than any other bond.

   5.   That if children come to bless the union, they are guaranteed a royal birth—a clean, unpolluted body.

   6.   That a marriage thus commenced is as eternal as love, the divinest attribute of the human soul.

   7.   That the family unit will remain unbroken throughout eternity.

May youth look forward to such a marriage and the building of a happy home. To make it so, each must lose himself or herself for the good of the other and for the welfare of the family.

MISSIONARIES

It is generally understood that every member of the Church should be a missionary. Neighbors are watching him. Neighbors are watching his children. He is a light, and it is his duty not to have the light hidden under a bushel, but it should be set up on a hill that all men may be guided thereby.

MORTALITY

Man's earthly existence is but a test as to whether he will concentrate his efforts, his mind, his soul upon things which contribute to the comfort and gratification of his physical instinct and passions, or whether he will make as his life's end and purpose the acquisition of spiritual qualities.

MOTHER

The noblest calling in the world is that of mother. True motherhood is the most beautiful of all arts, the greatest of all professions. She who can paint a masterpiece or who can write a book that will influence millions deserves the plaudits and admiration of mankind; but she who rears successfully a family of healthy, beautiful sons and daughters whose immortal souls will be exerting an influence throughout the ages long after painting shall have faded, and books and statues shall have been destroyed, deserves the highest honor that man can give.

PARENTS

A married woman who refuses to assume the responsibility of motherhood, or who, having children neglects them for pleasure or social prestige, is recreant to the highest calling and privilege of womanhood. The father who, because of business or political responsibilities, fails to share with his wife the responsibilities of rearing his sons and daughters, is untrue to his marital obligations, is a negative element in what might and should be a joyous home atmosphere, and is a possible contributor to discord and delinquency.

POLITICS

It is our duty, therefore, as citizens of this great republic, to exercise our right at the ballot box. It is our duty to see that men in both our great parties are chosen who will teach not only by precept, but also by example, obedience to law; that these men so elected will appoint men under them who will not scoff at the law, or who will not in any way protect these men or women who violate moral law.

PROGRESSION

Each one of us is the architect of his own fate, and he is unfortunate indeed who will try to build himself without the inspiration of God, without realizing that he grows from within, not from without.

READING

Reading material should be chosen wisely. As a man may be judged by the company he keeps, so his leanings for the highest and the best or the low and the vulgar in life are indicated by what he reads. "Evil communications corrupt good manners" and vile literature debases the soul.

REVERENCE

The principle of self-control lies at the heart of reverence. I place reverence as one of the objectives of nobility, indeed, one of the attributes of Deity.

SABBATH DAY

Is it better to cherish Church ideals on Sunday or to indulge in Sunday sports? This is simply a question of physical pleasure or spiritual development; and in that regard we should keep in mind the following: First, it is a day of rest, essential to the true development and strength of the body, and that is a principle we should publish more generally abroad; and we should practice it. A second purpose for keeping holy the Sabbath day is mentioned in one sentence of modern revelation: ". . . That thou mayest more fully keep thyself unspotted from the world. . . ." (D&C 59:9.) That is a glorious sentence! Third, keeping the Sabbath day holy is a law of God, resounding through the ages from Mount Sinai. You cannot transgress the law of God without circumscribing your spirit.

SPACE

For the first time in history man viewed the earth from outer space, and he saw that it was a bright, beautiful earth where he was privileged to dwell with his brothers. Man knows that our solar system is merely one tiny part of our Milky Way galaxy, and that our sun is but an average star among a spiral of one hundred billion other galaxies.

TEACHING

Teaching is the noblest profession in the world. Upon the proper education of youth depend the permanency and purity of home, the safety and perpetuity of the nation. The parent gives the child an opportunity to live; the teacher enables the child to live well. That parent who gives life and teaches his child to live abundantly is the true parent-teacher. The responsibility of the teacher, however, does not end in his duty to teach truth positively. He enters the realm of what-not-to-do as well as the realm of what-to-do.

TEMPTATION
Every temptation that comes to you and me comes in one of three forms: (1) a temptation of appetite or passion; (2) a yielding to pride, fashion, or vanity; (3) a desire for worldly riches or power and dominion over lands or earthly possessions of man.

TESTIMONY
Many people today wonder wherein lies the secret of the growth, stability, and vitality of the Church of Jesus Christ. The secret is this—that every true Latter-day Saint possesses individually the assurance that this is the work of God. . . . The secret lies in the testimony possessed by each individual who is faithful in the Church that the Gospel consists of correct principles.

TRUTH
Knowledge of the truth is not enough unless it is expressed by action.

YOUTH
In their yearning for a good time, young people are often tempted to indulge in the things which appeal only to the baser side of humanity, five of the most common of which are: first, vulgarity and obscenity; second, drinking and the using of narcotics and now the vicious LSD drug, especially among the young; third, unchastity; fourth, disloyalty; and fifth, irreverence.

Joseph Fielding Smith, Tenth President (1876-1972)

JOSEPH FIELDING SMITH

Tenth President of the Church

Born: July 19, 1876, Salt Lake City, Utah

Died: July 2, 1972, Salt Lake City, Utah (age 95)

President of the Church: January 23, 1970, to July 2, 1972
(2½ years)

Physical Characteristics: Five feet 10 inches tall, 165
pounds, pleasant features, medium build, gray hair,
blue eyes

Areas of Distinction: Prophet, writer, missionary,
historian, editor, theologian, genealogist

Family: Son of Joseph Fielding and Julina Lambson
Smith. Married Louie E. Shurtliff April 26, 1898
(she died March 30, 1908), two children; married
Ethel G. Reynolds November 2, 1908 (she died
August 26, 1937), nine children; married Jessie Ella
Evans April 12, 1938 (she died August 3, 1971).

Profile of Joseph Fielding Smith

"A solemn and religious regard to spiritual and eternal things is an indispensable element of all true greatness." This thought by Daniel Webster describes well the greatness of Joseph Fielding Smith.

Words used by the general public to describe him might include: fearless, forthright, scripturalist, orthodox, informed, tenacious, brusk, austere. Others who have known him well might choose: kind, loving, sympathetic, loyal, warm, understanding, dependable, charitable. His secretary of fifty years, Ruby Egbert, described him as "shy" and "independent":

> He wouldn't think of asking you to do something for him that he could do himself. He shakes hands with everyone on the elevator and on the floor where his office is. And the door to his office has always been open to anyone who needed his help. He loves children. He has a special voice for them, and will often go out in the hall to play with them or chat with them when they pass. (McConkie, *True and Faithful*, pp. 70-71.)

When Joseph Fielding Smith was born in Salt Lake City on July 19, 1876, Brigham Young was President of the Church. Thus his life spanned from pioneer days to the space age; it spanned the administrations of all of the Presidents of the Church save the first one, his great-uncle, the Prophet Joseph Smith.

He grew up on the family farm in Taylorsville, Salt

Joseph Fielding Smith, April 1910

Lake County. As a youth he loved to do farm chores; he herded cows near the Jordan River and learned to swim by diving from its banks. By nature quieter and more studious than his brothers, he habitually hurried with his chores so that he could go to his father's library and study. He enjoyed reading the scriptures and had read the Book of Mormon before the age of twelve.

In the pursuit and defense of truth he became a scholar and a writer. He criticized "modernists who reject the doctrine of the atonement of Christ, the resurrection of the Son of God and consequently the resurrection of mankind." He published twenty-five books and countless articles that define, clarify, and explain doctrine, and earned himself a place in Church history as a prolific gospel writer and staunch doctrinarian.

In 1898 Joseph Fielding Smith married Louie E. Shurtliff, and they had two daughters. She died in 1908.

Ethel G. Reynolds, whom he married in 1908 and who was the mother of their nine children, described her husband as follows:

> I have often thought when he is gone people will say, "He is a very good man, sincere, orthodox, etc." They will speak of him as the public knows him; but the man they have in mind is very different from the man I know. The man I know is a kind, loving husband and father whose greatest ambition in life is to make his family happy, entirely forgetful of self in his efforts to do this. He is the man that lulls to sleep the fretful child, who tells bedtime stories to the little ones, who is never too tired or too busy to sit up late at night or to get up early in the morning to help the older children solve perplexing school problems. When illness comes, the man I know watches tenderly over the afflicted one and waits upon him. It is their father for whom they cry, feeling his presence a panacea for all ills. It is his hands that bind up the wounds, his arms that give courage to the sufferer, his voice that remonstrates with them gently when they err, until it becomes their happiness to do the thing that will make him happy.
>
> The man I know is most gentle, and if he feels that he has been unjust to anyone the distance is never too far for him to go and, with loving words or kind deeds, erase the hurt. He welcomes gladly the young people to his home and is never happier than when discussing with them topics of the day—sports or whatever interests them most. He enjoys a good story and is quick to see the humor of a situation, to laugh and to be laughed at, always willing to join in any wholesome activity.
>
> The man I know is unselfish, uncomplaining, considerate, thoughtful, sympathetic, doing everything within his power to make life a supreme joy for his loved ones. That is the man I know. (*Improvement Era*, June 1932, p. 459.)

Following his second wife's death in 1937, President Smith married Jessie Ella Evans on April 12, 1938. A contralto, she had earlier turned down an operatic career

Joseph Fielding Smith, around 1921

after touring with the American Light Opera Company. She was a soloist with the Tabernacle Choir and thrilled crowds wherever she sang. To the delight of thousands, President and Sister Smith often sang duets as they traveled around the Church. She had a vivacious personality and did much to buoy President Smith in his many duties. She died on August 3, 1971.

President Smith as a family man was deeply concerned with his children's growth and development. At family evenings he enjoyed telling them stories from the scriptures or Church history. He never spanked his children, preferring to discipline them with love. When one

President Smith gets briefed on Air Force jet

of the children needed correction, he would discuss the problem with the offender, then put his hands on the child's shoulders and, looking into his or her eyes, softly say, "I wish my kiddies would be good."

He was interested in athletics. He often took his sons to the old Deseret Gym and let them choose which hand he would keep behind his back; then he would "beat the socks" off them in a game of handball. He played this strenuous game until his seventieth birthday. He also enjoyed watching softball.

In the Smith home the family always gathered together for family prayer. One of his children recalls, "It scared me every time I heard Dad pray that the purposes of the Lord 'would speedily come to pass.' "

Another family tradition was President Smith's birthday. On a Saturday near the date of his birthday, family members met in a park in Salt Lake City to play games, tell stories, sing, and enjoy a traditional dinner. Important on these occasions were his words of advice and the presents he distributed to each person—a procedure that eliminated the problem of his having to remember well over one hundred birthdays each year.

A lesser-known aspect of President Smith's personality was his sense of humor. For example, on a beautiful sunny holiday one of his sisters went to visit him only to find him busily working in his office. Concerned that he was working too hard, she scolded him for not taking the day off. He responded, "All my days are off." Ignoring this, she continued. "Now I want you to go home and take a nap. George Albert Smith, Stephen L Richards, and J. Reuben Clark always did, so you can too." "Yes," came the quick response, "and look where they are now." (McConkie, *True and Faithful*, p. 75.)

"My first assignment in the Church," President Smith told some interested listeners, "was to go with Brigham Young down to St. George to dedicate the temple there." He then quietly added, "I was one year old then."

He believed in strict observance of the Word of Wisdom, and he credited this principle for his good health and freedom from illness.

He believed it a privilege to be of service to others. He spent countless hours counseling others and wrote thousands of letters in answer to gospel questions. He supported missionaries, paid hospital bills for the unfortunate, and sent groceries to the hungry and destitute.

D. Arthur Haycock, executive secretary to President Smith, wrote this character sketch:

President Joseph Fielding Smith assumed the presidency of The Church of Jesus Christ of Latter-day Saints exceptionally well qualified by study, experience, and training. He had served for 60 years as an apostle under four Presidents of the Church, 19 years as President of the Quorum of Twelve and five years as a counselor in the First Presidency. . . .

It has been my privilege to accompany President and Sister Smith as they have traveled about the Church since he became President. I have observed the great love that the people, young and old, have for him, and I have seen him reciprocate by leaving a blessing upon the people. I have watched as he has picked up little children and held them in his arms and have seen the tenderness with which he has greeted them. . . .

Although he has been so blessed that he has never really been sick, he has great compassion for those who suffer. He has sat up at night with his own children when they were young, caring for them. This was not only to comfort them, but to relieve their mother, who had had a long and strenuous day and needed the rest. When shown a picture of a group of handicapped children to whom he and Sister Smith had recently spoken and sung a duet, tears came to his eyes as he reflected upon the circumstances of these wonderful young people.

I have found the President to be forthright, honest, and a fearless defender of the faith. He has always been a kind, compassionate, and loving father and a devoted, considerate, and gentle husband and companion. To know him is to love, honor, and respect him, not only as a man and as a friend, but as the Prophet of the Lord. (Heslop and Van Orden, *A Prophet Among the People,* p. 1.)

Elder Bruce R. McConkie of the Council of the Twelve has said:

President Smith is a doctrinal teacher, a theologian, a scriptorian, a preacher of righteousness in the full and true sense of the word. For 60 years he has raised a warning voice in the stakes and missions, at home and abroad, before the saints and the world.

Millions of words have come from his pen—explaining, expounding, exhorting, in the spirit and manner of the prophets of old. Few doctrinal books have been as widely studied as his *Way to Perfection,* and no treatise on Church history has been as widely read as his *Essentials in Church History.* . . .

In order to preach with power, to teach with wisdom, to write with inspiration, our new president has of necessity been a student of the standard works. Early and late he has poured over and pondered the words of the prophets and has sought the same Spirit which enabled them to write and speak the mind and will of the Lord. Of particular note is the fact that President Smith's study and teaching have been confined to the basic, sound, scriptural doctrines. Speculation about the mysteries has held little interest for him.

But President Joseph Fielding Smith's life has not been one of learning and teachings only. His study and gospel scholarship have been crowned by good words, by a life of conformity to gospel law. No one knows the hungry he has fed, the naked he has clothed, the missionaries he has supported, nor the sick he has healed. . . . (*Instructor*, March 1970, p. 78.)

On his ninetieth birthday, the First Presidency said:

A man of tenderness, a man of courage, decisive in action, alert to maintain the standards of the Church, but ready to forgive those who have erred and truly repented—these are among his sterling qualities. There is in him the peace that speaks of godliness, the certainty that comes of the Spirit's witness, the unflinching fidelity to duty that comes of self-discipline.

Those who have heard him pray have frequently heard him use the phrase "true and faithful." These words epitomize his life. (*Improvement Era*, July 1966, p. 613.)

After being sustained as President of the Church at the general conference in April 1970, President Smith stated:

I stand before you today in humility and in thanksgiving, grateful for the blessings which the Lord has poured out upon me, upon my family, upon you, upon all his people. . . .

I desire to say that no man of himself can lead this church. It is the Church of the Lord Jesus Christ; he is at the head. The Church bears his name, has his priesthood, administers his gospel, preaches his doctrine, and does his work.

He chooses men and calls them to be instruments in his hands to accomplish his purposes, and he guides and directs them in their labors. But men are only instruments in the Lord's hands, and the honor and glory for all that his servants accomplish is and should be ascribed unto him forever.

If this were the work of man, it would fail, but it is the work of the Lord, and he does not fail. And we have the assurance that if we keep the commandments and are valiant in the testimony of Jesus and are true to every trust, the Lord will guide and direct us and his Church in the paths of righteousness, for the accomplishment of all his purposes. (*Improvement Era*, June 1970, p. 26.)

It can truly be said of him that he lived for the Church and for his family and delighted wherever he saw spiritual development and growth.

The First Presidency, 1970-72: President Joseph Fielding Smith (center) and counselors, Harold B. Lee and N. Eldon Tanner

Interesting Facts and Contributions
of Joseph Fielding Smith

1. At the time of his birth, the Saints had been in the Salt Lake Valley only twenty-nine years; Brigham Young was still President of the Church.

2. His grandfather, Hyrum Smith, was martyred with the Prophet Joseph Smith at Carthage Jail. His great-grandfather, Joseph Smith, Sr., was the first Patriarch to the Church.

3. Joseph F. Smith (sixth President) and his son Joseph Fielding Smith were the only father and son to be Presidents of the Church.

4. He was one of the oldest men to serve as President of the Council of the Twelve (age 74) and was a member longer than any other man in this dispensation (sixty years). He served as President of the Twelve from April 9, 1951 to Jan. 23, 1970 (nineteen years). In the Council of the Twelve he served under four Presidents: Joseph F. Smith, Heber J. Grant, George Albert Smith, and David O. McKay.

5. He was the second General Authority to serve concurrently as President of the Council of the Twelve and counselor in the First Presidency.

6. He was the oldest man to become president—age ninety-three. He served for only two and a half years.

7. He was Church Historian longer than any other man—sixty-four years.

8. He served without pay as secretary to his father, Joseph F. Smith. After his regular work and during his free time, he helped his father with the growing correspondence of the Church.

9. When he became President, he used the same office desk that his father had used as President of the Church.

10. He was present at the dedications of eleven temples: St. George, Salt Lake, Hawaii, Alberta, Arizona, Idaho Falls, Los Angeles, London, Oakland, Ogden, and Provo (he presided at dedications of the last two).

11. He served as chairman of the Church reading committee and as such, read countless thousands of pages of manuscript for the priesthood, the auxiliaries, and other Church organizations and for individual authors.

12. His lifetime spanned the period from covered wagons to man's walk on the moon, and he lived during the time of all the Presidents except Joseph Smith.

13. He gave more than 125 talks in general conference sessions and participated in as many as 5,000 stake conferences.

14. He enjoyed music and often sang duets with his wife, Jessie, delighting thousands of Saints at stake conferences. He wrote the words to several hymns, including "The Best Is Not Too Good for Me," "Come, Come, My Brother, Wake!" "Does the Journey Seem Long?" and "We Are Watchmen of the Tower of Zion."

15. He wrote twenty-five books, more than any other President. These included: *Blood Atonement and the Origin of Plural Marriage, Essentials in Church History, Elijah the Prophet and His Mission, Salvation Universal, The Way to Perfection, The Progress of Man, The Life of Joseph F. Smith, Teachings of the Prophet Joseph Smith, Signs of the Times, The Restoration of All Things, Church History and Modern Revelation* (two volumes), *Doctrines of Salvation* (three volumes), *Answers to Gospel Questions* (five volumes), *Take Heed to Yourselves, Asael Smith of Topsfield, Origin of the Reorganized Church and the Question of Succession, Seeking After Our Dead, Seek Ye Earnestly,* and *Man: His Origin and Destiny.* For many years he wrote a monthly column, "Answers to Gospel Questions," in the *Improvement Era.*

16. During his administration, three new magazines began publication—*Friend, New Era,* and *Ensign,* replacing the *Improvement Era, Relief Society Magazine, Instructor,* and the *Children's Friend.*

17. During his administration new presidents were called to head Brigham Young University, Ricks College, and Church College of Hawaii, and a commissioner of education was named.

18. A program to bring the Aaronic Priesthood and the YMMIA into closer correlation was introduced, and personal achievement programs for boys and girls twelve to eighteen years of age were begun.

19. Other programs that received greater emphasis during his administration included social services, health services, and teacher development.

20. Missionary Representatives of the Council of the Twelve and the First Council of the Seventy were called to help supervise and direct proselyting efforts in missions of the Church. Additional Regional Representatives of the Twelve were also called, to direct leadership training of stake and ward leaders.

21. "All-Church" activities were discontinued, and greater emphasis began to be placed on stake, regional, and area activities, including athletic events, cultural events, and youth conferences.

22. New stakes were created in such distant places as Peru, Japan, South Africa, the South Pacific, and Brazil.

23. All five of President Smith's sons served on missions, and all of his living children were married in the temple.

24. His patriarchal blessing proclaimed: "It shall be thy duty to sit in counsel with thy brethren and to preside among the people."

25. During his administration the first area general conference was held in England and another one planned in Mexico.

26. He represented the last of the old generation in the leading councils of the Church. Never again will the Church have a prophet who can introduce a quotation by saying, "I want to read to you something I heard President Woodruff say."

27. He was an honorary brigadier general with the Utah National Guard and flew by plane on some of their missions.

Significant Dates and Events in Lifetime of Joseph Fielding Smith

Church Membership, 1970: 2,807,456   1972: 3,090,053
1972—Stakes: 581   Missions: 102   Temples: 15
U.S. Population, 1972: 209 million (est.)
World Population, 1972: 3.7 billion (est.)
U.S. President, 1970-72: Richard M. Nixon

1876	Born July 19 in Salt Lake City.
1895	Worked at ZCMI.
1898	Appointed to Salt Lake Stake YMMIA board. Married Louie E. Shurtliff.
1899-1901	Served mission to British Isles (age 22-24).
1901	Began working in the Church Historian's Office. Father was sustained as President of the Church.
1901-10	Home missionary in Salt Lake Stake.
1903-19	Member of the YMMIA general board.
1904	Became a member of the Salt Lake Stake high council.
1906	Appointed assistant Church historian.
1907	Began work with the Genealogical Society. Commissioned by the U.S. Department of Commerce and Labor to collect statistics of the Church for religious census being compiled at that time.
1908	Appointed director and librarian of the Genealogical Society. Married Ethel G. Reynolds.
1909	Appointed to the general board of Religion Classes. Named librarian and treasurer of the Genealogical Society.
1910	Ordained an apostle by Joseph F. Smith, April 7. Be-

came first associate editor and business manager of the *Utah Genealogical and Historical Magazine* (age 33).

1910-22   Secretary of the Genealogical Society.

1912   Appointed to board of trustees, Brigham Young University.

1915-35   Counselor in the Salt Lake Temple presidency.

1917   Appointed to the Church board of education.

1921   Named Church Historian (age 44).

1934   Named president of the Genealogical Society (age 57).

1938   Married Jessie Ella Evans, April. Toured California Mission.

1939   Toured European missions and supervised evacuation of American LDS missionaries throughout Europe except British Isles.

1945-49   President of the Salt Lake Temple (age 68).

1949   Gave baccalaureate sermon at Brigham Young University.

1950   Toured the Texas-Louisiana Mission. Was sustained as Acting President of the Council of the Twelve, September 30.

1951   Became President of the Council of the Twelve, April. Received honorary doctor of letters degree from Brigham Young University (age 75).

1955   Toured Japanese Mission. Dedicated Korea, Okinawa, Guam, and the Philippines for preaching the gospel, and divided the Japanese Mission to form the Northern Far East and Southern Far East missions.

1959   Visited stakes and missions in New Zealand and Australia.

1960   Named honorary brigadier general of the Utah National Guard. Visited missions in South America.

1963   Dedicated historical landmarks at Liberty and Kansas City, Missouri. Officiated at laying of cornerstone at Oakland Temple.

1965   Named counselor in the First Presidency, October 29, age 89.

1966   A collection of books and materials on American church history at Brigham Young University was named in his honor.

1970   Was sustained as President of the Church, January 23, with

Harold B. Lee and N. Eldon Tanner as counselors. Visited Mexico City and spoke at Benemerito de los Américas (Church school) and two stake conferences, July. Was Days of '47 marshal for parade in Salt Lake City July 24, after which he greeted President and Mrs. Richard M. Nixon. Set apart temple presidencies for the Arizona, Idaho Falls, Los Angeles, and St. George temples. Spoke at cornerstone ceremony for Ogden Temple. Visited in Hawaii and spoke at Church College of Hawaii and at ward and stake events. Family home evening was uniformly designated for Monday nights throughout the Church. The Mormon Pavilion at Expo 70 at Osaka, Japan, had more than four million visitors. More than two tons of Church welfare supplies were sent to Peru to aid victims of the worst earthquake in that country's history. Health services of the Church were organized under one corporation. The *Improvement Era, Instructor, Relief Society Magazine,* and *Children's Friend* ceased publication with the December issues. Tokyo Stake, the first stake in Asia, was organized. Transvaal Stake, the first stake in Africa, was organized.

The Vietnam conflict, terror bombings, airplane hijackings, inflation, drug abuse, pollution, and women's liberation were dominant issues in U.S. and world news. A cyclone and tidal wave killed more than 500,000 in Pakistan. Civil War erupted in Ireland.

1970-72 Missions opened: Japan East, Japan West, Spain, Pennsylvania, Ecuador, Taiwan, Nauvoo, Alabama-Florida, Italy North, Florida South, Georgia South, Quebec, Fiji, Georgia-South Carolina.

1971 President Smith spoke to nearly 10,000 youths at Utah State University Institute of Religion; 13,000 youths in Southern California. Gave the baccalaureate sermon at Ricks College, May 7. Spoke at cornerstone ceremonies for the Provo Temple, May 21. Dedicated the Laguna Hills (California) Ward chapel and the Independence (Missouri) Visitors Center. Presided and spoke at the first area general conference at Manchester, England, in August. Three new Church magazines—*Ensign, New Era,* and *Friend* —began publication. A teacher development program and a supervisory program were introduced to help train more effective teachers and provide inservice training for present teachers. A Churchwide training course for bishops was begun. Church membership reached three million. It was announced that more than 150,000 missionaries had been called since 1830.

Voting age was lowered to 18 in the U.S. America launched a satellite to explore Mars. Two more Apollo flights were launched, and astronauts walked on the moon. Pakistan declared war on India. Red China was admitted to the United Nations.

1972   The Ogden Temple was dedicated in January, at which time President Smith read the dedicatory prayer; he also presided at the Provo Temple dedication in February. He addressed the MIA June Conference on Sunday, June 25, his last public address. On Thursday, June 29, he spoke at the mission president's seminar in Salt Lake City, at which time a new program of supervision for the missions was announced. Mission Representatives of the Council of the Twelve and the First Council of the Seventy were called, as were additional Regional Representatives of the Twelve. President Smith died at 9:25 P.M. on Sunday, July 2. Funeral services were held in the Salt Lake Tabernacle on Thursday, July 6, and burial was in the Salt Lake City Cemetery (age 95).

Destructive floods caused considerable damage in Rapid City, South Dakota, where five Latter-day Saints were killed and many sustained damage to their homes and property, and in states along the eastern seaboard, particularly Pennsylvania, in June. President Richard M. Nixon made historic trips to China and Russia. The U.S. Supreme Court outlawed the death penalty.

1970-72   *Significant inventions: Super-fast typesetting machine (U.S.); Color T.V. from black and white films (U.S.); Device makes fast cancer detection (U.S.); Heart-lung Detector (U.S.); Liquid membranes purify streams (U.S.).*

The First Presidency

During Joseph Fielding Smith's Administration

First Counselor	President	Second Counselor
Harold B. Lee	Joseph Fielding Smith	N. Eldon Tanner
(1941)	(1910)	(1962)
1970-72	1970-72	1970-72

Council of the Twelve—April 1970

Spencer W. Kimball (1943)　　Richard L. Evans (1953)
Ezra Taft Benson (1943)　　Hugh B. Brown (1958)
Mark E. Petersen (1944)　　Howard W. Hunter (1959)
Delbert L. Stapley (1950)　　Gordon B. Hinckley (1961)
Marion G. Romney (1951)　　Thomas S. Monson (1963)
LeGrand Richards (1952)　　Boyd K. Packer (1970)

Died　　　　　　　　Added

1971—Richard L. Evans　　1971—Marvin J. Ashton

July 1972

Spencer W. Kimball (1943)　　Hugh B. Brown (1958)
Ezra Taft Benson (1943)　　Howard W. Hunter (1959)
Mark E. Petersen (1944)　　Gordon B. Hinckley (1961)
Delbert L. Stapley (1950)　　Thomas S. Monson (1963)
Marion G. Romney (1951)　　Boyd K. Packer (1970)
LeGrand Richards (1952)　　Marvin J. Ashton (1971)

Note: Dates in parentheses indicate date ordained member of the Council of the Twelve.

Testimony of Joseph Fielding Smith

As I stand now, in what I might call the twilight of life, with the realization that in a not-far-distant day I shall be called upon to give an account of my mortal stewardship, I bear testimony again of the truth and divinity of this great work.

I know that God lives and that he sent his beloved Son into the world to atone for our sins.

I know that the Father and the Son appeared to the Prophet Joseph Smith to usher in this final gospel dispensation.

I know that Joseph Smith was and is a prophet; moreover, that this is the Lord's church, and that the gospel cause shall roll forward until the knowledge of the Lord covers the earth as the waters cover the sea.

I am sure that we all love the Lord. I know that he lives, and I look forward to that day when I shall see his face, and I hope to hear his voice say unto me: "Come, ye blessed of my Father, inherit the kingdom prepared for you from the foundation of the world." (Matt. 25:34.) (*Ensign*, December 1971, p. 136.)

Personal Experience of Joseph Fielding Smith

A large crowd gathered at the General Authorities' exit of the Tabernacle following the general conference. The visitors, many from out-of-town, were anxious to get a glimpse of President Joseph Fielding Smith or perhaps a warm handshake from the new Church president.

From the crowd, wiggling between legs, came a small girl who made her way to President Smith. Soon she was in his arms for a little hug, and then back into the crowd so quickly that the *Deseret News* photographer was unable to get her name.

The picture, unidentified, appeared in the *Church News*. However, her proud grandmother, Mrs. Milo Hobbs of Preston, Idaho, recognized her and promptly wrote a letter to President Smith to share the information.

"I am so happy that we can identify her as our granddaughter, Venus Hobbs. She has a birthday on April 17 when she will be four years old," Grandmother Hobbs wrote.

On her birthday, little Venus Hobbs, who lives in Torrance, Calif., received a surprise "happy birthday" call and song from President and Mrs. Smith. President Smith was spending the week in California when he made the call.

The call was a thrill to the W. Odell Hobbs family. Mrs. Hobbs was touched with tears to think that the President of the Church was so kind. Venus was delighted with the song.

The letter went on to explain that she was with

two of her aunts, but she slipped away. They feared they had lost her in the crowd. When she returned they asked, "How did you get lost?"

"I wasn't lost!" she said.

"Who found you?" they asked.

"I was in the arms of the Prophet," was her reply. (*Church News*, April 25, 1970, p. 3.)

Quotations from Joseph Fielding Smith

ATONEMENT

Salvation comes because of the atonement. Without it the whole plan of salvation would be frustrated and the whole purpose behind the creating and populating of the earth would come to naught. With it the eternal purposes of the Father will roll forth, the purpose of creation be preserved, the plan of salvation made efficacious, and men will be assured of a hope of the highest exaltation hereafter.

CHILDREN

The revelations of the Lord to the Prophet Joseph Smith declare that all little children who die are heirs of the celestial kingdom. This would mean the children of every race. All the spirits that come to this world come from the presence of God and, therefore, must have been in his kingdom. Little children are redeemed by the Lord's decree from the foundation of the world through the ministry of Jesus Christ; every spirit of man was innocent in the beginning; and all who rebelled were cast out; therefore, all who remained are entitled to the blessings of the gospel. . . . Therefore, by what right or reason are we going to deprive innocent children whether they are black, brown, or yellow who die in their infancy—innocent and without sin—from entering the celestial kingdom?

CREATION

While it is true that all things were created spiritually, or as spirits, before they were naturally upon the face of the earth, this creation, we are informed, was in heaven. This applies to animals of all descriptions and also to plant life, before there was flesh upon the earth, or in the water, or in the air. The account of the creation of the earth as given in Genesis, and the Book of Moses, and as given in the temple, is the creation of the physical earth, and of the physical animals and plants. I think the temple account, which was given by revelation, is the clearest of all of these.

EARTH

Is this earth upon which we dwell going to be one-third celestialized, one-third terrestrialized, one-third telestialized? Are all the inhabitants of the earth going to dwell upon the earth? No. This earth is going to become a celestial body and is going to be a fit abode for celestial beings only; the others will have to go somewhere else, where they belong. This earth will be reserved for those who are entitled to exaltation.

EDUCATION

There is no knowledge, no learning that can compensate the individual for the loss of his belief in heaven and in the saving principles of the Gospel of Jesus Christ. An education that leads a man from these central truths cannot compensate for the great loss of spiritual things.

ETERNAL LIFE

When an elder of Israel dies, he does not go to some glorious place prepared to play a harp, and wait for the redemption to come at some future period when the Lord shall return to the earth. He has duties to perform. They go on. There is labor on the other side, just as there is labor here, and our brethren who have gone to the other side since the days of the Prophet Joseph Smith are organized, and they are carrying on their work over there as it has been assigned unto them to bring to pass the fulness of our Savior's mission.

HELL

The Church does teach that there is a place called hell. Of course, we do not believe that all those who do not receive the gospel will eventually be cast into hell. We do not believe that hell is a place where the wicked are being burned forever. The Lord has prepared a place, however, for all those who are to be eternally punished for the violation of his laws.

HOLY GHOST

There is a difference between the light of Christ and the gift of the Holy Ghost. The gift of the Holy Ghost is only given to those who are baptized for the remission of their sins and have hands laid upon their heads for the gift of the Holy Ghost. That is a far greater blessing. But the light of Christ will lead every soul to righteousness, to the keeping of the commandments of the Lord, if they will hearken to it.

LIFE

A wise man is the man who puts first things first. What are the first things? To know why we are here, where we came from and where we are going, and to discover the truths while we are here that will take us to the right place after we are gone. Anything short of that is folly.

MAN

We are informed that man was created in the image of God. This is repeated several times in the Book of Genesis in speaking of the creation of man. This is the answer to the evolutionist in relation to the descent of man, and to all religionists as well as scientists who ridicule the anthropomorphic nature of God. Man was created in the likeness of the body of God. We call him Father, we are taught that he is literally the Father of the spirits of men, and in the spirit they were created, or begotten, sons and daughters unto him.

MARRIAGE

Since marriage is ordained of God, and the man is not without the woman, neither the woman without the man in the Lord, there can be no exaltation to the fulness of the blessings of the celestial kingdom outside of the marriage relation. A man cannot be exalted singly and alone; neither can a woman. Each must have a companion to share the honors and blessings of this great exaltation. . . . If a man and his wife are saved in separate kingdoms, for instance, the celestial and terrestrial, automatically the sealing is broken; it is broken because of the sins of one of the parties. No one can be deprived of exaltation who remains faithful. In other words, an undeserving husband cannot prevent a faithful wife from an exaltation and vice versa. In this case the faithful servant would be given to someone who is faithful.

MARRIAGE

No woman will be condemned by the Lord for refusing to accept a proposal which she feels she could not properly accept. In my judgment it is far better for our good girls to refuse an offer of marriage when they think that the companionship of the man would be disagreeable, or if he is one they do not and believe they cannot learn to love. If in her heart the young woman accepts fully the word of the Lord, and under proper conditions would abide by the law, but refuses an offer when she fully believes that the conditions would not justify her in entering a marriage contract, which would bind her forever to one she does not love, she shall not lose her reward. The Lord will judge her by the desires of the heart, and the day will come when the blessings withheld shall be given, though it be postponed until the life to come.

MODESTY

The principle of modesty and propriety is still the same today as it was then. The standards expressed by the General Authorities of the Church are that women, as well as men, should dress modestly. They are taught proper deportment and modesty at all times. It is, in my judgment, a sad reflection on the "daughters of Zion" when they dress immodestly. Moreover, this remark pertains to the young men as well as to the young women. The Lord gave commandments that both men and women should cover their bodies and observe the law of chastity at all times.

MURDER

There is a growing notion in the world today that it is adding a crime to a crime to take the life of these who deliberately murder—a cruel retaliation which cannot benefit the murdered person and likewise the murdered can reap no benefits therefrom. The real purpose which the Lord gave for the taking of life has long been forgotten. The taking of the life of the murderer was never intended to be a benefit to the murdered person or even a benefit to humanity. It was intended to be a benefit to the murderer himself. There are sins which cannot be forgiven, except by the guilty person paying a price by the shedding of his blood. Capital punishment was to benefit the guilty to obtain a better resurrection when the sin had been one unto death.

PRAYER

It is not a difficult thing to learn how to pray. It is not the words we use particularly that constitute prayer. True, faithful, earnest prayer consists more in the feeling that rises from the heart and from the inward desire of our spirits to supplicate the Lord in humility and in faith, that we may receive his blessings. It matters not how simple the words may be if our desires are genuine and we come before the Lord with a broken heart and contrite spirit to ask him for what we need.

PRIESTHOOD

I do not care what office you hold in the Church—you may be an apostle, you may be a patriarch, a high priest, or anything else—but you cannot receive the fullness of the priesthood and the fullness of eternal reward unless you receive the ordinances of the house of the Lord; and when you receive these ordinances, the door is then open so you can obtain all the blessings which any man can gain.

PROFANITY
Filthiness in any form is degrading and soul-destroying, and should be avoided as a deadly poison by all members of the Church.

RACE
We are the children of God. He is our Father and he loves us. He loves all men whether they be white or black. No matter what their color, no matter what the conditions under which they were born and reared, the Lord looks upon all his children in mercy and will do for them just the best that he can.

SACRIFICE
Sacrifice does not mean that we are to inflict punishment upon ourselves. It does not mean that we are to be persecuted, or to deprive ourselves of comforts and blessings of mortal life, not in the least, but that we are willing to place upon the altar all things, even our lives, for the kingdom of God, and that we will accept in fulness all the principles of the gospel and put them into practice. Sacrifice of the world? Yes, if you want to call it such, and the things of the world, to a concentration of the mind and action upon the things of the kingdom of God.

SATAN
Satan's mission is to destroy. When he rebelled at the council in heaven, he determined to destroy the work of the Lord and subject all mankind to his power. It must be admitted that in a great measure he has accomplished his purpose, for he has persuaded the vast majority of the inhabitants of the earth to turn away from the divinely revealed truth. He will lay temptations in the path of every individual to cause him to commit sin. He has taught the world false doctrines under the guise of truth and many have followed him. We should be on guard always to resist Satan's advances. He will appear to us in the person of a friend or a relative in whom we have confidence. He has power to place thoughts in our minds and to whisper to us in unspoken impressions to entice us to satisfy our appetites or desires and in various other ways he plays upon our weaknesses and desires.

SERVICE
No man is independent. Put a man off by himself where he could communicate with none of his fellow beings or receive aid from them, and he would perish miserably. It is a mistake for us to draw within ourselves as does a snail into its shell. No man has had the priesthood as an ornament only. He is expected to use it in behalf of the salvation of others.

TESTIMONY

A testimony is a revelation to the individual who earnestly seeks one by prayer, study, and faith. It is the impression or speaking of the Holy Ghost to the soul in a convincing positive manner. It is something which is far more penetrating than impressions from any other source, but it cannot fully be described. . . . Its convincing power is so great that there can be no doubt left in the mind when the Spirit has spoken. It is the only way that a person can truly know that Jesus is the Christ and that his gospel is true.

YOUTH

The destiny of the Church rests with the youth of Zion. The Church is here to stay, and the young and rising generation shall rise up and direct the kingdom in due course with great power and glory. It is true that some of our youth may be led astray and fall into forbidden paths. But the generality of them will remain faithful.

Harold B. Lee, Eleventh President (1899-1973)

HAROLD B. LEE

Eleventh President of the Church

Born: March 28, 1899, Clifton, Idaho

Died: December 26, 1973, Salt Lake City, Utah (age 74)

President of the Church: July 7, 1972—December 26, 1973
(1½ years)

Physical Characteristics: Five feet eleven inches tall,
weighed 175 pounds, medium build, penetrating
hazel eyes, gray hair

Areas of Distinction: Prophet, educator, missionary,
business executive, writer, public official

Family: Son of Samuel M. and Louisa Bingham Lee.
Married Fern Lucinda Tanner November 14, 1923
(she died September 24, 1962); two children.
Married Freda Joan Jensen, June 17, 1963.

Profile of Harold B. Lee

Mohandas Gandhi, the leader of India, once said, "My life is my message." This can truly be said of President Harold B. Lee, prophet of the Lord. He was a pillar of faith and exerted a profound influence for good. He was a giant of strength and leadership in both spiritual and secular affairs.

Today the world needs people who are committed and involved in worthy causes. President Harold B. Lee was such a man. He was an example of righteous living and service to mankind. He was polished and refined, endowed with intelligence, energy, and initiative. He was skillfully gifted in human relations and with eloquence in teaching the glorious promises of God. He was a mighty instrument in carrying forward the eternal plan of salvation.

President Lee was recognized for his prophetic character and unusual administrative ability. He had a commanding personality and was known for his frankness and courage. His words inspired men to service and devotion, thus bringing joy into the heart.

The worth of a man can well be determined by the impact he makes on the lives of his associates. President Marion G. Romney stated:

Harold B. Lee is a powerful man in modern Israel. The source of his strength is in his knowledge that he lives in the shadow of the Almighty. To him, his Heavenly Father is a senior partner, daily giving him guidance. His contacts with heaven are direct and regular. (*Improvement Era*, July 1953, p. 504.)

Harold B. Lee, newest member of the Council of the Twelve in 1941

When he became President of the Church, the *Deseret News* wrote that "he is a farsighted innovator. Many of the new programs and administrative changes that have made such a profound impact on the Church in recent years have his stamp on them."

President Lee brought to the presidency of the Church years of distinctive service, highlighted by twenty-nine years as a member of the Council of the Twelve and two and a half years as first counselor in the First Presidency; he served as President of the Church for one and a half years. He made valuable contributions in civic affairs, education, and business. Before his call to the Council of the Twelve he served as schoolteacher and principal and was active in politics, serving as a Salt Lake City Commissioner. He was also associated with the boards of directors of major U.S. corporations.

To him there was in the gospel of Jesus Christ a solution to every human problem. "The dispensation in which you and I live," he said, "is intended to be a demonstration of the power and effectiveness of the gospel of Jesus Christ to meet everyday problems here and now." At general conference in October 1946, he said:

> I know there are powers that can draw close to one who fills his heart with . . . love. . . . I came to a night, some years ago, when on my bed, I realized that before I could be worthy of the high place to which I had been called, I must love and forgive every soul that walked the earth, and in that time I came to know that I received a peace and a direction, and a comfort, and an inspiration, that told me things to come and gave me impressions that I knew were from a divine source. (*Conference Report*, October 1946, p. 110.)

President Romney has written of him:

> Humility before God—and fearlessness before men—is the key to his character. His ministry is characterized by an uncommon originality and daring. He is not hampered and restricted by the learning of the world and the forms of men. We, who sit with him daily, are frequently startled by the scope of his vision and the depth of his understanding. With forthrightness, he separates the wheat from the chaff and comes directly to the truth. (*Improvement Era*, July 1953, p. 504.)

Church membership goes back several generations on both sides of Harold B. Lee's family. His ancestors came from the British Isles to Ohio and Indiana and then valiantly struggled to cross the midwestern plains to

Harold B. Lee, who led the Church from July 7, 1972, to December 26, 1973

settle first in southern Utah and then in southern Idaho. His great-grandfather moved his family from Liberty to Far West, and they were finally evacuated from Nauvoo.

Harold Bingham Lee was born March 28, 1899, in the farming community of Clifton, Idaho, one of six children of Samuel Marion and Louisa Bingham Lee. He benefited from the training and discipline of living in a rural community as a member of a large family.

Educated at Oneida Stake Academy, he entered Idaho's Albion State Normal School at the age of 17. He thrived on books and learning and was active in sports and music.

Early in his life President Lee studied the piano, and some of his most pleasurable hours have come in sharing music with his family. After he became a member of the Council of the Twelve, he would often accompany the brethren on the piano as they sang in their council meetings. Stake and ward officers have been surprised and pleased when he has offered to substitute for an absent organist. (*Improvement Era*, March 1970, p. 9.)

At the age of eighteen, President Lee was named principal of the school in Oxford, Idaho. In November 1920, he was called to serve on a mission in the Western States with headquarters in Denver. Following his mission, he moved to Salt Lake City, where he attended summer sessions at the University of Utah. From 1923 to 1928 he continued his education by correspondence courses and extension classes while serving as principal of the Whittier and then the Woodrow Wilson schools in the Granite School District, Salt Lake County.

On November 14, 1923, President Lee married Fern Lucinda Tanner in the Salt Lake Temple. They were blessed with two daughters, Maurine Wilkins (deceased) and Helen (Mrs. L. Brent Goates). In 1962 Sister Lee passed away, and in 1963 he married Freda Joan Jensen, a member of the Primary general board and a respected educator.

He had great regard for family life, his own and that of others. He reflected often in his teachings this thought: "The most important work you will do for the Church will be within the walls of your own home."

In the Church he has served as a high councilor, stake Sunday School superintendent, and stake president. In the latter capacity he instituted, with his counselors, a welfare program and established a warehouse for storing and distributing food and other commodities. This venture proved successful and was one of the beginnings of the general Church welfare program, of which he was appointed managing director in 1936.

As an educator, President Lee had a special interest

in supporting a strong educational program for the Church. He commented that "the best missionaries we have are the graduates of our institutes and seminaries and of the Brigham Young University and Ricks College." He said:

The five purposes of our church schools I would name are: First, to teach truth, secular truth, so effectively that students will be free from error, free from sin, free from darkness, free from traditions, vain philosophies and from untried, unproven theories of science. Second, is to educate youth, not only for time, but for all eternity. Third, is to teach the Gospel that students will not be misled by purveyors of false doctrines, vain speculations of faulty interpretations. Fourth, to prepare students to live a well rounded-out life. Fifth, to set the stage for students to acquire a testimony of the reality of God and of the divinity of His work. Set the stage and help youth to gain a testimony that God lives and that this work is divine. (*Church News*, August 21, 1953, p. 3.)

In an address to seminary students on Temple Square, President Lee admonished: "The most important thing you can do is to learn to talk to God. Talk to him as you would talk to your father, for he is your Father and he wants you to talk to him."

President Lee loved young people and was skillful in lifting them to greater heights of spirituality. He shared experiences with youth under many conditions as he loved and assisted them. He helped bridge the generation gap in many ways, one of which was a successful series of radio talks in 1945 over Radio Station KSL, titled "Youth and the Church." These talks were published in book form under that title and later reissued and revised in the book *Decisions for Successful Living.*

President Lee showed a special interest in young men called to serve their country, and served for several years as chairman of the Church's Servicemen's Committee. Thousands of military personnel throughout the world have testified to the contributions he made through his personal presence and inspirational messages.

During his presidency of the Church, President Lee's talks emphasized patriotism. He spoke often of his great love for and faith in America. To young people in particular, he said that despite the many trials and crises American may pass through, "this nation, founded as it was on a foundation of principle laid down by men whom God raised up, will never fail." (*Deseret News*, December 27, 1973.)

As a General Authority, President Lee traveled widely and was known as a true friend to members and non-members alike. Wherever he journeyed he helped build bridges across the stream of differences and misunderstandings.

President Lee addresses students at Brigham Young University, June 3, 1953

President Lee was a man of great spiritual power and strength. Fenton L. Williams, patriarch in the Sacramento California Stake, related an experience that illustrates this gift:

I have had many rich religious experiences in my life, but the single event that did the most to build my faith and make me want to shun evil was an afternoon with a member of the Council of the Twelve who was visibly inspired to perform his duties. That man was Elder Harold B. Lee.

Our stake had just been divided, and Elder Lee, then one of the Twelve, conducted a special Sunday afternoon meeting to set apart the high councilors, bishoprics, and other officers.

I knew these men well. . . . However, our visiting apostle knew none of them personally. . . . As a member of the older stake presidency I was invited to join the laying on of hands. . . . After the first two or three blessings, I found myself thinking, "He surely has read these men correctly—almost seems to know them."

As the blessings continued I began listening intently to every word, tears welling in my eyes, as I began to realize that the pronouncements had not been by chance but by prophetic inspiration.

Here was a new bishop's counselor who would need to "always be on guard" to "honor his priesthood and calling." How well I knew it. Then followed one who had been having a tithing and coffee problem. His blessing contained specific warnings against those weaknesses.

By this time, my tears flowed freely and I personally did some intense soul-searching about my worthiness to participate in that humbling hour. I bear witness that not in one instance did the servant of the Lord fail to strike home. Several of the men who received blessings that day have since borne witness, in my hearing, of the prophetic utterances of our inspired visitor. They were from God. (*Ensign*, February 1974, pp. 27-28. Used by permission.)

Yes, President Lee was a great instrument for the Lord in touching thousands of lives. He was not only a man dedicated to the Lord, but also a man who loved people and life. He touched people's lives in many ways, such as shaking hands, putting a loving arm around a shoulder to give reassurance, uttering a strengthening word, giving a prophetic blessing upon someone called to a new assignment, blessing sick souls, listening to problems.

Not only did President Lee touch lives in so many ways, but he also had sensitivity for those who had lost loved ones, for he had lost a wife and a daughter. He had a special gift for lifting the burden of the bereaved and for lighting their way with peace and hope. He said:

> The all-important thing is not that tragedies and sorrows come into our lives, but what we do with them. Death of a loved one is the most severe test that you will ever face, and if you can rise above your griefs and if you will trust in God, then you will be able to surmount any other difficulty with which you may be faced. (*From the Valley of Despair to the Mountain Peaks of Hope*, p. 10.)

The members of the Church were indeed to test their trust in God, as President Lee's own death came unexpectedly on December 26, 1973, stunning and shocking the Church. He died that evening in the LDS Hospital in Salt Lake City at 8:58 P.M. of lung and cardiac failure. At 74, he was the youngest Church president to die since the martyrdom of Joseph Smith. Although his death came unexpectedly to Church members, he had told his wife, Joan, just before the end, "God is very near."

The deep sorrow and profound sense of loss at his death were softened by the knowledge expressed by several General Authorities at his funeral—that his passing represented a mission completed.

His term of office was comparatively brief, but his influence was far reaching. He was recognized as a great administrator, a master planner, a man with extraordinary leadership abilities.

During his brief tenure as President of the Church, much was accomplished. Perhaps as never before it became evident to everyone that The Church of Jesus Christ of Latter-day Saints is a worldwide church. In his opening address at general conference on April 6, 1973, he said,

No longer might this church be thought of as the "Utah Church," or as an "American church," but the membership of the Church is now distributed over the earth in 78 countries, teaching the gospel in 17 different languages at the present time. (*Ensign*, July 1973, p. 5.)

Friends and leaders the world over began to take note as never before of the Mormon Church and this great leader. One of his friends, Dr. Norman Vincent Peale, minister of Marble Collegiate Church in New York, called President Lee "one of the most enlightened and creative religious leaders in this world."

Elder Gordon B. Hinckley of the Council of the Twelve said:

President Lee was frequently knocked down by circumstances during his long odyssey from farm to the office of Church president. But he stood up again where he had fallen and then moved on to greater achievement; for out of that chastening process, there came refinement, patience, a polish, an understanding, a grace beautiful to witness and marvelous in its expression. (*Deseret News*, December 29, 1973, p. A-8.)

Though President Lee's administration as president was brief, the gems of wisdom and direction he left the Church and the world are lasting and never to be forgotten.

One of his main themes as prophet was the home. He urged people everywhere to strengthen the home. He sought to help the world understand and appreciate parenthood. He once told of standing in a doorway in his home as a boy, amid a severe thunder and lightning storm. Without warning, his mother pushed him so vigorously that he went sprawling on his back out of the door. At that instant, lightening struck the home and traveled through the very doorway in which he had been standing. If he had remained in the doorway, he would have been killed.

He concluded the story with these words: "From my

experience, it would seem that faithful mothers have a special gift that we often refer to as mother's intuition. Father is the head of the home, but mother is the heart of the family home."

Another general theme of his administration was unity. As his months as prophet progressed, testimonies of Church members grew stronger, filled with love and support for their Prophet, Seer, and Revelator, and toward brotherhood and service.

But of all his counsel and emphasis, perhaps the

The First Presidency, 1972: President Harold B. Lee (front) and counselors N. Eldon Tanner and Marion G. Romney

greatest to all mankind—a central theme repeated again and again—was simply "Keep the commandments."

The fibers of Harold B. Lee's character were strengthened and woven into greatness because he did just that. With vigor and dedication he kept the commandments of the Lord. He was sensitive to the needs and problems of others. He was a peacemaker and a man of God who enriched, blessed, and healed innumerable lives. He was a persuader of people, a resolver of problems, a builder of confidence, a possessor of unusual spiritual insight and understanding. To journey with him was to be strengthened, challenged, inspired, and changed. He bore a strong personal witness to the divinity of the Lord Jesus Christ and the restoration of the gospel.

At his funeral, Elder Hinckley paid him this tribute:

Now he is gone. I am certain that his passing was as much the will of the Lord as was his preservation and preparation through the years for the high and holy calling which he filled so nobly. (*Church News*, January 5, 1974, p. 12.)

The words of Gandhi are likewise applicable to this great prophet-leader, for Harold B. Lee might also well have said, "My life is my message."

Interesting Facts and Contributions
of Harold B. Lee

1. He was a schoolteacher and a principal. He is the third President to have trained professionally as a teacher (the other two were Lorenzo Snow and David O. McKay).

2. His first teaching assignment was in the one-room "Silver Star School" near Weston, Idaho. He was seventeen, not much older than his students.

3. His interest in boys goes back to his school teaching days in Idaho, where he was an athletic coach and Scoutmaster. As a stake president he gave great attention to the Boy Scout and Cub Scouting programs.

4. He has received the Silver Buffalo—Scouting's highest award.

5. While in school, he participated in basketball and debating.

6. He enjoys music. He played in a school band and in a dance orchestra to earn money. An excellent pianist, he was organist for the Clifton (Idaho) Ward. He accompanied his daughter, who played the violin. He has also played at stake conferences when the regular organist has been absent, and accompanied the brethren in their council meetings.

7. He has received honorary doctorate degrees from three universities: Utah State University, Brigham Young University, and the University of Utah.

8. His calling as an apostle spanned the administrations of four Presidents: Heber J. Grant, George Albert Smith, David O. McKay, and Joseph Fielding Smith.

9. He is the first General Authority to have been

called as first counselor in the First Presidency and President of the Quorum of the Twelve at the same time.

10. He demonstrated great interest in and support for Church school programs, seminaries, and institutes.

11. He contributed much to the success and happiness of the youth of the Church. He gave numerous radio talks, as well as talks at firesides, seminaries and institutes, and on college and university campuses. He received an honorary Master M Man award in 1951 for his outstanding leadership and inspiration to youth.

12. He made broad changes in the MIA youth programs of the Church, bringing them "under the umbrella of the priesthood." These programs were given more fully into the hands of the young people themselves for planning and directing the activities, along with directions for more emphasis on service by youth. There was also the creation of a broad program for unmarried adult members. President Lee described the new MIA program as "potentially one of the most significant changes in the Church in our lifetime."

13. He was the chairman and master planner of the correlation program, which includes a training program for bishoprics, home teaching, family home evening, teacher development, and correlated curriculum.

14. He restructured the general auxiliary boards and priesthood organizations at the ward, stake, and regional levels, and created the internal and public communications departments.

15. He helped to organize the original Church welfare program. As a stake president, he found numerous members of his stake in need of help. In 1932, he instituted a stake welfare program to care for the needy and unemployed of his stake and established a warehouse. This was the beginning of the welfare plan as we know it today. He served as managing director of the welfare program until called to the Council of the Twelve, whereupon he became chairman of the General Welfare Committee.

16. He served as chairman of many important committees of the Church, included General Melchizedek Priesthood, Military Relations, and the General Music and Correlation committees; adviser to the Primary and Relief Society general boards and member of the executive committee of the Brigham Young University board of trustees. He was also a member of the General Appropriations Committee.

17. Under his leadership, the force of full-time missionaries reached an all-time high of more than 18,000.

18. He presided and spoke at the second area general conference in Mexico City in August 1972 (17,000 in attendance). It was the largest indoor conference ever held in the Church. He also presided at the third area general conference in Munich, Germany, in August 1973.

19. He was author of *Decisions for Successful Living*, a revision of the book *Youth and the Church*. Another book based on his sermons and writings, *Stand Ye in Holy Places*, was published in March 1974.

20. He was present at the dedications of the following temples: Idaho Falls, Swiss, Los Angeles, London, Oakland, Ogden, and Provo.

21. He traveled widely as a General Authority and as President of the Church. He traveled to Europe, Central and South America, South Africa, the Far East, the Holy Land, Greece, and throughout the United States.

22. In business and civic activities he served as a member of the boards of directors of the Union Pacific Railroad Company, the Equitable Life Assurance Company, and Beneficial Life Insurance Company. He was a member of the board of governors of the American Red Cross, as well as chairman of the board of directors of Zion's First National Bank. He also served as president of the Salt Lake Oratorio Society. He acted as chairman of the board for many of the Church-owned businesses, including Hotel Utah Company, the Utah-Idaho Sugar Company, Bonne-

ville International, and ZCMI. He also served as chairman of the board of Deseret Management Corporation.

23. He was made an honorary lifetime member of the Sons of the Utah Pioneers and an honorary colonel of the Utah National Guard. He was also given the Exemplary Manhood Award by the students of Brigham Young University in 1973.

24. In 1973, the main library at Brigham Young University was renamed in his honor the Harold B. Lee Library.

25. He was the youngest President in 40 years and served as President of the Church the shortest time of any of the Presidents (18 months). At 74, he was also the youngest President to die since the martyrdom of Joseph Smith.

Significant Dates and Events in
Lifetime of Harold B. Lee

Church membership, 1972: 3,090,053   1973: 3,360,190
1973—Stakes: 630   Missions: 110   Temples: 15
U.S. Population, 1972: 210 million (est.)
World Population, 1972: 3.8 billion (est.)
U.S. President, 1972-73: Richard M. Nixon

1899   Born in Clifton, Idaho, March 28.

1912-16   Enrolled in the Oneida Stake Academy.

1916   Entered Albion State Normal College, Idaho.

1917   Started teaching school near Weston, Idaho; later became a principal of a school at Oxford, Idaho, at age 18.

1920-22   Served mission to Western States.

1922   Attended summer sessions at University of Utah.

1923   Married Fern Lucinda Tanner in the Salt Lake Temple on November 23 (she passed away in 1962).

1923-28   Continued his education at University of Utah by correspondence and extension classes while serving as principal in Granite School District, Salt Lake County.

1926-29   Served as Pioneer Stake religion class superintendent, Sunday School superintendent, and counselor in the stake presidency.

1928-32   Was intermountain manager for the Foundation Press, Inc.

1930-37   Served as president of Pioneer Stake (age 31-38).

1932   Was appointed Salt Lake City commissioner (won reelection 1933). Established, with his counselors, a Pioneer Stake welfare program, with a warehouse for storing and distributing food and other commodities.

1937   Was called as managing director of the Church welfare program.

1941   Was ordained an apostle by President Heber J. Grant on April 10 (age 42).

1941-45 Traveled extensively to visit Latter-day Saint servicemen on military duty in World War II; served as chairman of the Church's Servicemen's Committee.

1945   Published *Youth and the Church.*

1946   Met with President Harry S Truman to discuss plans for sending aid to Saints in Europe.

1953   Received honorary doctor of humanities degree from Utah State Agricultural College (now Utah State University).

1954   Taught seminary and institute teachers at summer school at BYU. Visited the Orient—Japan, Korea, Okinawa, the Philippines, Guam.

1955   Received honorary doctor of Christian service degree from BYU.

1957   Was elected to board of Union Pacific Railroad (reelected in 1960).

1958   Became a member of the board of directors of Equitable Life Assurance Society. Toured South Africa Mission.

1959   Visited missions in South and Central America.

1960   Became a member of the board of Zion's National Bank. Delivered three talks in Churchwide youth fireside series, with about 120,000 persons assembled in 170 locations.

1961   Became chairman of the executive committee of the Church's new correlation program.

1963   Married Freda Joan Jensen. Was elected to the national board of directors, American Red Cross. Received the Silver Buffalo award of Boy Scouts of America.

1964   Became vice-chairman of the board of Beneficial Life Insurance Company.

1965   Received an honorary doctor of humanities degree from the University of Utah.

1967   Was named chairman of the board, Zion's First National Bank.

1970   Was sustained as first counselor in the First Presidency to President Joseph Fielding Smith and president of the Council of the Twelve Apostles, January 23 (age 70). Delivered baccalaureate addresses at Utah State University at Logan and Ricks College at Rexburg, Idaho, in May.

1971   Received distinguished service award from the LDS Student Association. Became chairman of the board of the Utah-Idaho Sugar Company. Spoke at commencement at Dixie College, St. George, Utah. Visited the Far East. Spoke at first area general conference held in Manchester, England, in August.

1972   Attended dedication of Ogden Temple (January 18-20) and Provo Temple (February 9). Was ordained as President of the Church on July 7 (age 73), with N. Eldon Tanner and Marion G. Romney as counselors. Spoke at the second area general conference in Mexico City. Was elected chairman of the boards of ZCMI, Beneficial Life Insurance Co., and Hotel Utah Company. Was named director of the Zion's Utah Bancorporation. New Sunday School reorganization was introduced to the Church. The 28-story Church Office Building was completed in Salt Lake City. Church Welfare Services were consolidated (Welfare, Social Services, and Health Services). The MIA program was restructured into the Aaronic Priesthood MIA and the Melchizedek Priesthood MIA. President Lee visited England, Switzerland, Italy, Germany, Greece, and the Holy Land; he organized a branch in Jerusalem in September. He dedicated the San Diego Area Visitor's Center in November; and spoke to 3,000 Young Adults in Mesa, Arizona. Church Music Department was reorganized, December.

"Skyjacking" attempts made big news and tougher tatics were adopted to try to stop them. Worldwide rise in crime, terror, and violence. Continued worldwide turmoil within Catholic and Protestant churches. U.S. Apollo 17 astronauts made the last exploration of the moon. Earthquake in Managua, Nicaragua (second worst in Americas), killed thousands in December.

1972-73 Missions opened: Quebec, Argentina East, International, Brazil North Central, Brazil South Central, Australia Northeast, Canada-Maritime, Japan-Naguya, Michigan, North Carolina, Thailand.

1973   Received Exemplary Manhood Award presented by BYU

Associated Students. Awarded Utah Army National Guard Minuteman Award for significant contributions to state, nation, and National Guard. Awarded honorary life membership in the Sons of the Utah Pioneers. Published *Decisions for Successful Living*, a revision of the book *Youth and the Church*. Spoke to seminary students at a meeting in the Assembly Hall on Temple Square (February). Spoke to the seminary and institute students in Pocatello, Idaho. Spoke to youth groups in Southern California. Presided and spoke at the third area general conference in Munich, Germany (August). The Mormon Tabernacle Choir performed in various European cities, including singing for the area general conference. President Lee spoke at Ricks College, calling for patriotism (October). The six hundredth stake of the Church was organized. Seoul (Korea) Stake was organized, the first on the continent of Asia; the Manila Stake was organized, the first in the Republic of the Philippines. Growth in the seminary and institute programs reached 250,000 students, registered in each of the fifty states in the United States and in 27 other countries. ABC and NBC television presented documentaries about the Church. Full-time missionaries reached an all-time high of more than 18,000. President Lee delivered his last sermon to the Church's employees and families on December 13. He died at 8:58 P.M. on Wednesday, December 26, of heart and lung failure.

American troops were withdrawn from Vietnam after 20-year involvement that had divided the American people. Mideast War: Syria and Egypt attacked Israel on Oct. 6. Watergate scandal: The 1972 burglary of the national headquarters of the Democratic Party became an international symbol of corruption and led to mass resignations and firings of members of the White House staff. Food and energy crises became national and international concerns, with the latter complicated by an Arab boycott of oil shipments to the United States and other nations. The United States continued its investigation of conditions in space with lengthy skylab missions. Vice-president Spiro Agnew pleaded no contest to charges of income tax evasion and resigned his office (October). Congressman Gerald R. Ford became the first U.S. Vice-president to be selected under the procedures of the 25th Amendment. He was confirmed in December.

1972-73 *Significant inventions: an artificial heart that can be implanted as total replacement for the human organ (U.S.); the pseudopod, which enables doctors to give germ-free treatment (U.S.); ultrasonic waves, a method for operating without cutting (U.S.); a computer that identifies voices (U.S.); a pilot collision warning system (U.S.) Tajmir—a nylon that acts like cotton (U.S.).*

The First Presidency

During Harold B. Lee's Administration

First Counselor	President	Second Counselor
N. Eldon Tanner	Harold B. Lee	Marion G. Romney
(1962)	(1941)	(1951)
1972-73	1972-73	1972-73

Council of the Twelve—October 1972

Spencer W. Kimball (1943)
Ezra Taft Benson (1943)
Mark E. Petersen (1944)
Delbert L. Stapley (1950)
LeGrand Richards (1952)
Hugh B. Brown (1958)

Howard W. Hunter (1959)
Gordon B. Hinckley (1961)
Thomas S. Monson (1963)
Boyd K. Packer (1970)
Marvin J. Ashton (1971)
Bruce R. McConkie (1972)

Note: Dates in parenthesis indicate year ordained member of the Council of the Twelve.

Testimony of Harold B. Lee

The Lord and Savior, Jesus Christ, is the head of this church. I happen to be the one who has been called to preside over his church at the present time here upon the earth.

There is no more powerful weapon that can be forged than the powerful teaching of the gospel of Jesus Christ.

There are two things that, when fully applied, would save the world. The first is to put the full might of the priesthood of the kingdom of God to work, and the second is the powerful teachings of the gospel of Jesus Christ.

No truly converted Latter-day Saint can be immoral; no truly converted Latter-day Saint can be dishonest, nor lie, nor steal. That means that one may have a testimony as of today, but when he stoops to do things that contradict the laws of God, it is because he has lost his testimony, and he has to fight to regain it again. Testimony isn't something that you have today and you keep always. Testimony is either going to grow to a brightness of certainty or it is going to diminish to nothingness, depending on what we do about it. The testimony that we recapture day by day is the thing that saves us from the pitfalls of the adversary.

Now, more than ever, I sense the great import of the Lord's revelation relative to the First Presidency. Three things are required of those who are called to this position. They must be ordained, they must be chosen by the Twelve, and, to me one of the most significant things, they must be upheld by the confidence, faith, and prayers of the Church. That means by the faith of the total individual membership of the Church.

With all sincerity I bear my witness to you that by a witness of the Spirit, more powerful than I have ever experienced before, I know that the Savior lives. As I have sought to live as close as I know how, to know his mind and will concerning matters, and to take the first steps during this last change in the Presidency of the Church, I need your faith and prayers. Pray for me. I plead with you to pray for me. (*Church News*, August 19, 1972, pp. 3, 5.)

Personal Experience of Harold B. Lee

Some years ago when I served as a stake president, we had a very grievous case that had come before the high council and the stake presidency that resulted in the excommunication of a man who had harmed a lovely young girl. After nearly an all-night session that resulted in that action, I went to my office rather weary the next morning, to be confronted by a brother of this man whom we had had on trial the night before. This man said, "I want to tell you that my brother wasn't guilty of that thing which you charged him with."

"How do you know he wasn't guilty?" I asked.

"Because I prayed, and the Lord told me he was innocent," the man answered. I asked him to come into the office and we sat down, and I asked, "Would you mind if I ask you a few personal questions?" and he said, "Certainly not."

"How old are you?"

"Forty-seven."

"What priesthood do you hold?"

He said he thought he was a teacher.

"Do you keep the Word of Wisdom?"

He said, "Well, no." He used tobacco, which was obvious.

"Do you pay your tithing?"

He said, "No"—and he didn't intend to as long as that blankety-blank-blank man was the bishop of the Thirty-second Ward.

I said, "Do you attend your priesthood meetings?"

He replied, "No sir!" and he didn't intend to as long

as that man was bishop. "You don't attend your sacrament meetings either?"

"No, sir."

"Do you have your family prayers?"

And he said, "No."

"Do you study the scriptures?"

He said, "Well, my eyes are bad and I can't read very much."

I then said to him: "In my home I have a beautiful instrument called a radio. When everything is in good working order we can dial it to a certain station and pick up a speaker or the voice of a singer all the way across the continent or sometimes on the other side of the world, bringing them into the front room as though they were almost speaking there. But, after we had used it for a long time, there were some little delicate instruments or electrical devices on the inside called radio tubes that began to wear out. When one of them wears out, we get a kind of a static—it isn't so clear. . . . If we don't give that attention, and another one wears out—well, the radio sits there looking quite like it did before, but something has happened on the inside. We can't get any singer. We can't get any speaker.

"Now," I said, "you and I have within our souls something like what might be said to be a counter-part of those radio tubes. We might have what we call a 'Go-to-Sacrament-Meeting' tube, 'Keep-the-Word-of-Wisdom' tube, 'Read-the-Scriptures' tube, and, as one of the most important, that might be said to be the master tube of the whole soul, we might call the 'Keep-Yourselves-Morally-Clean' tube. If one of these becomes worn out by disuse or is not active—we fail to keep the commandments of God—it has the same effect upon our spiritual selves that that same worn-out instrument in the radio in my home had upon the reception that we otherwise could receive from a distance.

"Now, then," I said, "fifteen of the best living men in the Pioneer Stake prayed last night. They heard the evidence and every man was united in saying that your brother was guilty. Now, you, who do none of these things, you say you prayed, and you got an opposite answer. How would you explain that?"

Then this man gave an answer that I think was a classic. He said, "Well, President Lee, I think I must have gotten my answer from the wrong source." And you know that's just as great a truth as we can have. We get our answer from the source of the power we list to obey. If we're keeping the commandments of the Devil, we'll get the answer from the Devil. If we're keeping the commandments of God, we'll get the commandments from our Heavenly Father for our direction and for our guidance. (Cox, *Our Leaders Speak*, pp. 152-54.)

Quotations from Harold B. Lee

ACTION

A truth of the Gospel is not a truth until you live it. You do not really believe in tithing . . . until you pay it. The Word of Wisdom to you is not a truth of the Gospel until you keep it. The Sabbath Day is not a holy day unless you observe it. Temple marriage does not mean anything unless you have a temple marriage. A friend is not a friend unless you defend him.

CHRIST

Before we can feel our kinship to our Savior and be influenced by his teachings in all our thoughts and deeds, we must be impressed by the reality of his existence and the divinity of his mission.

CHURCH

An uninvolved member, with no office and no calling, and no opportunity to serve, only shrinks in his own strength; but, the more deeply involved members become accustomed to doing without his contribution, hence the system is less perfect. We need appropriate involvement for every individual, because there is little individual progress without participation; for it is participation by everyone which permits us to apply the principles of the gospel. . . . The Church is built upon the foundation of Apostles and Prophets, Jesus Christ, himself, being the chief cornerstone; but, the Church is incomplete, in a sense, without all its members being involved. We must do all that we can to see that we build those analogies in a way to see that we are "fitly joined together."

CHURCH LEADERS

I want to bear you my testimony that the experience I have had has taught me that those who criticize the leaders of this Church are showing signs of a spiritual sickness which, unless curbed, will bring about eventually spiritual death. I want to bear my testimony as well that those who in public seek by their criticism, to belittle our leaders or bring them into disrepute, will bring upon themselves more hurt than upon those whom they seek thus to malign. I have watched over the years, and I have read of the history of many of those who fell away from this Church, and I want to bear testimony that no apostate who ever left the Church ever prospered as an influence in his community thereafter.

COMMANDMENTS

The greatest message that one in this position could give to the membership of the Church is to keep the commandments of God, for therein lies the safety of the Church and the safety of the individual. Keep the commandments. There could be nothing that I could say that would be a more powerful or important message today.

CONFESSION

Those in sin must confess. "By this ye may know if a man repenteth of his sins—behold, he will confess them and forsake them." (D&C 58:43). That confession must be made first to the person who has been most wronged by your acts. A sincere confession is not merely admitting guilt after the proof is already in evidence. If you have offended many persons openly, your acknowledgment is to be made openly and before those whom you have offended that you might show your shame and humility and willingness to receive a merited rebuke. If your act is secret and has resulted in injury to no one but yourself, your confession should be in secret, that your Heavenly Father who hears in secret may reward you openly. Acts that may affect your standing in the Church, or your right to privileges or advancement in the Church, are to be promptly confessed to the bishop whom the Lord has appointed as a shepherd over every flock and whom the Lord has commissioned to be a common judge in Israel.

CONVERSION

To become converted, according to the scriptures, means having a change of heart and the moral character of a person turned from the controlled power of sin into a righteous life. It means to "wait patiently on the Lord" until one's prayers can be answered. . . . Conversion must mean more than just being a "card carrying" member of the Church with a tithing receipt, a membership card, a temple recommend, etc. It means to overcome the tendencies to criticize and to strive continually to improve inward weaknesses and not merely the outward appearances.

FAITH

By faith in God you can be attuned to the Infinite and by power and wisdom obtained from your Heavenly Father harness the powers of the universe to serve you in your hour of need in the solution of problems too great for your human strength or intelligence.

HYPOCRITES

We have people who pray in private places and then publicize the fact that they pray. We sometimes are more concerned about publicizing ward teaching and sacrament meeting attendance for the sake of comparative statistics than in improving the spiritual qualities of our performance. We sometimes in some places publicize convert baptisms to make a record rather than concern ourselves principally with the salvation of human souls. I fancy the Master, if He were among us, would say of all such—and I am talking of members of the Church who do things like this—"Moreover when you fast, when you pray, when you worship, when you pay tithing, when you do your ward teaching, attend sacrament meeting, when you baptize, be not as the hypocrites. Verily, if you publicize it and dramatize it you have your reward already." This is but another way of repeating what the Master previously warned.

LAW

If there were no opposition to good, would there be any chance to exercise your agency or right to choose? To deny you that privilege would be to deny you the opportunity to grow in knowledge, experience, and power. God has given laws with penalties affixed so that man might be made afraid of sin and be guided into paths of truth and duty.

MARRIAGE

If Satan and his hosts can persuade you to take the broad highway of worldly marriage that ends with death, he has defeated you in your opportunity for the highest degree of eternal happiness through marriage and increase throughout eternity.

ORDER

There are frequent requests from sealers in one temple who want to perform sealings in another temple. When we tell them that their work must be confined to the temple for which they have been set apart, they ask why. And we tell them that there must be order in the kingdom of God. Sometimes a former temple president asks years after his release if he can have permission to go back into the temple to perform another sealing, perhaps for a grandchild.

His request is denied because that isn't God's way. When a member releases the keys that he formerly held, the keys do not belong to him anymore. They belong to somebody else, and he doesn't have the authority he once had because there is order in the Church.

PROPHETS
In the history of the Church there have been times or instances where counselors in the First Presidency and others in high station have sought to overturn the decision or to persuade the President contrary to his inspired judgment, and always, if you will read carefully the history of the Church, such opposition brought not only disastrous results to those who resisted the decision of the President, but almost always such temporary persuasion was called back for reconsideration, or a reversal of hasty action not in accordance with the inspired feelings of the President of the Church, and that, I submit, is one of the fundamental things that he must never lose sight of in the building of the Kingdom of God.

RELIGION
It is not the function of religion to answer all the questions about God's moral government of the universe, but to give one courage, through faith, to go on in the face of questions he never finds the answer to in his present status.

SIN
One may not wallow in the mire of filth and sin and conduct his life in a manner unlawful in the sight of God and then suppose that repentance will wipe out the effects of his sin and place him on the level he would have been on had he always lived a righteous and virtuous life. The Lord extends loving mercy and kindness in forgiving you of the sins you commit against him or his work, but he can never remove the results of the sin you have committed against yourself in thus retarding your own advancement toward your eternal goal. There are no successful sinners.

TEMPLE
When you enter a holy temple, you are by that course gaining fellowship with the saints in God's eternal kingdom where time is no more. You have no time for man-made secret societies, if you do your duty as a faithful Church member.

TESTIMONY
This should be the only objective of instructors and teachers in this Church—to teach "Jesus Christ, and him crucified." We need

not the "excellency of speech nor of wisdom," but we need "the testimony of God."

WAR

On each side, people believe that they are fighting for a just cause, for defense of home and country and freedom. On each side they pray to the same God in the same name for victory. Both sides cannot be wholly right; perhaps neither is without wrong. God will work out in his own due time and in his own sovereign way, the justice and right of the conflict. But he will not hold the innocent instrumentalities of the war—our own brethren in arms—responsible for the conflict.

WOMAN

To be what God intended you to be as a woman depends on the way you think, believe, live, dress, and conduct yourselves as true examples of Latter-day Saint womanhood, examples of that for which you were created and made. To be thus merits the deepest respect of your sweetheart and your husband. Righteous indignation should be felt by every pure woman when she sees in pictures, on the screen, and in song a vulgar portrayal of a woman as something a little more than a sex symbol. . . . The woman who is too scantily dressed, or immodestly dressed, oftimes is the portrayal of one who is thus trying to draw the attention of the opposite sex when her natural adornments do not, in her opinion, suffice. Heaven help any woman so minded for drawing such attention. For a woman to adopt the mode of a man's dress, it is said, is to encourage the wave of sexual perversion, when men adopt women's tendencies and women become mannish in their desires. If a woman will preserve and properly maintain her God-given identity, she can captivate and hold the true love of her husband and the admiration of those who admire natural, pure, lovely womanhood. What I am saying to you sisters first of all, then, is to be what God intends you to be, a true woman.

YOUTH

You are a wise youth if you see in your play not an end in itself but a means to a divine purpose that conduces to the advancement of your eternal nature. Don't "go slumming." The youth who seeks constantly for a thrill in his pleasures is following a dangerous road. He is hunting for the rapture of the moment and in so doing he may lose the peace of years.

Spencer W. Kimball, Twelfth President (1895-   )

SPENCER W. KIMBALL

Twelfth President of the Church

Born: March 28, 1895, Salt Lake City, Utah

President of the Church: December 30, 1973

Physical Characteristics: Five feet six and one-half
   inches tall, weighs 165 pounds, medium build,
   brown eyes, gray hair

Areas of Distinction: Prophet, banker, farmer,
   businessman, writer, civic leader, Scouter

Family: Son of Andrew and Olive Woolley Kimball.
   Married Camilla Eyring November 16, 1917; four
   children

Profile of Spencer W. Kimball

The hour was late. It had been a long and busy day for Spencer W. Kimball. Even now he was running behind schedule as his secretary entered his office. Would he be willing to meet with an unscheduled couple for a few minutes? she asked. They said they must see him. He nodded his assent. Suddenly the other demands of the day faded, as President Kimball directed his energies toward two people in need, sincerely concerned to help them if he could.

As the couple walked in, there were tears in their eyes, and it was apparent they urgently needed counseling. After more than an hour with President Kimball they departed—this time with eyes clear, full of faith and confidence.

This scene is not unusual in the office of President Spencer W. Kimball. It has been repeated thousands of times as this servant of the Lord comforts and counsels Church members in their efforts to reshape their personal lives.

Spencer W. Kimball is a prophet of the Lord. Perhaps the greatest tribute that could be paid him would be simply: he is a servant of the people. His life is literally based on Paul's admonition: "Bear ye one another's burdens, and so fulfil the law of Christ." (Galations 6:2.)

As a young boy Spencer W. Kimball loved the Lord and His work. He was a boy with a destiny to perform.

Spencer W. Kimball as a missionary, May 24, 1915

His father, who had received the gift of prophecy, once said to his neighbor:

> That boy Spencer is an exceptional boy. He always tries to mind me, whatever I ask him to do. I have dedicated him to be one of the mouthpieces of the Lord—the Lord willing. You will see him someday as a great leader. I have dedicated him to the service of God, and he will become a mighty man in the Church. (*Conference Report*, October 1943, p. 17.)

Certainly that prophecy has been fulfilled. President Kimball stands as the mouthpiece of the Lord as the twelfth President and prophet of the Church. His voice is the voice of the Lord. He is the one whom the Saints trust to reveal new truths, new solutions, and new programs by the inspiration of the Lord. He is a man of humility and a great teacher of truth. He has gained love and respect throughout the world, and in all his doings he radiates spiritual fervor and enthusiasm.

Spencer W. Kimball was born with a rich heritage. His paternal grandfather was Heber C. Kimball, apostle and counselor to Brigham Young. His maternal grandfather, Edwin D. Woolley, served 28 years as a bishop in Salt Lake City, and his father, Andrew Kimball, served for 26 years as a stake president in Arizona.

The sixth of eleven children, Spencer W. Kimball was born March 28, 1895, in Salt Lake City, a son of Andrew and Olive Woolley Kimball. Three years after Spencer was born, his father was called to be a stake president in the Gila Valley of Arizona. He had previously served ten years as president of the Indian Territory. While listening to Indian stories and songs at his father's knee, young Spencer developed a great love for the Indian people, which later sustained him through 25 years as head of the Church Indian Committee.

> My patriarchal blessing, given at age 11, told me I would preach to man, but especially to the Indians. When my mission call was to the Swiss-German Mission I could not see how I would be teaching the Indians. Then because of the World War I, I was sent to the Central States Mission, but not to the Indians. This worried me a little, until I was called to the Council and was asked to work with President George Albert Smith, then a member of the Twelve, as he labored to revive the Indian work. I have always loved those people and I know that the day of the Lamanite has come. (*Church News*, February 26, 1972, p. 13.)

In his high school days in Thatcher, Arizona, he was student body president, honor student, and athlete. During his school years and summers, he worked at dairying and farming. As soon as he was graduated from high school at the Church's Gila Academy, he was called to serve a mission.

As a missionary in the Central States, he showed resourcefulness in his missionary work. One day while tracting in St. Louis, Missouri, he saw, through a partly opened door, a new piano. To the woman who was closing the door in his face, he pointed to the piano and asked if it was a Kimball piano. She indicated that it was. He told the woman that was also his name. "Would you like me to sing and play for you?" The door opened wider and she said: "Surely. Come in." He sat down and played and sang for her. This led to a number of gospel discussions.

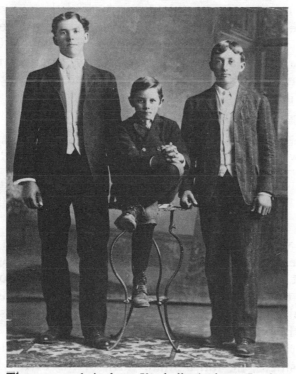

Three sons of Andrew Kimball: Andrew Gordon, Spencer W., and Delbert G., in about 1906

President Kimball says missionary work is "a great character builder" and believes every young man should aspire to fill a mission. "My mission was a stabilizer and an organizer and a spiritualizer," he says. "It strengthened my testimony. It solidified my character and my life. It was a great experience. It was a time of personal growth." (*Church News*, January 5, 1974.)

Upon returning home, he began college. The next year he was called home to enter military service. The Armistice was signed before the contingent to which he was assigned was activated.

After his mission, Spencer had acquired summer work mining water for a large ranch. He and his co-worker camped in a tent on a mountain, cooked their own food, and once a week got the local newspaper. One week, the paper showed a beautiful girl on the front page—Camilla Eyring, a new teacher at Gila Academy. Spencer read all the information about her and then said, "I am going to marry that girl."

President Kimball recalls:

As soon as I got back down in the valley and was finished with the well work, I looked her up and a courtship was started. I was in the military service, waiting to be called, so my courtship was mostly in a khaki uniform. But she seemed not to be too much offended by my appearance. We were married in November 1917. (*Church News*, January 5, 1974, p. 4.)

As an Arizona businessman, he began first in a bank as a teller and bookkeeper and then branch manager and assistant cashier. He resigned after eight years to form and manage the partnership of Kimball-Greenhalgh Insurance and Realty Company, in which he sold his interest at the time of his call to the Council of the Twelve.

During those early years of laboriously building up a new business, he ran a small farm of his own where he raised cotton and alfalfa. He also found time for civic, professional, and community work, including Scouting, local government, Chamber of Commerce, and Rotary

International. In the latter organization he became a district governor; and in Scouting he was director and vice-president of the council.

Two months after his marriage, he was called as stake clerk and served for six and a half years under his father, the stake president. When his father died, Spencer, still in his twenties, was called by Heber J. Grant to be a counselor in the new stake presidency; he served 12 years in that position, much of the time functioning as stake clerk also. When the stake was divided, he served five and a half years as the president of the newly created Mt. Graham Stake. In this position he directed use of the Church welfare program in achieving the rather spectacular rehabilitation of Church members at Duncan, Arizona, after a disastrous flood in the upper Gila Valley in 1938.

Spencer W. Kimball was called to be a member of the Council of the Twelve on July 8, 1943. He remembers the almost reverential awe that he held as a boy for General Authorities who stayed in the Kimball home when his father was stake president. Little did he know that years later, President J. Reuben Clark, Jr., would call him on the telephone with the words: "Spencer, I hope you have a chair near you. The brethren agree that you would be a great apostle of the Lord, and I am calling you to that position."

Throughout his whole life, Spencer W. Kimball has been devoted to the service of the Lord. For most of his 30 years as an apostle, he was in charge of conference assignment schedules; among other assignments he headed the Church Missionary Committee, the Budget Committee, and for 25 years the Church Indian Committee. Because of his great work with the Lamanites, many Church members link his name with programs designed to meet their needs; he has been instrumental in securing for the Indians many social, religious, and educational opportunities, including the Indian Student Placement Program.

President Kimball is a powerful and persuasive

speaker. He speaks from the heart and communicates so all understand. He is noted for his frank, wise, and relevant messages. His son, Edward L. Kimball, describes his father's speaking and purpose:

> In the many sermons he has delivered over the years there are several repeated strains. One is the Church Indian program. Another reflects his feeling of responsibility to speak forthrightly to members of the Church about sexual sins, warning of the approaches to them, emphasizing the seriousness of succumbing to the near-universal temptations, and pointing out the road back for those who have erred and yearn for reconciliation with the Lord. This is a difficult and unpleasant task, but one he has not shirked. His objective has not been to be popular, or to please the ear, but to preach repentance. It is true, however, that his directness, his earnestness, his careful statement of the problem and solution, and his obvious love and concern for those to whom he speaks have made him one of the most respected speakers of his generation. What he says is not intended to be entertaining, but almost always is worth hearing and rehearing. (Kimball, *Faith Precedes the Miracle,* Deseret Book Company, 1972, p. xx.)

Throughout President Kimball's life, from childhood, hard work has played a vital part. At age five, he did farm chores that were no small job for a young boy. At age 16, he supported himself by milking between 18 and 28 cows twice a day. Since there were no machines, he also had to separate the cream, bottle the milk, wash the cans and bottles, feed the cattle, and clean out the manure. President Kimball has never been one to spare himself of work, especially the work of the Lord. A work day of 16 or 18 hours is not unusual for him. His great concern for people and his deep compassion for them is demanding on his time.

Although he works hard, he realizes that there must be time for relaxation. From the age of seven he has chosen music as a diversion. He has served as a choir director and organist and sang often in a chorus or quartet. His singing ended when surgery removed most of his vocal chords in 1957, but he still enjoys playing the piano. He enjoys walking in the hills or woods and especially on the beaches of California. When he was younger he played handball regularly and for many years enjoyed square dancing. He believes that exercise is important—exercise of the muscles, of the mind, and of the spirit. He chooses simple food.

Perhaps Spencer and Camilla Kimball's favorite pasttime is reading. They both share a great love for books and are often found during leisure hours immersed in the thoughts of a good book. They feel that children will generally follow the pattern of their parents in choosing what to read. They also believe that the family that make good books their companions have found one of the joys of life.

President and Sister Kimball state:

The Lord would have us know the gospel truths first, but would not limit us to the scriptures.

He has indicated that our reading should be of a general nature, including material in every legitimate field.

As we yearn and plan and program our lives to become gods, it is apparent that we must have full knowledge of all the fields which affect a world. ("The Power of Books," *Relief Society Magazine*, October 1963, p. 726.)

To watch Spencer W. Kimball at work or recreation, one would never know of the trials that have filled his life. When he was seven, he nearly drowned. At ten, he suffered Bell's palsy, a facial paralysis. At 11, his mother died. At 12, he had typhoid fever. Later he was stricken with years of boils, Bell's palsy again, a major heart attack, and cancer of the throat, resulting in the removal of most of his vocal cords and in subsequent radiation treatments. Forced to redevelop his ability to speak, he talks today with a deep, deliberate voice. In April 1972, at age 77, he had open heart surgery. But in overcoming all these obstacles and persevering, he has found a faith unwavering and a solidarity with his Heavenly Father.

When called a "modern miracle," President Kimball replies, "Haven't you read in the scriptures that men will be strengthened even to the renewing of their bodies if they are doing the work of the Lord?"

As the mantle of president and prophet came upon him, he said, "I doubt if anyone in the Church has prayed harder and more consistently for a long life and the general welfare of President Lee than my Camilla and I. I had expected that I would go long before he would go."

In his work as a Church official, he is one of the most widely traveled General Authorities in the Church today. He has visited many countries in the world. He has toured most missions, has visited most stakes, and has created many of them. He has interviewed thousands of missionaries. His years spent as a stake clerk have made him sensitive to pertinent details and the importance of follow-through on these details as he visits the stakes of Zion.

There were 120 stakes in the Church when President Kimball was called to preside over the new Mt. Graham (Arizona) Stake in 1938. When he was called to the Council of the Twelve on July 8, 1943, there were 143 stakes. When he became President of the Church, there were 630 stakes.

President Kimball feels that family worship can ease the world's ills. "We would go a long way to curing the world's ills if the families could follow the same pattern of living as that laid down by my father." That pattern which the Kimball family followed was to have family prayer morning and night, have a family home evening at least once a week, and go to their meetings as a family.

I was fortunate that I grew up in a good home. My father was sent into the Arizona territory to preside there when I was only three. As long as I can remember, my father was stake president.

My father was kind; he took me with him to conferences in the stake, and once I came to Salt Lake City with him to attend general conference. I think closeness with your children pays off. My mother died when I was 11, but I always had a mother to come home to. My

The Kimball family at the time of his call to be a General Authority. In front, Sister Kimball, Elder Kimball, and daughter Olive Beth. Back, Edward, Spencer L., and Andrew.

second mother was very special; she died shortly after I was married. My third mother died after my father did.

I was one of 11 children in the family, and this meant everyone had to help on our small family farm.

I feel that's the problem today. Young people don't have enough to do to keep out of mischief, and in many cases the mothers are not home to guide the children. (*Church News,* July 15, 1972, p. 10.)

President and Sister Kimball are the parents of one daughter and three sons: Olive Beth (Mrs. Grant M. Mack), Spencer LeVan, Andrew Eyring, and Edward Lawrence. They have 27 grandchildren and 10 great-grandchildren. For President and Sister Kimball, their family remains a central concern in their life. President Kimball is a devoted father and husband and insists that under normal circumstances "the place of women is in the home."

President Kimball is a builder of character in youth. He has been very much aware of their needs and problems and has also been involved in their happinesses and joys.

He is known for his talks concerning dating, morals, modesty, and marriage.

He has been in great demand as a counselor to people. He is a good listener, and when he does talk, he often draws diagrams to clarify his points. He listens, he watches reactions, he comforts, he may even reprimand, but his love is apparent in his conversation.

Many years ago as members came to President Kimball for advice and counsel, he would write down a scripture reference or a note to help them remember the counsel. The note became a list, and then a sheet of information. Soon he was duplicating several sheets of scripture reference and direction.

"I thought I would write a little message of encouragement and counsel. That message became 23 chapters in a book." The book is *The Miracle of Forgiveness*, which has sold tens of thousands of copies. It is a common occurrence for him to receive letters of appreciation from members who have read the book. Many bishops use the book as a text in working with transgressors. The income from the book is largely given to the missionary program, especially for Indian missionaries. President Kimball says:

> I have had many experiences in dealing with transgressors, especially those involved in sexual sins, both inside and outside of marriage. . . . To cure spiritual diseases which throttle us and plague our lives, the Lord has given us a sure cure—repentance. . . . Having come to recognize their deep sin, many have tended to surrender hope, not having a clear knowledge of the scriptures and of the redeeming power of Christ. . . . Man can be literally transformed by his own repentance and by God's gift of forgiveness which follows for all except unpardonable sins. It is far better not to have committed the sin; the way of the transgressor is hard; but recovery is possible. (*The Miracle of Forgiveness*, Bookcraft Inc., 1969, pp. ix-xi.)

Another outstanding book, *Faith Precedes the Miracle*, drawn from his sermons and writings, has also proven to be very helpful and inspiring to its readers.

To Church members worldwide, Spencer W. Kimball

is seen as a servant of the Lord filled with a deep love and concern for his fellowman. His kindness and love are epitomized in the story of a visit to a stake conference shortly before he became President of the Church.

It was a Friday evening, and President Kimball was staying in the stake president's home when the young grandchildren telephoned to see if they might shake hands with President Kimball. The stake president began telling them that it was too late and President Kimball had worked all day. However, President Kimball, overhearing the conversation, interrupted and said, "Have them come down." The hour was late, but 12 grandchildren hurried to their grandfather's home to see an apostle of the Lord. As they arrived, President Kimball scooped up the two-year-old in his arms and said, "Now I think that with all these lovely children here, we ought to have a party." Then he gathered them around the piano, and he played and sang with them for more than an hour. Those 12 children thrill at that memory and call him their "special president."

President N. Eldon Tanner, who now serves as President Kimball's first counselor in the First Presidency, has said:

> I feel honored to be a counselor to President Kimball. He has been prepared for over 30 years. He has been prepared as well as a man could be prepared. Besides his natural abilities, he has the Spirit of the Lord for guidance. We believe and know that men are fore-ordained and that his experience in the world has prepared him for this position. We have no doubt but that the work of the Lord will go forward.

Whether it be laughing young school children or teary-eyed young couples, Spencer W. Kimball has captured hearts the world over. Because of his abiding love, he indeed "bears the burdens" of his fellowmen. He believes a man has two duties: to master himself and to help others achieve perfection.

The prophecy of President Kimball's father has come

true. For through his committed and diligent service, his love for mankind, his courage, faith, and patience over great adversity, and his strong testimony of Jesus Christ, Spencer W. Kimball has become a mighty man in the Church. Today he is the voice of the Lord, his spokesman on earth, and a beloved prophet-president.

President and Sister Kimball in Munich, Germany, August 1973.

Interesting Facts and Contributions
of Spencer W. Kimball

1. He served the second shortest period of time as an apostle (thirty years) before becoming President of the Church. Brigham Young had the shortest period—twelve years.

2. His paternal grandfather was Heber C. Kimball, apostle, missionary, and counselor to Brigham Young.

3. His maternal grandfather, Edwin Dilworth Woolley, was the business manager for President Brigham Young and for 28 years was bishop of the 13th Ward, in which President Heber J. Grant lived as a boy.

4. His calling as an apostle spanned the administration of five Presidents: Heber J. Grant, George Albert Smith, David O. McKay, Joseph Fielding Smith, and Harold B. Lee.

5. He is the oldest man to be ordained an apostle and then become president—age 48. From Brigham Young to Harold B. Lee, the average age has been 32 years.

6. On July 7, 1972, at age 77, he became the oldest man to serve as President of the Council of Twelve Apostles and then later become President of the Church.

7. Only Wilford Woodruff (age 82), Lorenzo Snow (age 84), and Joseph Fielding Smith (age 93) were older when they became President; President Kimball's age—78.

8. He is the author of two books: *The Miracle of Forgiveness* and *Faith Precedes the Miracle*, as well as many articles and pamphlets.

9. He has been involved for more than twenty-five years in helping develop the Church Indian program, including the Indian Student Placement Program. Perhaps

no aspect of Church work is so definitely identified with his name.

10. As President of the Council of the Twelve, he was the chairman of the executive committee of the Church Missionary Committee.

11. He has served in many positions as a General Authority: as chairman of the Missionary Committee, the Indian Committee, and the Budget Committee; a member of the Expenditures Committee and the Correlation Committee; and a member of the board of trustees of the Brigham Young University and of the board of education of the Church Schools, and chairman of the executive committee of these institutions. He made extensive efforts toward youth development and was an organizer of the girls' program; he also helped develop the Youth Rehabilitation Committee, later to become the Church Social Services.

12. He has been present at the dedications of the following temples: Arizona, Idaho Falls, Swiss, Los Angeles, Oakland, Ogden, and Provo.

13. In his sermons there have been several major themes such as the Church Indian Program, avoidance of sexual sin, repentance, and the family.

14. He has been involved and committed in working for the success and happiness of youth in the Church. He has given numerous talks and written numerous articles that have helped to guide them to seek happy marriages with worthy partners, performed in the temple.

15. "All his sermons are kept in volumes and are indexed by subject. He also has kept a personal journal since he was a very young man, and these too, are kept in volumes. His journals carry descriptions of the myriad of places he has visited, with pictures and descriptions and identification of the people he has met in these places. He says that every person should keep a personal journal, so posterity can know of ancestry." (*Church News*, July 15, 1972, p. 10.)

16. He and President Harold B. Lee were born on the same date, March 28—President Kimball in 1895 and President Lee in 1899.

17. At age seven, he sang often at home and church. Later he was in musical plays. He earned extra money playing piano in a dance band. He served as a choir leader and organist in local wards, and was a member of choruses and quartets, performing at funerals, conventions, and other functions. The singing had to stop when surgery removed part of his vocal cords in 1957, but he is always a willing accompanist.

18. His life has been filled with many illnesses, including typhoid fever, smallpox, Bell's palsy, years of boils and carbuncles, a major heart attack, cancer of the throat resulting in the removal of most of his vocal cords, recurrence of cancer requiring radiation treatment, heart disease requiring open-heart surgery to replace a valve and transplant an artery, and most recently Bell's palsy again. (See *Faith Precedes the Miracle*, pp. xi-xii.) At the time he became President, his doctor certified that he was in good health, perhaps better than he had enjoyed in the previous twenty years.

19. In 1969 Brigham Young University awarded him the honorary degree of Doctor of Laws. LDS Institute students at Snow College in Ephraim, Utah, gave him the honorary title, "Gardener of Souls."

20. He has traveled extensively throughout the Near East, the Far East, Southeast Asia, South America, Central America, Mexico, Europe, Canada, United States, South Pacific, New Zealand, Australia, and South Africa.

21. As a youth he was a leader in athletic, social, and educational areas. At Gila Academy (a high school), he played on the basketball team and was student body president. For many years he enjoyed handball.

22. He has been active in civic and business circles. He has participated in the following activities: Scouting, school boards, member of city councils, Rotary

Club, director of the Association of Insurance Agents, as director of the Utah Home Fire Insurance Company and of the Beneficial Life Insurance Company, and director of AYUDA, an organization of professional men carrying medical help to deprived people in Central and South America. He worked as a youth in water mining, dairying, and farming.

23. He was elected a district governor of Rotary International. He was also director and vice-president of a Scout council.

24. He was one of the organizers, owners, and operators of the Gila Broadcasting Company, KGLU, the first station in Gila (Arizona) Valley. He was a secretary of irrigation canals of the Gila Valley and of the Gila Valley Irrigation District and secretary of the Arizona Pima Cotton Growers' Association.

25. He was an official in local banks for eight years and then for sixteen years was the co-owner and manager of the Kimball-Greenhalgh Insurance and Realty Company in southern Arizona.

Significant Dates and Events in Lifetime of Spencer W. Kimball

Church membership, 1973: 3,360,190
Stakes: 630   Temples: 15   Missions: 110
U.S. Population, 1973: 210 million (est.)
World Population, 1973: 3.8 billion (est.)
U.S. President, 1973: Richard M. Nixon

1895	Born in Salt Lake City, Utah, March 28.
1898	Moved to Thatcher, Arizona, where his father had been called as president of St. Joseph Stake.
1906	From Samuel Claridge, received his patriarchal blessing, which said he would one day preach the gospel to the Lamanites.
1914	Was graduated from Gila Academy (a Church-operated high school) with highest honors and as student body president.
1914-16	Was called to Swiss-German Mission but served in Central States Mission because of World War I (28 months).
1917	Attended the University of Arizona at Tucson. While waiting for his World War I military contingent to be called up, he married Camilla Eyring of Pima, Arizona. Contingent was never called to active duty (age 22).
1917-26	Started his career in banking as teller, bookkeeper, then branch manager and assistant cashier.
1918	Was called as stake clerk of St. Joseph Stake, serving under his father. Was sealed to his wife, Camilla, in the Salt Lake Temple.
1924	Was called as second counselor in the St. Joseph Stake presidency, continuing to serve for several years as stake clerk. Became a member of the Gila College board of education.
1927	Became president and manager of Kimball-Greenhalgh Insurance and Realty Co.

1935   Became secretary of the Gila Valley Irrigation Co. Organized and became part-owner of Gila Broadcasting Co., station KGLU.

1938-43 Served as president of the newly organized Mount Graham Stake (ages 42-48).

1943   Was called to the Council of the Twelve on July 8. Was ordained an apostle by President Heber J. Grant on October 7 (age 48).

1946   Was called by President George Albert Smith on special assignment to work with the Lamanites, thus fulfilling in part his patriarchal blessing. Named to serve as chairman of the Church Indian Committee.

1952   Traveled to Mexico and Central America; dedicated the land to proselyting; divided the Mexican Mission; and organized the Central American Mission.

1954   Toured missions in Canada.

1955   Toured the missions of Europe; visited 116 cities in the Norwegian, Swedish, Danish, Finnish, British, Netherlands, French, Swiss-Austrian, East German, and West German missions; attended the dedication of the Swiss Temple.

1957   Underwent surgery for a malignancy in his throat, losing one vocal cord and part of another, along with temporary loss of his voice.

1958   Received honorary Master M Men award, and his wife received honorary Golden Gleaner award during June MIA Conference. Toured Spanish-American West Mission.

1959   Toured missions in South America.

1960   Delivered talks in Churchwide youth fireside series, with about 120,000 persons assembled in 170 locations.

1961-62 Traveled to the Holy Land and in Europe (December to February).

1961-62 Traveled to the Holy Land and European Stake conference (December to February).

1964   Toured missions in Brazil and Uruguay.

1965   Named Council of the Twelve supervisor for South American missions.

1966 Toured Chile, Argentina, Uruguay, and Brazil. Delivered commencement address at Brigham Young University.

1967 Received "The Gardener of Souls" award from the Institute of Religion student body at Snow College in Ephraim, Utah.

1968 Named Council of the Twelve supervisor for British Mission.

1969 Received honorary Doctor of Laws degree from Brigham Young University. His book *The Miracle of Forgiveness* was published.

1970 Was sustained as Acting President of the Council of the Twelve Apostles, January 23 (age 75). Was honored by Indian students of BYU.

1971 Was presented with the Pursuit of Excellence award at the sixth annual conference of the Latter-day Saints Student Association at the University of Utah Institute of Religion. Spoke at first area general conference in Manchester, England (August).

1972 Underwent open heart surgery (April). Was sustained as President of the Council of the Twelve Apostles, July 7 (age 77). His book *Faith Precedes the Miracle* was published. Spoke at the second area general conference in Mexico City.

1973 Spoke at the third area general conference in Munich, Germany (August). Visited Church members in South Africa (September). Was ordained as President of the Church on December 30, with N. Eldon Tanner and Marion G. Romney as counselors (age 78).

The First Presidency
During Spencer W. Kimball's Administration

First Counselor	President	Second Counselor
N. Eldon Tanner	Spencer W. Kimball	Marion G. Romney
(1962)	(1943)	(1951)
1973-	1973-	1973-

Council of the Twelve—December 1973

Ezra Taft Benson (1943)
Mark E. Petersen (1944)
Delbert L. Stapley (1950)
LeGrand Richards (1952)
Hugh B. Brown (1953)
Howard W. Hunter (1959)

Gordon B. Hinckley (1961)
Thomas S. Monson (1963)
Boyd K. Packer (1970)
Marvin J. Ashton (1971)
Bruce R. McConkie (1972)

Note: Dates in parenthesis indicate year ordained member of the Council of the Twelve.

Testimony of Spencer W. Kimball

Recently a prominent doctor, knowing of my surgeries and cancer treatments, exhibited a little surprise at my assuming this great responsibility of presidency. He was not a member of the Church and evidently had never known the pull and pressure one feels who has a positive assurance that the Lord is not playing games but has a serious program for man for his glory. The Lord knows what he is doing and that all his moves are appropriate and right. And I was surprised also that any man would wonder and question the work of the Lord.

We who have the positive assurance and testimony of the divinity of this work do not question the ways or determinations of the Lord.

I know without question that God lives, and I have a feeling of sorrow for those people living in the world of doubt who do not have such assurance.

I know that the Lord Jesus Christ is the Only Begotten Son of our Heavenly Father and he assisted in the creation of man and all that serves man, including this earth and all that is in the world, and that he was the Redeemer of mankind and the Savior of this world, the Author of the plan of salvation for all men, and the Exalter of all who live all the laws he has given.

He it is who organized the true vehicle, this church, and called it after his own name: The Church of Jesus Christ of Latter-day Saints, and that in it are all the saving graces. I know that there is contact of the Lord with his prophets and that he reveals the truth today to his servants as he did in the days of Adam, Abraham, Moses, and Peter, and the numerous others throughout time. God's messages of *light* and *truth* are as surely given to man today as in any other dispensation. Since Adam and Eve were placed in the garden, the Lord has been eager to reveal truth and light to his people, but there have been many times when man would not listen, and of course "where there is no ear there is no voice." I know the gospel truths will save and exalt mankind if men will accept the truth and fully live up to their commitments and covenants.

I know this is true, and I bear this testimony to all the world. I urge all men to seriously accept and conform their lives totally to the precepts of the gospel. I bear this witness in all soberness and in the name of Jesus Christ. Amen. (February 1974.)

The First Presidency in 1974: President N. Eldon Tanner, first counselor; President Spencer W. Kimball; and President Marion G. Romney, second counselor.

Personal Experience of Spencer W. Kimball

I feel extremely humble in this calling that has come to me. Many people have asked me if I was surprised when it came. That, of course, is a very weak word for this experience. I was completely bewildered and shocked. I did have a premonition that this call was coming, but very brief, however. On the eighth of July, when President Clark called me, I was electrified with a strong presentiment that something of this kind was going to happen. As I came home at noon, my boy was answering the telephone and he said, "Daddy, Salt Lake City is calling."

I had had many calls from Salt Lake City. They hadn't ever worried me like this one. I knew that I had no unfinished business in Salt Lake City, and the thought came over me quickly, "You're going to be called to an important position." Then I hurriedly swept it from my mind, because it seemed so unworthy and so presumptuous, and I had convinced myself that such a thing was impossible by the time that I heard President [J. Reuben] Clark's voice a thousand miles away saying: "Spencer, this is Brother Clark speaking. The brethren have just called you to fill one of the vacancies in the Quorum of the Twelve Apostles."

Like a bolt of lightning it came. I did a great deal of thinking in the brief moments that I was on the wire. There were quite a number of things said about disposing of my business, moving to headquarters, and other things to be expected of me. I couldn't repeat them all!; my mind seemed to be traveling many paths all at once. I was dazed, almost numb with the shock; a picture of my life spread out before me. It seemed that I could see all of the people before me whom I had injured, or who had fancied that I had injured them, or to whom I had given offense, and all the small petty things of my life. I sensed immediately my inability and limitations and I cried back, "Not me, Brother Clark! You can't mean that!" I was virtually speechless. My heart pounded fiercely.

I recall two or three years ago, when Brother Lee was giving his maiden address as an apostle of the Lord Jesus Christ from this stand, as he told us of his experience through the night after he had been notified of his call. I think I now know something about the experience he had. I have been going through it for twelve weeks. I believe the brethren were very kind to me in announcing my appointment when they did so that I might make the necessary adjustments in my business affairs; but perhaps they were more inspired to give me the time that I needed for a long period of purification, for in those long days and weeks I did a great deal of thinking and praying and fasting and praying. There were conflicting thoughts that surged through my mind—seeming voices saying: "You can't do the work. You are not worthy. You have not the ability." And always finally came the triumphant thought: "You must do the work assigned; you must make yourself able, worthy, and qualified." And the battle raged on.

I remember reading that Jacob wrestled all night, "until the breaking of the day," for a blessing; and I want to tell you that for eighty-five nights I have gone through that experience, wrestling for a blessing. Eighty-five times the breaking of the day has found me on my knees praying to the Lord to help me and strengthen me and make me equal to this great responsibility that has come to me. I have not sought positions nor have I been ambitious. Promotions have continued to come faster than I felt I was prepared for them.

I remember when I was called to be a counselor in the stake presidency. I was in my twenties. President Grant came down to help to bury my father, who was the former stake president, and reorganize the stake. I was the stake clerk. I recall that some of my relatives came to President Grant, unknown to me, after I had been chosen, and said, "President Grant, it's a mistake to call a young man like that to a position of responsibility and make an old man of him and tie him down." Finally, after some discussion, President Grant said very calmly, but firmly, "Well, Spencer has been called to this work, and he can do as he pleases about it," and, of course, when the call came, I accepted it gladly, and I have received great blessings therefrom.

A few days ago one of my well-to-do clients came to me and said, "Spencer, you're going away from us?" "Yes," I said. "Well, this is going to ruin you financially," he continued. "You are just getting started well; your business is prospering. You are making a lot of money now and the future looks bright yet. I don't know how you can do this. You don't have to accept the call, do you?"

And I said, "Brother, we do not have to accept any calls, but if you understand the Mormon way of life, those of us who have been reared in the Church and understand the discipline of the Church, we just always do accept such calls." And I further said to him: "Do you remember what Luke said, '. . . for a man's life consisteth not in the abundance of the things which he possesseth' (Luke 12:15), and all the bonds, lands, houses, and livestock are just things that mean so little in a person's abundant life."

In these long weeks since July 8 I can tell you that I have been overwhelmed and have felt that I was unable to carry on this great work; that I was up against a blank wall. And in that interim I have been out in the desert and in high mountains alone, apart, and have poured out my soul to God. I have taken courage from one or two scriptures that constantly came to my mind and of which people continued to remind me. One was from Paul, and as I felt so foolish, small, and weak, I remembered that he said: "Because the foolishness of God is wiser than

men; and the weakness of God is stronger than men. For
ye see your calling, brethren, how that not many wise men
after the flesh, not many mighty, not many noble, are
called: But God hath chosen the foolish things of the
world to confound the things which are mighty. . . . That
no flesh should glory in his presence." (1 Corinthians
1:25-27, 29.)

When my feeling of incompetence wholly overwhelmed me, I remember the words of Nephi when he
said: "I will go and do the things which the Lord hath
commanded, for I know that the Lord giveth no commandments unto the children of men, save he shall prepare a way for them that they may accomplish the thing
which he commandeth them." (1 Nephi 3:7.) I want to tell
you that I lean heavily on these promises, that the Lord
will strengthen and give me growth and fit and qualify me
for this great work. (*Conference Report*, October 1943, pp.
15-18.)

Quotations from Spencer W. Kimball

CELESTIAL LIFE

Celestial life may be had by every soul who will fulfill the requirements. To know is not enough. One must do. Righteousness is vital and ordinances are necessary.

CHURCH LEADERS

I hope you get your copy [the *Ensign*—containing General Conference discourses of the General Authorities] and underline the pertinent thoughts and keep it with you for continual reference. No text or volume outside the standard works of the Church should have such a prominent place on your personal library shelves.

DESTINY

It is the destiny of the spirits of men to come to this earth and travel a journey of indeterminate length. They travel sometimes dangerously, sometimes safely, sometimes sadly, sometimes happily. Always the road is marked by divine purpose.

ETERNAL LIFE

To doubt the wisdom and justice of the passing of a loved one is to place a limitation on the term of life. It is to say that it is more important to continue to live here than to go (forward in progression). To continue to grieve without faith and understanding and trust when a son goes into another world is to question the long-range program of God, life eternal with all its opportunities and blessings.

FAITH

It takes faith—unseeing faith—for young people to proceed immediately with their family responsibilities in the face of financial uncertainties. It takes faith for the young woman to bear her family instead of accepting employment, especially when schooling for the young husband is to be finished. It takes faith to observe the Sabbath when "time and a half" can be had working, when profit can be made, when merchandise can be sold. It takes a great faith to pay tithes when funds are scarce and demands are great. It takes faith to fast and have family prayers and to observe the Word of Wisdom. It takes faith to do home teaching, stake missionary work, and other service, when sacrifice is required. It takes faith to fill full-time missions. But know this—that all these are of the planting, while faithful, devout families, spiritual security, peace, and eternal life are the harvest.

FAMILY

Have your family as the Lord intended. Of course, it is expensive, but you will find a way, and besides, it is often those children who grow up with responsibility and hardships who carry on the world's work. And, . . . do not limit your family as the world does. I am wondering now where I might have been had my parents decided arbitrarily that one or two children would be enough, or that three or four would be all they could support, or that even five would be the limit; for I was the sixth of eleven children. Don't think you will love the later ones less or have fewer material things for them. Perhaps, like Jacob, you might love the eleventh one most. Young people, have your family, love them, sacrifice for them, teach them righteousness, and you will be blessed and happy all the days of your eternal lives.

FORGIVENESS

Forgiveness is the miraculous ingredient that assures harmony and love in the home or the ward. Without it there is contention. Without understanding and forgiveness there is dissension, followed by lack of harmony, and this breeds disloyalty in homes, in branches, and in wards. On the other hand, forgiveness is harmonious with the spirit of the gospel, with the Spirit of Christ. This is the spirit we must possess if we would receive forgiveness of our own sins and be blameless before God.

INDIANS

I present to you a people who, according to prophecies, have been scattered and driven, defrauded, and deprived, who are a branch of the tree of Israel—lost from its body, wanderers in a strange land, their own land. I give you nations who have gone through the deep waters of the rivers of sorrow and anguish and pain; a people who have had visited upon their heads the sins of their fathers not unto the third and fourth generations but through a hundred generations. I bring to you a multitude who have asked for bread and have received a stone, and who have asked for fish and have been given a serpent. (See 3 Nephi 14:9-10.) This people ask not for your distant, far-away sympathy, your haughty disdain, your despicable contempt, your supercilious scorn, your turned-up nose, your scathing snobbery, your arrogant scoffing, nor your cold, calculating charity.

It is a people who, unable to raise themselves by their own boot straps, call for assistance from those who can push and lift and open doors. It is a people who pray for mercy, ask forgiveness, beg for membership in the kingdom with its opportunities to learn and to do.

It is a good folk who ask for fraternity, a handclasp of friendship, a word of encouragement; it is a group of nations who cry for warm acceptance and sincere brotherhood. I give you a chosen race, an affectionate and warmhearted people, a responsive but timid and frightened folk, a simple group with childlike faith. I point you to a people in whose veins flows the blood of prophets and martyrs; a people who have intelligence and capacity to climb to former heights but who need the vision and the opportunity and the assistance of the nursing parents.

LOVE

What is love? Many people think of it as mere physical attraction and they casually speak of "falling in love" and "love at first sight." This may be Hollywood's version and the interpretation of those who write love songs and love fiction. True love is not wrapped in such flimsy material. One might become immediately attracted to another individual, but love is far more than physical attraction. It is deep, inclusive and comprehensive. Physical attraction is only one of the many elements, but there must be faith and confidence and understanding and partnership. There must be common ideals and standards. There must be a great devotion and companionship. Love is cleanliness and progress and sacrifice and selflessness. This kind of love never tires or wanes, but lives through sickness and sorrow, poverty and privation, accomplishment and disappointment, time and eternity. For the love to continue, there must be an increase constantly of confidence and understanding, of frequent and sincere expression of appreciation and affection. There must be a forgetting of self and a constant concern for the other. Interests, hopes, objectives must be constantly focused into a single channel.

MARRIAGE

A basic reason for eternal marriage is that life is eternal; and marriage, to be in harmony with eternal purposes, must be consistent with life in duration. Marriage by civil officers, or by Church officers outside of the temples, is made for time only, "till death do you part" or "so long as you both shall live." It terminates with death. Only celestial marriage extends beyond the grave. Eternal marriage is performed by the prophet of the Lord or by one of the very few to whom he has delegated the authority. It is performed in holy temples erected and dedicated for that purpose. Only such marriage transcends the grave and perpetuates the husband-wife and parent-child relationships into and through eternity.

MODESTY

One contributing factor to immodesty and a breakdown of moral values is the modern dress. I am sure that the immodest clothes that are worn by some of our young women, and their mothers, contribute directly and indirectly to the immorality of this age. Even fathers sometimes encourage it. I wonder if our young sisters realize the temptation they are flaunting before young men when they leave their bodies partly uncovered. They frequently wear short skirts and body-revealing blouses and sweaters that seem to be worn to draw attention to the form of the girls and to emphasize sexuality.

MOTHER

How can mothers justify their abandonment of home when they are needed so much by their offspring? Rationalization must take over as they justify themselves in leaving home and children.

Of course, there are *some* mothers who *must* work to support their children, and they are to be praised, not criticized, but let every working mother honestly weigh the matter and be sure the Lord approves before she rushes her babies off to the nursery, her children off to school, her husband off to work, and herself off to her employment. Let her be certain that she is not rationalizing herself away from his children merely to provide for them greater material things. Let her analyze well before she permits her precious ones to come home to an empty house where their plaintive cry, "Mother," finds no loving answer.

PRAYER

We pray for the poor and needy. . . . If we pray we are more likely to pay our fast offerings, contribute to the welfare program, and pay our tithing, for out of these tithes and offerings comes much of the assistance to the poor and needy. . . . We pray for the missionaries. Children who have petitioned to "bless the missionaries" are most likely to be desirous of filling missions and of being worthy for such service.

We pray for our enemies. This will soften our hearts, and perhaps theirs, and we may better seek good in them. . . . We pray for the Church leaders. If children all their days in their turn at family prayers and in their secret prayers remember before the Lord the leaders of the Church, they are quite unlikely to ever fall into apostasy. . . .

When boys speak to the Lord concerning their bishop, they are likely to take very seriously the interviews with the bishop in which priesthood advancements and mission and temple blessings are being discussed. And girls too will have a healthy respect for all church proceedings as they pray for the leaders of the Church. . . .

We pray for our own family members, their incomings and out-goings, their travels, their work, and all pertaining to them. When children pray audibly for their brothers and sisters, it is likely that quarreling and conflict and jarrings will be lessened.

RACE
From a church whose membership was for the first hundred years largely confined to the white nations of America and Europe, we have grown to a worldwide force, embracing men of all colors and cultures. And we must learn the lesson that our fellowship is as universal as God's love for all men.

REPENTANCE
Repentance is a kind and merciful law. It is so far-reaching and all inclusive. It has many elements and includes a sorrow for sin, a confession of sin, an abandonment of sin, a restitution for sin, and then the living of the commandments of the Lord, and this includes the forgiveness of others, even the forgiving of those who sin aginst us.

REVELATION
The burning bushes, the smoking mountains, the Cumorahs, and the Kirtlands were realities but they were the exceptions. The great volume of revelation came to Moses and to Joseph and come to to-day's prophet in the less spectacular way—that of deep impressions but without spectacle or glamour or dramatic events. Always expecting the spectacular, many will miss entirely the constant flow of communication.

RIGHTEOUSNESS
Peace, joy, satisfaction, happiness, growth, contentment—all come with the righteous living of the commandments of God. The one who delights in all of the worldly luxuries of today at the expense of spirituality is living but for the moment.

SATAN
Satan never sleeps—he is diligent and persevering. He analyzes carefully his problem and then moves forward diligently, methodically to reach that objective. He uses all five senses and man's natural hunger and thirst to lead him away. He uses his natural and proper

desires and passions to distort and pervert man. He anticipates resistance and fortifies himself against it. He uses time and space and leisure. He is constant and persuasive and skillful. The useful things such as radio, television, the printed page, the airplane, the car, he uses to distort and damage. He uses the gregariousness of man, his loneliness, his every need to lead him astray. He does his work at the most propitious time in the most impressive places with the most influential people. He overlooks nothing that will deceive and distort and prostitute. He uses money, power, force. He entices man and attacks at his weakest spot. He takes the good and creates ugliness. He takes beautiful art and gives it sensualness. He takes divine music and changes it to excite passion and lewdness. He uses sacred things to divert. He uses every teaching art to subvert man.

SEXUAL MORALITY

Illicit sex is a selfish act, a betrayal, and is dishonest. To be unwilling to accept responsibility is cowardly, disloyal. Marriage is for time and eternity. Fornication and all other deviations are for today, for the hour, for the "now." Marriage gives life. Fornication leads to death. Premarital sex promises what it cannot possibly produce or deliver. Rejection is often the fruit as it moves its participants down the long highway of repeated encounters.

When we talk of sex, our first thought is adultery or fornication; but our second one, and close on its heels, is the sex stimulation to self and others, sometimes called "petting." It is a damaging and a damning transgression in its own right, and then, of course, it is also the gateway to the final acts of fornication and adultery.

SUCCESSION

Significant to us is the fact that there has never been one minute since April 6, 1830, that the Church has been without divine leadership. No deceased President has ever taken the keys and authorities into the spirit world away from the Church on the earth.

Since the death of his servants is in the power and control of the Lord, he permits to come to the first place only the one who is destined to take that leadership. Death and life become the controlling factors. Each new apostle in turn is chosen by the Lord and revealed to the then living prophet who ordains him.

Joseph Smith bestowed upon the twelve apostles all the keys and authority and power that he himself possessed and that he had received from the Lord. He gave unto them every endowment, every washing and anointing, and administered unto them the sealing ordinances.

YOUTH

We must develop these precious youth to know the art of statesmanship, to know people and conditions, to know situations and problems, that all the men will be trained so thoroughly in the arts as their future workers, and in the basic honesties, and integrities and spiritual concepts that there will be no compromise of principle.

Name	Born	Birthplace	Date Ordained Apostle	President Council of Twelve
Joseph Smith 1805-1844	Dec. 23, 1805	Sharon, Vermont	May 1829 (age 23)	*First Elder*
Brigham Young 1801-1877	June 1, 1801	Whittingham, Vermont	Feb. 14, 1835 (age 33)	Apr. 14, 1840
John Taylor 1808-1887	Nov. 1, 1808	Milnthorpe, England	Dec. 19, 1838 (age 30)	Oct. 6, 1877
Wilford Woodruff 1807-1898	Mar. 1, 1807	Avon (now Farmington) Connecticut	April 26, 1839 (age 32)	Oct. 10, 1880
Lorenzo Snow 1814-1901	April 3, 1814	Mantua, Ohio	Feb. 12, 1849 (age 34)	April 7, 1889
Joseph Fielding Smith 1838-1918	Nov. 13, 1838	Far West, Missouri	July 1, 1866 (age 27)	no record
Heber Jeddy Grant 1856-1945	Nov. 22, 1856	Salt Lake City, Utah	Oct. 16, 1882 (age 25)	Nov. 23, 1916
George Albert Smith 1870-1951	April 4, 1870	Salt Lake City, Utah	Oct. 8, 1903 (age 33)	July 1, 1943
David Oman McKay 1873-1970	Sept. 8, 1873	Huntsville, Utah	April 9, 1906 (age 32)	Sept. 30, 1950
Joseph Fielding Smith 1876-1972	July 19, 1876	Salt Lake City, Utah	April 7, 1910 (age 33)	April 9, 1951
Harold Bingham Lee 1899-1973	Mar. 28, 1899	Clifton, Idaho	April 10 1941 (age 42)	Jan. 23, 1970
Spencer Woolley Kimball 1895-	Mar. 28, 1895	Salt Lake City, Utah	Oct. 7 1943 (age 48)	July 7, 1972

Sources: Smith, Joseph Fielding. *Essentials in Church History.* Deseret Book Co., 1971, and Church Historical Department

THE PRESIDENTS

Age & Day Sustained as Pres.	Served as President	Years as Pres.	Years as General Authority		Age at Death	Church Membership	Stakes	Missions	Temples
24 Apr. 6 26 Jan. 25	*1830-1832* 1832-1844	*1 +* *9 mos.* 12½	14	June 27, 1844	38	1844 35,000 (est.)	9	3	2
46 Dec. 27	1847-1877	30	42	Aug. 29, 1877	76	1877 155,000 (est.)	20	9	1
71 Oct. 10	1880-1887	6 + 9 mos.	49	July 25, 1887	78	1887 192,000 (est.)	31	12	3
82 Apr. 7	1889-1898	9½	59	Sept. 2, 1898	91	1898 228,032	40	20	4
84 Sept. 13	1898-1901	3	52	Oct. 10, 1901	87	1901 278,645	50	21	4
62 Oct. 17	1901-1918	17	52	Nov. 19, 1918	80	1918 495,962	75	22	4
62 Nov. 23	1918-1945	26½	63	May 14, 1945	88	1945 979,454	155	38	7
75 May 21	1945-1951	6	48	April 4, 1951	81	1951 1,147,157	191	43	8
77 Apr. 9	1951-1970	18 + 9 mos.	64	Jan. 18, 1970	96	1970 2,807,456	499	88	13
93 Jan. 23	1970-1972	2½	62	July 2, 1972	95	1972 3,277,790	581	102	15
73 July 7	1972-1973	1½	32	Dec. 26, 1973	74	1973 3,360,190 (est.)	630	110	15
78 Dec. 30	1973-								

APPENDIX I

Questions About the Presidents

1. Who was the first President to visit or travel outside the United States as President?
2. Who were the only father and son who both served as President?
3. Which President lived the longest?
4. Which President lived the shortest time?
5. Which President was born a British subject?
6. Who was the first President born in the western part of the United States?
7. Who was the first President to be born into the Church?
8. Who was the first President to speak on radio?
9. Who was the first President to speak on television?
10. Which President published the most books?
11. Which Presidents served more than sixty years as General Authorities?
12. Which President traveled most during his term as President?
13. Which President, as a member of the Council of the Twelve, helped establish the Scouting program in the Church?
14. Which President served as an apostle at the same time his father was an apostle?
15. Which President pioneered the welfare program as a stake president?
16. Which three Presidents were trained as professional schoolteachers?
17. Which President became President after serving as first counselor in the First Presidency?
18. Which two Presidents became Presidents after serving as second counselor in the First Presidency?
19. Which President served the longest in the Council of the Twelve?
20. Who was the tallest President?
21. Who was the shortest President?
22. Which President, as a boy, walked across the plains to the Great Salt Lake Valley?

23. Which President was shot four times in Carthage Jail and witnessed the killings of Joseph Smith and Hyrum Smith?

24. Which President, while presiding over the Church, also became mayor, army general, social reformer, candidate for president of the United States, pioneer in adult education?

25. Which President served the longest as President of the Council of the Twelve?

26. Who was the youngest man to be ordained an apostle?

27. Under which President did the Church see the greatest growth in membership?

28. Which President served the shortest time?

29. Who served the longest term as President?

30. Who was the last President to have been closely associated with the Prophet Joseph Smith?

31. Which Presidents served in public office during their lifetimes?

32. Which President issued the Manifesto, discontinuing polygamy?

33. Which President was known as "Lion of the Lord"?

34. Which President was known as "A Preacher of Righteousness"?

35. Which President was known as "The Champion of Liberty"?

36. Which President gave the prophecy concerning the Civil War and the Saints' settling in the Rocky Mountains?

37. Which President, while serving as a missionary to the Sandwich Islands (Hawaii) was virtually raised from the dead?

38. Which President worked on the inspired revision of the Bible?

39. Which President was noted for helping preserve historical trails as landmarks?

40. Which President dedicated the most temples during his presidency?

41. Which President had the most children?

42. Which President made the statement that later became a principle of eternal progression: "As man is, God once was; as God is, man may be."?

43. Which President made the statement: "No other success can compensate for failure in the home"?

44. Which President was the youngest to die since the martyrdom of Joseph Smith?

45. Which President kept a daily journal for more than 62 years, which journal later served as part of the Church's history?

46. Under which President was the first stake outside the intermountain area organized?

47. Which President was noted for helping to get the Church out of debt?

48. Which President served as counselor to four Presidents and then became President himself?

49. Which Presidents did not die in Salt Lake City?

50. Who was the oldest man to become President?

51. Which President made the first voice recording?

52. Which men served in the First Presidency and later became President?

53. Which two men served the shortest time as apostles before becoming President?

54. Under which President were Assistants to the Council of the Twelve added?

55. Which President was a friend to the Indians and had this as his policy: "It is better to feed them than to fight them"?

56. Which President said: "I teach them correct principles and let them govern themselves"?

57. Which President was faced with more than forty lawsuits but acquitted on all but one?

58. Which Presidents served jail sentences?

59. Which of the Presidents was the oldest when ordained an apostle?

60. Hollywood made a motion picture of which President?

61. Which Presidents served five missions?

62. Who was the only President to have sons serve with him in the First Presidency?

63. What was the average age of nine of the Presidents from John Taylor to Harold B. Lee when they assumed office?

64. Which Presidents served the longest time in the First Presidency?

65. Which Presidents were noted for their work with the Lamanites?

66. Which President suffered an unusual number and variety of illnesses?

67. Who became chairman of the correlation committee prior to being President?

68. Who was the only President whose wife was not living during his presidency?

Answers

1. Joseph F. Smith (to Europe)
2. Joseph F. Smith, sixth President, and Joseph Fielding Smith, tenth President
3. David O. McKay (96 years)
4. Joseph Smith (38 years)
5. John Taylor
6. Heber J. Grant
7. Joseph F. Smith
8. Heber J. Grant (1922)
9. George Albert Smith (1949)
10. Joseph Fielding Smith (25 books)
11. David O. McKay (64 years), Heber J. Grant (63 years), Joseph Fielding Smith (62 years)
12. David O. McKay (more than two million miles)
13. George Albert Smith (1912)
14. George Albert Smith (father: John Henry Smith)
15. Harold B. Lee
16. Lorenzo Snow, David O. McKay, Harold B. Lee
17. Harold B. Lee
18. Joseph F. Smith, David O. McKay
19. Joseph Fielding Smith (60 years)
20. David O. McKay (6 feet 1 inch)
21. Lorenzo Snow (5 feet 6 inches)
22. Joseph F. Smith
23. John Taylor
24. Joseph Smith
25. Joseph Fielding Smith (19 years)
26. Heber J. Grant (age 25)
27. David O. McKay
28. Harold B. Lee (1½ years)
29. Brigham Young (30 years)
30. Lorenzo Snow
31. Joseph Smith, Brigham Young, John Taylor, Wilford Woodruff, Lorenzo Snow, George Albert Smith, Harold B. Lee

32. Wilford Woodruff
33. Brigham Young
34. Joseph F. Smith
35. John Taylor
36. Joseph Smith
37. Lorenzo Snow
38. Joseph Smith
39. George Albert Smith
40. David O. McKay (5)
41. Brigham Young (56)
42. Lorenzo Snow
43. David O. McKay
44. Harold B. Lee—age 74
45. Wilford Woodruff
46. Wilford Woodruff (Alberta, Canada, 1895)
47. Lorenzo Snow
48. Joseph F. Smith
49. Joseph Smith (Carthage, Illinois), John Taylor (Kaysville, Utah), Wilford Woodruff (San Francisco, California)
50. Joseph Fielding Smith (age 93)
51. Wilford Woodruff
52. Lorenzo Snow, Joseph F. Smith, David O. McKay, Joseph Fielding Smith, Harold B. Lee
53. Brigham Young, 12 years; Spencer W. Kimball, 30 years
54. Heber J. Grant, 1941
55. Brigham Young
56. Joseph Smith
57. Joseph Smith
58. Joseph Smith, on a variety of false charges, and Lorenzo Snow, on a plural marriage charge
59. Spencer W. Kimball—age 48
60. Brigham Young
61. Lorenzo Snow and Joseph F. Smith
62. Brigham Young (sons John and Brigham, Jr.)
63. Age 75
64. Joseph F. Smith (38 years) and David O. McKay (almost 36 years)
65. George Albert Smith and Spencer W. Kimball
66. Spencer W. Kimball
67. Harold B. Lee
68. George Albert Smith

APPENDIX II

Works Cited and Acknowledgments of Quotations

Andrus, Hyrum L. *Joseph Smith, the Man and the Seer*. Salt Lake City: Deseret Book Company, 1970.

Brooks, Melvin R. *LDS Reference Encyclopedia*. Salt Lake City: Bookcraft, 1960.

Colliers Encyclopedia. New York and London: Crowell-Collier Publishing Company, 1966.

Cowley, Matthias. *Wilford Woodruff*. Salt Lake City: The Deseret News, 1909.

Cox, Soren. *Our Leaders Speak*. Salt Lake City: Deseret Book Company, 1957.

Dictionary of American Biography. New York: Charles Scribner's Sons, 1937.

Durham, Reed C., Jr., and Stephen H. Heath. *Succession in the Church*. Salt Lake City: Bookcraft, 1970.

Evans, John Henry. *Joseph Smith, An American Prophet*. New York: Macmillan, 1933.

Grant, Heber J. *Gospel Standards*. Comp. G. Homer Durham. Salt Lake City: Improvement Era, 1941.

Green, Forace (comp.). *Testimonies of Our Leaders*. Salt Lake City: Bookcraft, 1958.

Heslop, J M., and Dell R. Van Orden. *A Prophet Among the People*. Salt Lake City: Deseret Book Company, 1971.

Hinckley, Bryant S. *Heber J. Grant, Highlights in the Life of a Great Leader*. Salt Lake City: Deseret Book Company, 1951.

Hinckley, Bryant S. *The Faith of Our Pioneer Fathers*. Salt Lake City: Deseret Book Company, 1956.

Jenson, Andrew. *Latter-day Saint Biographical Encyclopedia*. Salt Lake City: Andrew Jenson Historical Company and Andrew Jenson Memorial Company, 1901, 1920, 1936.

Journal of Discourses (JD). Salt Lake City: The Church of Jesus Christ of Latter-day Saints. 26 volumes.

Kimball, Spencer W. *Faith Precedes the Miracle*. Salt Lake City: Deseret Book Company, 1972.

Kimball, Spencer W. *The Miracle of Forgiveness*. Salt Lake City: Bookcraft, 1969.

Lee, Harold B. *From the Valley of Despair to the Mountain Peaks of Hope*. Salt Lake City: Deseret Book Company, 1971.

Lee, Harold B. *Youth and the Church*. Salt Lake City: Deseret Book Company, 1945.

McConkie, Joseph F. *True and Faithful.* Salt Lake City: Bookcraft, 1971.

McKay, David O. *Gospel Ideals.* Salt Lake City: Improvement Era, 1953.

Morrell, Jeanette McKay. *Highlights in the Life of President David O. McKay.* Salt Lake City: Deseret Book Company, 1966.

Nibley, Preston. *Brigham Young and His Work.* Salt Lake City: Deseret Book Company, 1936.

Nibley, Preston. *The Presidents of the Church.* Salt Lake City: Deseret Book Company, 1971.

Roberts, B. H. *Life of John Taylor.* Salt Lake City: Bookcraft, 1963.

Romney, Thomas C. *The Life of Lorenzo Snow.* Salt Lake City: Deseret News Press, 1955.

Schluter, Fred E. *A Convert's Tribute to President David O. McKay.* Salt Lake City: Deseret News Press, 1964.

Smith, George Albert. *Sharing the Gospel.* Comp. Preston Nibley. Salt Lake City: Deseret News Press, 1948.

Smith, Joseph. *History of the Church* (also referred to as *Documentary History of the Church; DHC*). Salt Lake City: The Church of Jesus Christ of Latter-day Saints. 7 volumes.

Smith, Joseph F. *Gospel Doctrine.* Salt Lake City: Deseret Book Company, 1971.

Smith, Joseph Fielding. *The Way to Perfection.* Salt Lake City: Genealogical Society of The Church of Jesus Christ of Latter-day Saints, 1953.

Smith, Joseph Fielding. *Man: His Origin and Destiny.* Salt Lake City: Deseret Book Company, 1954.

Smith, Joseph Fielding. *Answers to Gospel Questions,* vol. 3. Salt Lake City: Deseret Book Company, 1960.

Smith, Joseph Fielding. *Doctrines of Salvation,* vol. 3. Comp. Bruce R. McConkie. Salt Lake City: Bookcraft, 1956.

Smith, Joseph Fielding. *Essentials in Church History.* Salt Lake City: Deseret Book Company, 1972

Smith, Joseph Fielding, *Life of Joseph F. Smith.* Salt Lake City: Deseret Book Company, 1969.

Snow, Eliza R. *Biography and Family Record of Lorenzo Snow.* Salt Lake City: Deseret News Company, 1884.

Stewart, John J. *Remembering the McKays.* Salt Lake City: Deseret Book Company, 1970.

Talmage, James E. *Jesus the Christ.* 32nd edition. Salt Lake City: Deseret Book Company, 1962.

Taylor, John. *Gospel Kingdom.* Selected and arranged by G. Homer Durham. Salt Lake City: Bookcraft, 1943.

Tullidge, Edward. *Life of Brigham Young or Utah & Her Founders.* New York: Tullidge and Crandall, 1877.

Werner, Morris R. *Brigham Young.* London: Jonathan Cape, Ltd., 1925.

Widtsoe, John A. *Priesthood and Church Government.* Salt Lake City: Deseret Book Company, 1965.

Widtsoe, John A. *Discourses of Brigham Young.* Salt Lake City: Deseret Book Company, 1961.

World Book Encyclopedia. Chicago: Field Enterprises Educational Corporation, 1972.

Periodicals

Brigham Young University Speeches of the Year, 1954-72.

Church News, section of the *Deseret News.*

Conference Report, official proceedings of the annual and semiannual conferences of The Church of Jesus Christ of Latter-day Saints, issued each April and October.

Liahona, or *Elders Journal,* vol. 4, 1895.

Millennial Star, periodical of The Church of Jesus Christ of Latter-day Saints, 1840-1970.

The Ensign of The Church of Jesus Christ of Latter-day Saints, 1971-72.

The Improvement Era, periodical of The Church of Jesus Christ of Latter-day Saints, 1897-1970.

The Instructor, periodical of The Church of Jesus Christ of Latter-day Saints, 1866-1970.

The New Era, periodical of The Church of Jesus Christ of Latter-day Saints, 1971-72.

The Relief Society Magazine, periodical of The Church of Jesus Christ of Latter-day Saints, 1915-70.

Index of Quotations

General Index